SEBASTIAN & SONS

T.M. Krishna is a vocalist in the Karnatik tradition. Uncommon in his rendition of music and original in his interpretation of it, he is at once strong and subtle, manifestly traditional and stunningly innovative. Krishna is also a prominent public intellectual, writing and speaking on issues of structural inequality and culture. He is the driving force behind the Chennai Kalai Theru Vizha (formerly Urur Olcott Kuppam Vizha) and the Svanubhava initiative. He has been part of inspiring collaborations, such as Chennai Poromboke Paadal, performances with the Jogappas who are traditional transgender musicians, the Karnatik Kattaikuttu that brought together art forms from two ends of the social spectrum, and an enduring poetic partnership with Tamil writer Perumal Murugan.

Krishna is the author of *A Southern Music: The Karnatik Story* (HarperCollins, 2013), which won the 2014 Tata Literature Award for best first book, and *Reshaping Art* (Aleph, 2018). He also co-authored *Voices Within: Carnatic Music—Passing On an Inheritance.*

T.M. KRISHNA

SEBASTIAN & SONS

A Brief History of Mrdangam Makers

cntxt

First published by Context, an imprint of Westland Publications Private Limited, in 2020

Published by Context, an imprint of Westland Books, a division of Nasadiya Technologies Private Limited, in 2022

No. 269/2B, First Floor, 'Irai Arul', Vimalraj Street, Nethaji Nagar, Allappakkam Main Road, Maduravoyal, Chennai 600095

Westland, the Westland logo, Context and the Context logo are the trademarks of Nasadiya Technologies Private Limited, or its affiliates.

ISBN: 9789395073585

10 9 8 7 6 5 4 3 2 1

Typeset by SÜRYA, New Delhi
Printed at Nutech Print Services-India

To
Sandanam,
Madhavan,
Gnaneshwaran,
and many like them we have chosen to forget

'The drums were still beating, persistent and unchanging. Their sound was no longer a separate thing from the living village. It was like the pulsation of its heart. It throbbed in the air, in the sunshine, and even in the trees, and filled the village with excitement.'

—*Things Fall Apart*, Chinua Achebe

CONTENTS

A BRIEF NOTE

In Karnatik music, the mrdangam is a king among percussion instruments. Through strokes of varying intensity on its multi-layered surfaces, the artist is able to reconfigure time, speed and gait, and produce a spectrum of tones. Intricate fingering techniques embellish the melody and construct mind-boggling arithmetic patterns. There are, of course, other percussion instruments, among them the ghatam, kanjira and the morsing. More often than not, however, they play second fiddle to the mrdangam, the flagship definer of rhythm. Although Karnatik music is aesthetically voice-driven, concerts can also be led by a flautist, vina artist or a violinist. But no performance scenario is considered complete without a mrdangam. Over the past century, it has become not just the dominant concert partner, but one that has given direction to the melodic narrative.

The official hierarchy on stage is evident in the Karnatik concert announcements published in newspapers. After naming the lead singer or instrumentalist, the advertiser mentions the name of the violinist (who is the only melodic partner on stage). This is followed by the name of the mrdangam artist, and only then are other percussionists listed. But ask any vocalist or instrumentalist who her accompanists are for any given concert, and the chances are she will instinctively name the mrdangam artist first. This comes from a long-established belief that mrdangam artists can make or break a concert. It is not much of a stretch to say that the mrdangam is the most distinctive Karnatik sound—perhaps overpoweringly so. Even on the casual listener, it leaves an indelible mark.

This dominance results in everyone, consciously or unconsciously, demanding that the mrdangam sounds 'just right'. Seeking this unspecified perfection is the mrdangam artist's duty. But this constant pursuit is not in his control as much as it is in the hands of the mrdangam maker.

In the case of the tambura/tanpura (the instrument used as the drone in Karnatik and Hindustani music), once it is bought, I have very little reason to go back to its maker. I take care of most minor adjustments and change the strings on my own. Unless there is drastic damage, such as a crack in the wood, it is just me and my tambura. My relationship with the maker is essentially severed, to be renewed only when I go back to buy another tambura. Even in the case of a vina or violin, instruments that require more maintenance inputs from the maker, the need is not constant; everyday dependency is non-existent. This is equally true of percussion instruments such as the ghatam or kanjira. It is difficult to find a pitch-perfect ghatam with that indescribably sweet ring to it. But once you have acquired such a gem, there is very little to worry about.

Now, the mrdangam is quite another kettle of fish. 'Maintaining a mrdangam is like managing a naughty child' is how a mrdangam artist described it to me. It calls for constant attention, care, sensitivity, monitoring and readjusting—all of which requires the player to call on the maker. A bond between the two is unavoidable, and in many cases leads to long-term dependency. This relationship is aesthetically, emotionally and intellectually intimate.

Through this book, it is my hope that the reader gets a glimpse of the histories, lives, the minds and artistry of the makers. And an understanding of the complex relationship between the mrdangam maker and the player.

1

THE ORIGINS IN THANJAVUR

Finding F. Selvaraj's house was no simple task.

First, there is the suburb of Nanganallur to negotiate. Situated southeast of National Highway 48, and across the road from Chennai airport's runway, Nanganallur is a congested urban village. More specifically, a brahmin enclave within a village. Narrow streets crisscross it, traffic pouring in from every direction. Small provision stores, homes built on tiny plots of land, multistorey flats nearly toppling on to the road ... colonies within colonies within colonies. Nestled amidst these uncertainties are innumerable temples.

I've always thought of Nanganallur as a poor man's Mylapore, that clichéd symbol of brahminism. Through the 1970s, 1980s and 1990s, Nanganallur had become home to brahmins from lower income groups and for government employees who could not afford, or were unable to find a place in, the larger Mylapore area, or the even more exclusive Alwarpet—an ungated yet walled locality. In Chennai, upper-caste habitations have continued to follow a century-old model. The socially privileged have almost always moved towards the south or southwest, and Nanganallur was one more wave of south-bound movement.

During the British Raj, the 'town' was the centre of all business activity in Madras; it was the heart of the city. The pin code 600001 is still assigned to the area. The city's administration (then and now) is not too far away, and the stunning Indo-Saracenic-style buildings of the High Court are close by. Places north of town were undesirable. Loaders, coolies and labourers belonging to the lower castes lived there. Upper castes who were in business or law situated themselves in town, while the middle-class brahmin neighbourhoods were south, built around two iconic temples in Triplicane and Mylapore. After establishing themselves in suburbs such as Vepery, Kilpauk, Chetpet and Egmore that were west of 'town', the English elite moved southward towards the Adyar river. This demographic movement continued after Independence too. The upper-caste rich, including those who lived in town, took over the British elite locations. The workers occupying places north of town became more marginalised still, while those who needed to work in the homes of upper castes, or provided them services, took to the backstreets all over the city. Therefore, new habitation for caste elites took the south or south-western trail.

I have performed often at Nanganallur's revered Anjaneyar temple, the more modest Lakshmi Hayavadana Perumal temple and for various sabhas,[1] such as Krishna Fine Arts or the older

---

1. Organisations that promote the performing arts, especially Karnatik music, Bharatanatyam and urban Tamil theatre.

NSTSS (the unwieldy abbreviation by which Nanganallur Sri Thyagaraja Sangeetha Samajam is known). Several visits later, I still struggled with directions to these venues, often reaching just in the nick of time, sometimes a few minutes late. Google Maps, that urban saviour, made things easier, but it had yet to master the labyrinth that is Nanganallur's agraharam.[2] Then there was that notorious railway crossing that arbitrarily regulated vehicular entry. Now, of course, underpasses and flyovers—Chennai's favourite and perpetual preoccupation— have eased travel to the area.

For all this talk of inaccessibility and distance, Nanganallur is only 13 kilometres from my home in Alwarpet, a mere forty-five-minute drive away, even accounting for Chennai traffic.

Selvaraj had moved to Nanganallur, and I had been planning this meeting for a while. Travelling with me was a colleague who had initiated me into the nuances of the mrdangam and its making. For over six months, he had been sending me literature and tutoring me on the instrument and its history.

Perhaps I should begin this book with a mrdangam 101.

The mrdangam is a cylindrical two-faced drum, the primary percussion instrument used in Karnatik music performances and Bharatanatyam recitals. Its body is a hollow resonating chamber fashioned from the wood of a jackfruit tree. The frame is curved, and narrows towards the ends. On the dominant side of the frame (which faces the audience) are three layers of hide, intricately braided together. The top layer of cow skin is cut out as an annular circle that leaves bare the goat skin

---

2. A brahmin quarter usually centred around a temple.

right below, in the centre of this drum face. Below these two playing layers is a much narrower supportive circular strip of cow skin. On the exposed goat skin (second layer), a black or dark reddish paste—made from a mixture of boiled rice and a specific kind of powdered stone—is applied. Between the two upper membranes, tiny strips of sticks cut from a variety of grass (usually used to make brooms) or small granules from the stone mentioned earlier are placed to provide resonance and tonality.

On the other side of the frame are also three layers of skin: two from buffalo and one from goat. The two layers of buffalo skin are cut out together and form one thick annular strip, but on this side, much more of the goat skin below is exposed in the centre, providing a larger indented playing surface. The two buffalo skins are braided together, while the goat skin below is simply tied to them with small knots on the inner side. Traditionally, the leather membranes on either side are tied and tightened together with ropes made of buffalo skin. All of this, of course, barely begins to describe either the process of making a mrdangam, or the complexity of the instrument itself—both of which we will explore further.

My curiosity about the mrdangam began when I realised that we rarely, almost never, speak about these master makers. My book, *A Southern Music: The Karnatik Story*, explored caste discrimination in, what I hoped was, some depth, but I had entirely excluded instrument makers from the discourse. And amongst makers, those who deal with skin have always remained at the very edge—a fact I was well aware of. But when I wrote about caste and its implications within Karnatik society, I failed them.

As a practitioner of vocal music, I have met some of them over the years and have heard folklores of their abilities. But they were not an integral constituent of Karnatik music's history or mythology. We knew very little about the people, their lives, struggles or, indeed, their creativity and workmanship. Little did I realise then that this was going to be a far more complex and messy investigation that I had envisaged.

That's how I set out in search of Selvaraj, at any rate. Selvam, as he is known, was a third-generation mrdangam maker, the oldest living member of a renowned Thanjavur family. He was the stalwart who gave maestros such as Palghat Mani Iyer the flawless medium through which they could express their rhythmic mastery.

As we turned left just past a market, a turning I had often missed before, I noticed a man hailing us. He was wearing a veshti, an orange shirt and a shawl draped around his neck and down a shoulder. Selvaraj was waiting for us on the main street to ensure we did not lose our way. He instructed me to park the car right there and walk with him. My first impression was of a frail, old man. But his steady stride and authoritative tone forced me to quickly reverse my judgement. As we followed him, I remembered that Selvaraj was missing an arm, and that he had lost it in a freak accident. F. Melgies, his brother, described the incident when we met later. 'He was coming back from Mayavaram after finishing some mrdangam work. You see, on the highway, there weren't any dividers. If two buses go side by side, they are really close. He was sitting with his hand out of the window and the bus hit it. It was a government bus. He got money from the government as compensation.' Selvaraj had lost his right hand, his working hand, the hand that made him who he was. Perhaps the white shawl covered his physical and emotional scars.

A few lanes down, we arrived at his home, a compact structure with a couple of small rooms. The walls were pink, the paint coming off here and there—a worn-out square den that put me in mind of old village tenements. He had laid out two mats for us to sit. On the wall behind him was a poster of Mother Teresa and, in another corner, the wooden shell of a mrdangam.

AS I WRITE ABOUT SELVARAJ, I imagine his sharp eyes, mischievous smile and his casual but knowing confidence. A confidence backed by generations of knowledge, strengthened by the waters of the Kaveri. That Kaveri metaphor came to mind unbidden. It is often used by brahmins from Thanjavur who believe that Karnatik music is in their very being because they grew up drinking the waters of that sacred river—the water that nourished this musical land.

Ruled by the Cholas, the Nayakas and the Marathas at various periods, prosperous Thanjavur has long been considered Tamil Nadu's cultural nerve centre. Why, though? Madurai, Tirunelveli or Ramanathapuram are no less 'cultural'. For me, this association comes from the many stories I heard as a child of Karnatik musicians who lived in and around Thanjavur.

The notion that this area is extra-special is not one I questioned for most of my life. Certain parts of Tamil Nadu do not find prominent mention in the state's cultural annals—say Kongu Nadu, comprising the state's northwestern districts. I have no doubt that this is because Thanjavur culture's upper-caste and -class associations sit comfortably with what the dominant sections of society have deemed to be 'culture'—or 'high culture' anyway. Even during the colonial era, the district was controlled by powerful brahmins and other upper-caste, land-owning communities, giving the art forms associated with it social gravitas.

According to F.R. Hemingway's *Madras District Gazetteers: Tanjore*, published in 1906, 'Brahmins are proportionately more numerous in Tanjore than any other district except Ganjam and South Canera, where the members of this caste are less orthodox than usual. They number no less than one in every fifteen of the inhabitants, and consequently brahmin influence is predominant in social and religious matters.' He goes on to write, 'Vedic sacrifices are performed on the banks of its streams; Vedic chanting is performed in a manner rarely rivalled; philosophical treatises are published in Sanskrit verse; and religious associations exist, the privilege of initiation into which is eagerly sought for and the rules of which are earnestly followed even to the extent of relinquishing the world.'

Is it surprising then that this area was once the beating heart of Karnatik music? The home of the holy trinity—Thyagaraja, Muthusvami Dikshitar and Syama Sastri—Thanjavur has an unbroken tradition of Karnatik music, Harikatha, Namasankirtana and Bharatanatyam (or Sadir, as it was in its earlier form practised by the devadasis).

But this so-called high culture has needs that must be met, necessities that it keeps hidden away from the spotlight.

Stretching one or multiple leather membranes on either side of a hollow shell to produce tone and rhythm is a universal idea, one present in civilisations across the world. In southern India, ancient texts speak of instruments such as the tannumai, which is similar to the mrdangam—and presented as early prototypes of the modern instrument, proof of its antiquity. But in visual form, there are frescos from the late Nayak and early Maratha period which show the mrdangam, as we know it, accompanying devadasis performing Sadir.

After Aliya Rama Raya's defeat in the Battle of Talikota in 1565, the Vijayanagar Empire collapsed. This led to the Telugu Nayak dynasties of Madurai and Thanjavur operating independently. Subsequent internal squabbles between the two provided the Maratha Ekoji, Shivaji's half-brother, entry into Thanjavur. In 1676, Ekoji became the first Maratha ruler of Thanjavur.

Along with the change in governance came the Maharashtrian cultural influx. The Naradiya tradition of Harikatha became a mainstay in the brahmin quarters of Thanjavur and its surrounding areas. At these presentations, mrdangam artists of Maratha origin used to accompany the kirtankar. The earliest mrdangam artist we know of, and to whom we can trace the instrument, is Narayanasvami Appa—a descendant of one of the families that migrated to Thanjavur when the Marathas were in power. He is considered the father of mrdangam-playing. However, there already existed a mrdangam-playing tradition that was influenced by the tavil, which was and continues to be the only percussion accompaniment for nadasvaram ensembles. This deliberate 'forgetfulness' about the older style is caused by the fact that, by the mid-twentieth century, the Maratha-influenced Thanjavur tradition became the brahmin style, while the tavil- and Sadir-inspired Pudukkottai tradition became associated with the isai vellalar aesthetic. In those older times, of course, it was unthinkable for brahmins to be playing this skin instrument. The mrdangam was played by the isai vellalar community—consisting of nadasvaram and tavil artists, male conductors of Sadir performances and devadasis—or Maratha non-brahmin musicians.

Soolamangalam Vaidyanatha Bhagavathar, a well-respected Harikatha exponent of the early twentieth century, describes Narayanasvami Appa's style of playing and specifically mentions the care he took of his instrument and its tuning. But who made, maintained and repaired the mrdangam? Who were its caretakers? Where did they come from? What techniques did they employ? It has been hypothesised by some mrdangam artists that the instrument makers too came along with the migrating musicians and passed on their knowledge to the locals.

The first mrdangam maker whose name appears in oral history is Arogyam. I am not certain of the name because some people also refer to him as Adaikalam. But one of his great-great grandsons is named Arogyam, and given that names tend to repeat in Indian families, we could assume that this was indeed his name. None of his descendants remember what the family vocation was before Arogyam's time. Nonagenarian mrdangam artist T.K. Murthy suggests that Arogyam, assisted by his son Sevittian (Sebastian), probably did some work for Narayanasvami Appa and his illustrious contemporary Tukkaram Appa. It is indeed possible that Arogyam had an association with those musicians, but it must have been a very young Sevittian watching and helping his father.

At any rate, Selvaraj entirely negates this version of the family history. According to him, it was Ratnam (who graces the cover of this book) from Madurai who convinced Sevittian to make mrdangams. Until then, Arogyam worked exclusively on the tavil, providing his services to famous tavil virtuosi such as Palani Muthiya Pillai and Needamangalam Meenakshisundaram Pillai. This places Arogyam in the early twentieth century, certainly not earlier.

Madurai Ratnam's father Silvamuthu and Arogyam must have been brothers, making Ratnam and Sevittian first cousins. Ratnam migrated to Madurai at a very early age and, since there were many drama groups there, he worked mainly on the tabla and, in Selvaraj's words, did some 'low-level mrdangam work'. During a visit to Thanjavur, Ratnam persuaded Arogyam and Sevittian to change track to mrdangam work because many mrdangam artists lived in the area. Thus began this family's involvement with the crafting of the instrument. It is, therefore, Sevittian—nudged in that direction by Madurai Ratnam—who truly developed the area's mrdangam-making tradition: the Thanjavur Bani.

When I asked mrdangam players about the ancestry of the makers, one word cropped up repeatedly: 'converted'. They seemed to feel the need to ascribe an original Hindu-ness to the Thanjavur mrdangam makers, or point to reasons for their conversion.

Senior mrdangam artist Trichy Sankaran had this to say: 'The whole family comes from the Scheduled Caste. I don't want to get into that much, but they were converted Christians.' There was definitely a special emphasis on 'converted'—the result of a peculiarity of Indian thinking, where Christians from the West are natural Christians but Indian Christians are converts. K.S. Kalidas, a disciple of the legendary mrdangam artist Palani Subramania Pillai, echoed this: 'They are all people from the most backward classes. And most of them have been converted to Christianity also. Missionaries were active and gave financial incentives. There are still Hindus amongst them. And a lot of them go to both temples and churches.' In other words, their Hindu roots are strong.

The octogenarian mrdangam artist and vocalist T.V. Gopalakrishnan, on the other hand, recognised socio-cultural mobility as a probable reason. 'About seventy or eighty years ago, most of them converted and became Christians because it gave them an elevated status from what they were.'

Mrdangam-making involves skinning, cutting and curing hides, and hence this work was almost never done by the mrdangam artists. In the established caste order, skin-work has always been allotted to the lowest of castes. Even a century ago, when the conversions began, the procuring of hide and the making of the mrdangam would have been executed by caste groups that worked with skin and leather, and were considered 'untouchable'.

The term 'adi dravida' has a complex history. Tamil politician and anti-caste campaigner M.C. Rajah coined it in the early twentieth century to stop the use of the casteist pejorative paraiyan or pariah, which referred to a deeply discriminated and marginalised caste group. Among the depressed castes (another word introduced in the early twentieth century to refer to the 'untouchable' castes), the paraiyars were the most socio-economically and politically mobile group. They had already established working relationships with the Europeans. By the late eighteenth century, irrespective of whether they converted to Christianity or not, paraiyars had joined the army and also worked as butlers in European homes. In addition to this vertical mobility, conversion too gave them access to education.

Soon, people of other marginalised castes too began using the term 'adi dravida'. Hence a pallar or chakkiliyar could get an adi dravida caste certificate. Within each caste, there are sub-groups that further complicate this discussion. Therefore, in a few generations, adi dravida subsumed multiple caste identities. The members of Sevittian's family only said they were adi dravida. According to Hemingway's *Madras District Gazetteers: Tanjore*, 'the paraiyars outnumber any other caste in Thanjavur district amounting to no fewer than 310,391 persons'.

As early as 1570, the Italian traveller Caesaro Federici had this to say about Christians in Thanjavur: '… Christians are well intreated there, and have their churches there with a monasterie of Saint Francis order, with great devotion and very well accommodated, with houses round about.' In the sixteenth century, St Francis Xavier travelled around south India, preaching and converting many. Catholic Christianity has had roots in the Tamil region since the mid-sixteenth century. We know, for instance, that the Marian shrine in Nagapattinam has been worshipped since the sixteenth century, though the basilica itself came up later.

But around the later part of the seventeenth century, the position of the Jesuits—until then the most powerful Christian missionaries—weakened. The Protestant movement began to rise especially in the Thanjavur region, getting a boost when Christian Friedrich Schwartz (1726–1798), a German Lutheran missionary, built the Christ Church in Tiruchirapalli in 1766, and in 1787, established what came to be known as provincial schools in many villages in and around Thanjavur. Schwartz was powerful and respected equally by the Thanjavur king Tulaja II (r. 1763–1787) and the British. Tulaja even appointed him as guardian to the crown prince Serfoji II (r. 1798–1832). Schwartz was also a political emissary for British parleys with Haidar Ali (1720–1782). But by the mid-nineteenth century, constant wars and uncertainty had led to the general decline of Christianity, and I quote Hugald Grafe from his book *The History of Christianity in Tamilnadu from 1800 to 1975*: 'There was hardly any church of whatever affiliation or tradition that was not affected by the long military strife in the country and the resulting disorder. In addition, the ties of the Churches of Tamil Nadu to their supporting Churches in Europe had been severed or seriously weakened. This was a result politically of the continued decline of Portuguese power, of the French Revolution and of the European wars in its aftermath.'

In the early nineteenth century, it was the Protestants, especially the Lutheran and Anglican denominations, that were rejuvenated, and this meant the Catholics had to respond because they had begun losing membership to the Protestants. And newly initiated structural changes within the Catholic establishment also helped it gain momentum.

In the late nineteenth century, there was a spike in the number of people converting to Christianity in Thanjavur district. According to Geoffrey A. Oddie, who authored *Hindu and Christian in South-East India*, between 1871 and 1901, while the population of Thanjavur rose by 13.8 per cent, the proportion of Christians in it rose by 31 per cent. Many converts belonged to the depressed classes. Oddie writes that, in 1871, 49.1 per cent of the area's Christians were from the depressed castes. They would form an even greater share of the converts over the next few decades. And paraiyars converted in much larger numbers than any other caste. Considering all this, it is likely that the Thanjavur mrdangam makers belonged to the paraiyar caste.

It does appear from missionary narratives that refuge, safety and education were all impetus for conversion, along with a possible realisation of self-worth and rights as oppressed communities came into contact with a new culture and new ideas. These mass conversions would have made upper-caste Hindu society uncomfortable. We see echoes of discomfort in a comment by Umayalpuram K. Sivaraman, an octogenarian maestro of mrdangam-playing: 'Before that (conversion), they were dalit and Hindus only.' There is a suggestion here that dalits later became Christians. This is a subconscious conflation of dalit culture and Christianity that he might have picked up as a young boy growing up in the brahmin clusters of Thanjavur district. After all, most converts in his region were dalits.

As far as we are able to surmise, Sevittian was a second- or third-generation Christian. The Portuguese Jesuit missionary Saint John de Britto—Arulanandar in Tamil—was martyred in

1693, was beatified in 1853 and declared the patron saint of Madurai Roman Catholic Mission in 1854. And behind what used to be Sevittian's home lies an Arulanandar church. This has been their family church, what they call pangu kovil, for at least five generations now. The St Antony church on Sunnambukara Street just a few blocks away is older and, according to Melgies, many males in the family were named Antony after the saint. We cannot be sure, but it is quite possible that either Arogyam or his father converted to Christianity sometime in the late nineteenth or early twentieth century.

AS YOU ENTER THANJAVUR FROM Kumbakonam, the CRC bus depot falls on the left. A right at the next junction takes you to Sunnambukara Street, and a little further down, Keethukara Street. This locality is referred to as Vadakuvasal, meaning 'Gate to the North'. Keethukara Street (the name means 'the street where people live in thatched homes') is outside this entry gate to the old fort city of Thanjavur. It looks like any backstreet in Tamil Nadu's numerous little towns. It was here that Sevittian's three sons—the siblings who ruled the mrdangam-making industry—were raised. The oldest, S. Shengol; the second, S. Parlandu (Fernandes); and the youngest, S. Antony (whom everyone knew as 'Shetty'). I learnt that 'shengol' is the staff that Jesus the Shepherd carries, and Antony was nicknamed Shetty because of his paunch, thanks to the stereotype of potbellied Chettiars, the banking community.

Selvaraj told me that Sevittian's family originally lived a few streets away, but that was 'not a good place', and so his grandfather's brother-in-law, who had already moved to

Keethukara Street, suggested that they shift here. He helped Sevittian acquire a piece of land. Until his death, Sevittian's three sons lived in the home he built there, under his watchful eye.

But this family story includes one more man—still a boy of about thirteen or fourteen in 1925-26, when he visited Thanjavur from his home in Palakkad. He was accompanying his father as part of a Namasankirtana ensemble. After the performance, they went in search of mrdangam artist Mylatur Sami Ayyar's house. The boy wanted to meet and hear Thanjavur Vaidyanatha Ayyar, but they did not know him. Instead, they were seeking out Sami Ayyar, whom they knew. Father and son stopped their bullock cart near the Venkatesa Perumal temple, where a concert was in progress, and asked for directions to Sami Ayyar's house. Perhaps the man they were speaking to noticed the mrdangam in the cart, and enquired who they were and the purpose of their visit. Having heard about the prodigy from Palakkad, this man told them that, since it was late, they could spend the night at his house and go to Sami Ayyar's the next day. By the morning, the youngster was taking mrdangam lessons from their host—Thanjavur Vaidyanatha Ayyar. This boy would go on to become the revered Palghat Mani Iyer, the man who is said to have redefined the mrdangam.

About seven years later, a little eight year old entered Vaidyanatha Ayyar's home—T.K. Murthy from Trivandram, whose only dream was to be mentored by the maestro. In the decades that followed, Murthy would become M.S. Subbulakshmi's most trusted percussionist. He lived with Ayyar and studied the mrdangam, while Mani shuttled back and forth from Palakkad, spending a few days with his teacher whenever he had concerts in the vicinity. Since Thanjavur was the hub of Karnatik music at the time, this would have been quite often.

Vaidyanatha Ayyar was not a prolific stage performer, though he had accompanied many leading musicians of his time, like Konerirajapuram Vaidyanatha Bhagavathar, and was a regular at Namasankirtana performances. But he was known to have organised and systematised mrdangam learning and performance. He had learnt the art from Das Rao, a Marathi-speaking Thanjavurian, and Kannusami Pillai, who belonged to the isai vellalar community.

According to S. Arulraj (Antony's son), there could not have been serious mrdangam workmanship before Vaidyanatha Ayyar's time. 'They would have put skin on both sides. They would not have known much about pitch, etc.' Madras A. Kannan, a Madras-based mrdangam artist, said something interesting: 'In Narayanasvami Appa's time, singers sang to the pitch of the mrdangam.' Essentially, it was the singer or instrumentalist who had to make the adjustment, tune their voice or instrument to the mrdangam's pitch.

Selvaraj is also quite sure that specialised mrdangam work did not exist before then. 'In my grandfather's period, there was no specialisation or individualisation as per the needs of the mrdangam artist or the singer. Work was just done in villages, along with what was done for local dance and drama.' With this observation, he was also clearly establishing artistic hierarchy.

Their testimonies contradict Soolamangalam Vaidyanatha Bhagavathar's account of Narayanasvami Appa's mrdangam, where he mentions tuning of the instrument.

From all that I could gather, I believe the craft of making, tuning and maintaining the instrument was in its nascent stages at that time, and it is quite possible that mrdangam artists had instruments tuned to only certain pitches, forcing the singers to adjust accordingly. This was before the advent of the microphone, a time when men sang at pitches natural to women.

T.K. Murthy asserts that it was Vaidyanatha Ayyar who taught Sevittian and his sons everything about mrdangam-making. While they might have been first-generation makers and Ayyar would have guided them in the nuances of the music that the instrument produced, their own knowledge of skin, its texture, nature and versatility would have been vast, while Ayyar's would have been non-existent. Arogyam was already a tavil maker and Madurai Ratnam had worked on a few techniques for the construction of a mrdangam. It is unacceptable that they are reduced to the status of mere executors, while Vaidyanatha Ayyar is credited with all the intellectuality.

Yet, to date, accomplished mrdangam artists stake claim to all the knowledge behind the making, leaving makers with credit only for the 'dirty work'. Some blatantly say, 'We can't do that', implying that someone else will have to do the undesirable and that it is, after all, low-grade work that anyone can do. Mrdangam artists don't want to be associated with the act of killing, skinning or cutting. And rarely will they publicly and unambiguously acknowledge the mrdangam maker's contribution to the improvement in their own playing or performance—or, indeed, to the development of the instrument's calibre. These people are not acknowledged as equal creative partners in the process of this artistic engagement. Trichy Sankaran had this to say: 'When the craftsmanship improved and fine-tuning evolved, the playing also changed.' When I prodded further to ask if it was fair to say that the craftsmanship improved the playing, he first responded, 'Not necessarily. I am saying that they go hand in hand,' and then said, 'I must reword what I said: it might have influenced the playing. That is the proper word.'

In Vaidyanatha Ayyar's time, all the skin-related work was carried out in Keethukara Street, while the final fine-tuning was done at his house, 941 Pandamanikkappa Street, within the precincts of the old fort. The Venkatesha Perumal temple was nearby, and the Bangaru Kamakshi Amman temple—where the venerated Syama Sastri had been a priest around a century earlier—was a short walk away.

'Sevittian would not even enter the house; he would stand at the corner of the street,' said T.R. Rajamani, Palghat Mani Iyer's son. Selvaraj, Parlandu's son, offers a similar description of his father at work. 'When my father worked for Thanjavur Vaidyanatha Ayyar, he would stand at the entrance. T.K. Murthy would keep all the mrdangams that needed to be worked on outside. He would work outside or tie the mrdangam in a piece of cloth and bring it back home.' Selvaraj used a phrase that fits this context: 'The boss is always the boss; the worker is always the worker.' The inference being that both remain, or must remain, in their respective socio-economic locations.

Murthy gave me the impression that his teacher allowed the makers into his home and had them dine inside too. This seems highly improbable since no one from the makers' family so much as hints at this possibility. If anything, they only reiterate the separation that existed. The mere presence of Sevittian or his sons within the inner enclave of Thanjavur would have been disconcerting enough for the upper-caste neighbourhood. Umayalpuram Sivaraman, who learnt from Vaidyanatha Ayyar, substantiated Selvaraj's account. 'Vehicles could not enter that street. There would be a stone right in the middle of the road, so you were forced to walk. You could also come from the Kamakshi Amman kovil. They would bring two mrdangams, one on each shoulder, and the mrdangam would be outside in the porch.'

Vaidyanatha Ayyar, nevertheless, was an unusual man. He taught a Muslim lad and a female student by the name Thirukokarnam Kanakabhujam who, according to Murthy, was a brilliant player. It is important to acknowledge these anomalies in human behaviour. While we cannot speak for a long-dead person, it is safe to assume that, within each one of these uncommon relationships, Ayyar had set regulations for both himself and the student, and these allowed him to maintain his own notion of 'purity'.

Sevittian's fame soon spread, and other artists, such as Thanjavur Ramdas Rao, Mahalinga Ayyar, Pakkriya Pillai and Mylatur Sami Ayyar, began employing him. Even the formidable Pudukottai Dakshinamurthy Pillai, a champion of the mrdangam and kanjira, called him over for some work. Shengol and Parlandu were apprentices when Sevittian worked for Vaidyanatha Ayyar. According to Selvaraj, the age difference between the two brothers was six to seven years, while Antony was about five years younger than Parlandu. Very soon, the older siblings had established their own market. Shengol operated in the Thiruvarur, Mannargudi, Needamangalam and Nagapattinam regions, while Parlandu remained in Thanjavur, taking over the reins of their father's business. As the youngest, Antony was slow to find his footing.

Other members of the family also established themselves in towns in and around Thanjavur. Ayyakannu, Sevittian's cousin, was a force in Kumbakonam. Mrdangam-playing elders, such as Azhaganambi Pillai and Sengottai Rangu Iyengar, depended on him. His son, Picchaimuthu, assisted him. Picchaimuthu's son, P.T. Martin, also joined the family business, possibly the last of his line to do so.

I first visited Keethukara Street in 2017 with K. Soosainathan, Parlandu's grandson from his daughter, as my companion. As he and I walked down, to my right were a few concrete two-storeyed structures and to the left a green-coloured house with a tiled roof. Many homes were painted green, pink or blue, most likely a sign of upward mobility, identity and financial growth. Or perhaps it was just the style here. Dogs roamed freely and children played and chattered, glancing at me. Parlandu's home was at the corner where Keethukara Street veers left. Situated under the shade of a large neem tree, it was a single-storeyed pucca house, with a blue front door, a small wooden window and a terrace covered with thatch. It was the only building here that retained an old-world charm. Quite likely, the mrdangam work was carried out on the terrace. Perhaps the neem tree germinated around the time Parlandu was born. Today, it watches over the home of the greatest-ever mrdangam maker.

A large pile of construction stones in front of the house, a broken roof and an unruly interior did nothing to quiet my imagination. If we had listened carefully, I am certain we would have heard the three legendary brothers argue over the choice of hide, and watched with astonishment as Parlandu gave finishing touches to a new mrdangam. Visiting Parlandu's house was like a pilgrimage to Thiruvaiyaru, Thyagaraja's resting place.

Behind that house was the home of Shengol, now an under-construction modern building belonging to A.S. Johnson Kennedy, Antony's youngest son. We retraced our steps and turned right at Parlandu's house. The adjacent property was Antony's village home, now owned by his second son, A. Jesudass. The door grille had a prominent mrdangam-shaped motif, and above it, the following words were shaped in metal:

Parlandu's house on Keethukara Street

'Shetty Ranjitham thunai', or seeking the blessings of Shetty (Antony) and Ranjitham, Antony's wife. To its right, were the words 'J. Edwin illam', the home of Edwin, Jesudass's son.

As we walked deeper into the colony, the streets got narrower. A number of aluminium basins and buckets were piled up outside one house; in another, jute sacks were stitched together to serve as a curtain. At every turn, Soosainathan reeled off names of family members, many of whom were also mrdangam makers. At the end of one lane was the small Sowriar kovil, the church of St Xavier. Every street has its own little shrine, the deity of which is taken out in a procession at a yearly celebration. Behind the Xavier's kovil was the Arulanandar church, their family temple. And just around a bend, the ubiquitous black Sintex water tank dominated the landscape.

A young, aspiring musician who accompanied me on this field trip wrote to me later to say, 'Though these individuals have been an integral part of the music ecosystem for generations, they seem so far removed from it. Their world is completely different from that of the musicians. There is a very small overlap, but I suppose that too is very transactional. It is saddening. They speak of musicians and have had close relations working with many for generations. Walking through the village in Thanjavur, I heard Soosainathan and his parents utter names that are legendary in the field of mrdangam-playing, but it seemed so unlikely that there was any connection between those musicians and this place. Why? I don't know.'

Speaking of Keethukara Street, Rajamani said, 'That place where they used to stay, you should not go there in the night'; he was alluding to the possibility of being attacked by drunkards. T.R. Rajaram, Palghat Mani Iyer's younger son, once accompanied his father there. 'I went with my father to the cheri (slum) searching for Parlandu. For my father, if some work has to be done by Parlandu, it has to get done. He will go to any extent.' Going to the slum was, to his mind, pushing the limits of his boundaries. But more often than not, Kitta Ayyar, Mani Iyer's right-hand man and a teacher at a government school, served as messenger. On one occasion, when he went to summon Parlandu for some urgent work at Mani Iyer's home, he was shooed away: 'You get lost, Ayyare, you have no other work.'

Yet, in spite of the bond that love of the mrdangam wrought between Mani Iyer and Parlandu, and despite the dependence of musicians on makers, the stigmas of caste remained unchallenged.

It was in this spirit of things that Vaidyanatha Ayyar did not pay Sevittian or Parlandu according to the work they did. He would give them money to cover basic expenditure and keep the rest in safe custody. As the benevolent feudal lord in a casteist structure, he provided for his workers but controlled their socio-economic power.

Sevittian died sometime in the early 1940s, after which the property was divided among the three brothers. Vaidyanatha Ayyar advised the family in this partition. He told Shengol that Mani Iyer and he would like to pay for a concrete house for Parlandu on his portion of the land, and that the other brothers must not misunderstand. Parlandu was their favourite, as Shengol knew only too well. He agreed to abide by whatever Ayyar decided. After some wheeling and dealing, the three brothers established individual residences. A few makers said that either Vaidyanatha Ayyar or Mani Iyer bought Parlandu some farmland.

According to Sivaraman, when Ayyar died, Parlandu would not leave the cremation ground, and kept vigil all night. Was it loyalty, gratitude, dependence, love or a complex web of emotions entrenched and normalised in the socialisation of both men?

Even after what was an evidently uncomfortable partitioning of property, the brothers worked side by side. The kitchen was common, but their earnings were kept separate. The jute-rope cots outside their homes served as a waiting room for junior students of the mrdangam artists who had to wait for the work to be completed. What part of the work was permitted within the compound of the mrdangam artist's house and what needed to be done far away from his sight was well understood by all.

A tectonic shift took place in 1954. The superstar of percussion, Palghat Mani Iyer, decided to move to Thanjavur. He was drawn out of his hometown to this ancient city only because Sevittian's sons, especially Parlandu, were based in Thanjavur. According to Mani Iyer's sons, the makers in Palakkad were no match for the Thanjavur family. Mani Iyer would reminisce about his days in Palakkad, recalling that the mrdangam would look nice and shiny but he had no clue what they had actually done in terms of mrdangam work.

Until he moved to Thanjavur, Mani Iyer had an interesting system in place. His close friend and music aficionado Kittappa Ayyar was the proprietor of Ananda Lodge, which was the Thanjavur home for most travelling musicians, including Iyer. Right next door was a sattiram, a wedding hall. In those days, sattirams were essentially thatched sheds. Mani Iyer would arrive with the instruments that needed adjustment or repair. A message would have already gone out to the entire Sevittian family that the king was on his way. Shengol, Parlandu, Antony, cousins such as Alkattan and his son Gnanaprakasam, and others—like Manickam and Munro (a name that became popular after the time of Thomas Munro, Governor of Madras Presidency from 1820 to 1827) from Madurai, and Thomas from Trichy—would all find their way to the kottai, or shed. Selvaraj and Rajamanickam (Shengol's son) would go there directly after school to observe their elders at work and to help with odd jobs. Mani Iyer would often walk in and check the progress. If a complete makeover was required (that is, an entirely new set of membranes needed to be selected, cured, fitted and braided), the mrdangam would be left behind in Thanjavur and taken home by the makers. They would be brought back here for the final touches whenever Iyer stopped by again.

Mani Iyer was in search of an elusive tone, nadam—an obsession with the unattainable that would drive him to extreme lengths. No one but he knew what he was looking for; it was in his head. Rajaram said, 'He gave his life for it. He would want more, better sound. Not loudness but a tone. He wanted to see whether he could improve the sound even more every time.' And in order to achieve this, he was willing to do everything in his power, and everybody became tools in this endeavour.

Perhaps Parlandu knew what Iyer had in his mind, and maybe that is why the maestro moved lock, stock and barrel to Thanjavur?

After years of experimenting and putting any number of people through all sorts of hardships, pressures, and hours and hours of physical labour, hoping for that 'ideal sound', Iyer came to the conclusion that there was, in fact, nothing to be done. The person who invented the mrdangam was so super-intelligent, he surmised, that the instrument could not be improved upon. It is complete, he noted in his diary.

This is a deeply disturbing statement. It is, in my opinion, an act of leveraging social privilege—especially because the statement was absolutely untrue. We know for a fact that Mani Iyer was part of the changes that were made to the instrument. His observation presents itself as humility but, unfortunately, it does two things. It allows Iyer to negate all the work done by those with whom he had ideated and collaborated—the hugely creative artists who actually put these ideas into practice: the makers. By denying that innovations and modifications had indeed been made, Iyer was removing the makers from the discourse entirely. And this meant that he was silently arrogating to himself the credit for everything that went into the instrument's growth, yet basking in the glow of humility.

Mani Iyer first moved into 173, North Main Street, and rented the house opposite it for all the mrdangam work. But, within a couple of years, he had shifted to 807, East Main Street. These houses were between 0.8 and 1.5 kilometres respectively from Keethukara Street. But it is not the distance that separated them; it was access that defined each one. 'Parijatham', the East Main Street home, had a large compound surrounded by walls. The house itself was deep inside that compound, leaving a lot of area free in front. There were steps that led up to the compound, which had a garden on the left, and on the right was a thatched shed just for his mrdangam work.

'That shed was not an ordinary one,' explains Rajaram. 'It was very well built; one could run a family in it. The thatch was very low (that is, the slope) to prevent rain from coming in. The mrdangams couldn't be exposed to rain. The shed also had a three-foot compound wall, which was jagged, not straight. There was a nice entrance also. The shed was built on proper cement pillars, not bamboo.' Inside were three benches in the shape of the Tamil letter 'Pa'.

Whenever Iyer travelled, he left instructions for Parlandu, Rajamanickam and Shengol. He also had a room on the first floor of the main building, where all his mrdangams were stored and was the other space that the makers worked.

By the mid-1950s, Parlandu was unable to work due to ill-health. Selvaraj, his son, was still in school. 'I had passed eighth at Thanjavur Maharaja School. Our family situation was not great (financially). Appa was not working because of his diabetes. I told my father that, though I wanted to study, I should get a job, but he responded rudely. In anger, I sold my books and went away to Thiruvaiyaru. There, Thiruvaiyaru Krishna Ayyar, a mrdangam artist and brother of Annaswami Bhagavathar, heard me out and brought me back to the church opposite my house. He advised my father to find me a job. I soon joined as a punkah-boy in the collector's office and was later moved to the R-section, where pensions were handled. I worked there for two or three months. Around that time, Mani Iyer asked my father to bring me along. He was sitting on a bench in the mrdangam shed, playing. I sat down on the floor next to him. He enquired about my education and wanted to know if I knew this job. I said that, though I had not really worked, I had learnt from observing my father and uncle. I was then getting Rs 60 per month plus a few rupees that came as tips. Mani Iyer offered me Rs 150 per month as a salary, and I agreed. When I joined, he told me very clearly that his wife and he were my parents. His son, Rajamani, took care of the things I needed, and my salary was given to my father twice a month, on the first and the fifteenth. This was 1958 or 1959, when I was around twenty years old,' Selvaraj told me.

He went to Iyer's house that week and was directed upstairs by Kitta Ayyar, where he waited outside the mrdangam room for the master to come. Thus began Selvaraj's relationship with Iyer. I have heard that Mani Iyer had anything between twenty

Courtesy: T.R. Rajamani

Selvaraj working on a mrdangam

and forty mrdangams, but Selvaraj swears that the number on the day he joined was precisely fifty-nine!

On the face of it, things had changed for Sevittian's family. In terms of access to a mrdangam artist's home, they had gone from standing at the street corner to waiting outside on the porch, and now to spaces demarcated within the household. There were no overt lines now, but all parties knew they existed. Sankaran put it succinctly thus, 'In my opinion, each one knew their limit and where to draw the line.'

I will let Selvaraj speak; nothing could describe these 'lines' better.

'I am saying this because Ayya (Iyer) was an honest person. Even his children did not know his needs and inner honesty. His food, clothing habits, everything I knew. I was only scared of Amma (Iyer's wife). I used to behave how one needs to in a brahmin house.'

But what did that mean? 'Respect. If master was sitting alone, I would go and do work. If Rajamani came, I would go inside because I should not intrude. I never fought or argued with Ayya on any issue. I would stay in the room (mrdangam room) unless called. If he came for anything (implying non-mrdangam-related work), I would come out.'

Selvaraj reiterated that Mani Iyer treated him like a son. Was the mere access to spaces that were normally out of bounds for his community such a huge step that it was being equated to a father–son relationship, I wondered. Arulraj was blunt. 'Those who were in this line of work were allowed access to the homes of the mrdangam artists; no one else.'

From Sankaran's point of view, these were the lines: 'As a staunch brahmin, I will stay away from him if there is some religious function at home. Not that I am asking him to stay out or anything. We will adjust to maintain that sacredness.'

Selvaraj had more to say: 'I did not eat with him. In Madras, when Mani Iyer stayed at the Woodlands Hotel, I used to eat his leftovers. He knew that and would keep some for me. In Thanjavur, Amma or his daughter would call at lunch time. I would go to the rear portion and, even if Amma said come in, I would not. I would eat outside; they gave me a plate; that was my plate. I would wash it and keep it separately. But, with coffee, tumblers were the same.'

When Mani Iyer went to Madras for the music season, Selvaraj would follow too. 'We used to stay in the rooms in Woodlands and Selvaraj in the shed outside. That shed was even called Selvam's (Selvaraj) shed. He used to work on mrdangams and stay there,' said Rajaram.

There were also lines between behaviour in the house and during travel. 'At home, I will not do "that" with Mani Iyer. Only when we travel will I socially mingle with him.' Selvaraj saw a difference between the way Iyer and his wife treated him. 'At home, the difference existed. Amma thought like that, but master was never like that.' Master needed Selvaraj and his services, the wife did not. Iyer had to share space, time and his mrdangam with Selvaraj—he had no choice. His need, which was aesthetic and emotional, smudged some boundaries, and this may be why Selvaraj felt his employer treated him differently.

Some practices did not change, however. 'The major skin-related work was all done at the makers' homes. So when they headed home in the evening, they would take two or three mrdangams on a bullock cart,' said Rajamani.

And social hierarchies were maintained in speech and action. 'I have heard that Parlandu and others would first tie their upper-body cloth around their hips and only then speak,' Melgies said. Soosainathan added, 'Even much later, I have seen Shetty address the mrdangam artists only as sami (literally meaning god).' Both attributed this behaviour to respect towards brahmins, saying that all this was missing today. T.K. Murthy too spoke of it as respect. Melgies added, 'It must be said that they (brahmin mrdangam artists) also did a lot and helped these workers (makers).'

Every anecdotal line is identical to what we would hear from a domestic help in a benevolently casteist household. My own home was no exception. Employees would speak about how they fed and bathed their employers' children, saw them grow up, cared for their well-being and were treated like family members. They would also express gratitude that the employer took care of their own children's education. But we all know that caste remains entrenched and they are never truly family members. Caste is not just a physical obstacle; it limits the relationship, reduces human respect, equality and, above all, results in a 'forgetting'. It is a violent dehumanisation that is not easily overcome.

This was the environment that every mrdangam maker operated within. He had to work in an environment that was simultaneously confining and advancing, and somehow find a way to make peace with how things were. The complicating element in these maker–player relationships was the fact that, no matter how talented a maker might have been, appreciation of his abilities rarely translated to true respect.

Palghat Mani Iyer is an etched memory in the national cultural consciousness, but Parlandu, Antony and Selvaraj are always on the periphery, if at all they exist there.

Arulraj was far more combative when speaking of the past and suggested that his father did manage to bring about some change. 'In the big hall, we would sit in a corner and work,' he said. 'That was insulting, ugly for us; pushing us to a corner. Those who earn name and fame because of our efforts were discriminating against us, so we made them bring the work to our homes. My father was the first to do this. Until then, we were going and coming; then the work shifted to our homes.'

I have not heard this from anyone else, but it is quite possible that Arulraj is speaking of work done for the not-so-powerful mrdangam artists. There must have been different categories of players, and in the case of the less eminent ones, perhaps the makers were able to force some change.

Within the Dalit Christian community of makers, there was, and still is, a sense of pride in being able to work with and within brahmin homes. As Melgies's wife, Arogyamary, said to me, 'Listen to me for a minute. He gets special respect among our people if he works at an Ayyar's house. "Oh, Ayyar veetla velai seyarangla!" (Oh, is he working in an Ayyar's house!), they say. Because of that, automatically, he gets a special stature and respect. At my father's place, they respect him a lot. In the beginning, they used to fight, saying it was a cheap job, working with skin and all that for mrdangam. But now it has changed ... they all say respectfully that their mama is working in Madras with mrdangams. They don't know ...' This incomplete 'they don't know' is loaded.

ONLY ONE MRDANGAM ARTIST POSED a challenge to Palghat Mani Iyer's dominance—Palani Subramania Pillai. There was undoubtedly a competitive spirit between them, perhaps something a bit more. They maintained a respectful camaraderie, but there was an ongoing 'soft war' underlying it. Their competitiveness was about skill, dexterity, musical insight, performance, popularity, and equally about the makers and controlling them.

Palani lived in Madras, except for a brief spell in Trichy. Though he employed mrdangam makers based in Madras, Palani too wanted members of Sevittian's family to work with him. But Iyer lived in the heart of Thanjavur, and was able to control and regulate the availability of the Thanjavur makers. Parlandu was Iyer's first choice, but he had also done some work for Iyer's rival. Eventually, it was Antony who became Palani's go-to man. Another maker whose attention the two musicians vied for was Shengol's son Rajamanickam. At one point, Palani complained that Iyer placed Rajamanickam on a monthly contract only so that he would not have time to take up any of Palani's work. In other words, Iyer was ensuring that he got the best mrdangams made. When he found it hard to access Thanjavur-based makers like Parlandu and Rajamanickam due to their bond with Iyer, Palani had Antony and people like Thomas in Trichy and Moses from Tirunelveli work for him.

Palani's students are peeved at the well-established notion that Mani Iyer was single-handedly responsible for the improved quality of the mrdangam. Makers also echo this idea. Kalidas vehemently objected, 'People say that Palghat Mani Iyer had a wood workshop and worked on mrdangams there. But Palani also did the same work without all these nomenclatures attached to him.'

Palani was not a brahmin; he belonged to the isai vellalar community. It has been said that Palani was discriminated against because of his caste. He expressed this to his students, and it is quite widely known but almost never discussed—or acknowledged—within the Karnatik establishment.

Trichy Sankaran is Palani's most prominent disciple. 'Until the 1920s and 1930s, it was the pillaimars (isai vellalars) who dominated the mrdangam. Maybe because it was an instrument made of skin, and touching skin was taboo for brahmins, they were not encouraged to take it up. But I can say one more thing, maybe, I don't know if I want to, but I want to say that my guru felt, when the brahmin dominance came, he was sidelined, he felt deeply.' This feeling of being sidelined and discriminated against was real, and manifested itself in so many ways that went beyond the dais.

Kalidas had this story to narrate about Rajamanickam Pillai, a much-respected violinist belonging to the isai vellalar community. 'Concerts in Pudukkotai were arranged by Ramaswamy Ayyar, a local dignitary. When food was served, in the first batch, Semmangudi Srinivasier (the legendary singer) and others would eat. Even Rajamanickam Pillai's disciples would eat in the first batch because they were brahmins. Rajamanickam Pillai would eat in the second batch and, as compensation, Ramaswamy Ayyar's wife would personally serve him food.'

Palani's career was resurrected only because the grand old man of Karnatik music, Chembai Vaidyanatha Bhagavathar, promoted him as challenger to Palghat Mani Iyer. Chembai was an outlier in the Karnatik field and is remembered to this day for his open-mindedness. Someone who went against the grain, even if it meant questioning hardened social mores. He is often described as a 'suddhatma', a pure soul.

I was curious about whether the relationship between Palani and the mrdangam makers was any different, both because the caste dynamic was slightly altered and also since Palani himself had felt wronged because of his caste. But caste does not work that way, does it? On every step of the ladder, the occupiers are expected to treat those below with an 'othering'.

Sankaran explained, 'Just because Palani and others belonged to the pillai caste, he did not treat the craftsmen any different. In my guru's time, the makers had to leave the mrdangam and stand outside. He will examine the mrdangam inside and give advice; we, the students, will then go outside and hand over the mrdangam to them. The makers were not even allowed to come into the main hall. It was like that. In the concerts, the makers did not sit next to the artists but in a corner, and had to be at their beck and call.'

Kalidas tried to present a different picture. 'It was a professional relationship,' he said.

But was there caste discrimination, I enquired.

'No, nothing like that. Palani used to have a hut on Boag Road. These people would work there. Food for them would go from his house only.'

I interjected at this point: 'But they have to eat in the hut only?'

'Yes, but not because of caste discrimination. This is where their entourage is. There were usually two or three disciples along with these people. There was no rule against touching them or anything like that.' Perhaps the repeated use of 'these people' by Kalidas points to his own subconscious sense of caste.

Against this backdrop, it is startling to hear an entirely different register originating from Madurai. Madurai Ratnam moved to Madurai between 1920 and 1925, when he was in his twenties. He set up an establishment there, working with tabla for the theatre and some mrdangam work. As I mentioned earlier, he inspired Sevittian to enter the mrdangam-making fold.

Normally, Ratnam's work would not have translated to great financial success. But Madurai J.M.S. Britto, his grandson, shares a starkly different narrative. Unlike his Thanjavur-based cousins and nephews, not only did Ratnam not live in poverty, he was relatively affluent. What makes this more intriguing still is that the mrdangam players I spoke to had very little to say about Ratnam or his work. They knew him and did some work with him and it ended there.

Ratnam's success did not depend on professional musicians, it appears, but various samasthanams, or princely states, in the southern districts of Tamil Nadu, such as Sivagangai and Ramanathapuram. His market extended so far as Sri Lanka. Britto explains, 'He was a different person even then. When he went out, he would wear a coat, turban and shoes and rings and gold chains. He would not walk but take horse carriages to attend concerts. My grandfather was rich. He built a bungalow.' He points to a picture of his grandfather in a suit adorned with medals. 'He was given those medals for his work in those samasthanams. There were Bharatanatyam performances there and he used to work for those artists. He also sent mrdangams to Kandy in Sri Lanka. This was pre-Independence.'

Britto tells me that Ratnam was well known in his own town too. He was friends with mrdangam artist

C.S. Murugabhoopathy and Sakthivel (M.S. Subbulakshmi's brother, who was also a mrdangam player). 'When my parents got married, they were feted in Shanmukhavadivu's (Subbulakshmi's mother) house. M.S. and Sakthivel presented them with a silver kudam. This was 1954.' In 1954, M.S. Subbulakshmi had left Madurai far behind, and her association with her family there had been nearly severed. In all likelihood, it was only Sakthivel who presented the gift.

Madurai Ratnam

Chennai-based mrdangam makers tell us that handsome earnings only come from producing for music stores, NRIs, dance-mrdangam artists and the various music schools that conduct mrdangam classes. When you work exclusively with concert professionals, there is greater prestige and the work is harder and more complex, but the returns are considerably less. It is possible that Ratnam cracked this business reality before anyone else did. He concentrated on bulk orders that came from the samasthanams, music teachers and international markets of his time. If this was indeed true, he was an enterprising and shrewd entrepreneur. There is one thing I can vouch for. In the photographs, Ratnam looks assertive, self-assured, impeccably dressed and proud. In some photographs, he has a large moustache, and the image of him posing with the mrdangam (he was left-handed), a cross hanging down his neck and covering a large part of his chest, is truly majestic. It does seem certain that Ratnam was more prosperous by far than any of his better-known family members 300 kilometres to the east. But after Ratnam's demise, the family lost their wealth.

The arrangements between musicians and makers in Thanjavur had changed somewhat, but all of that was a minuscule development compared to what was about to happen. From the turn of the century, slowly but surely, Karnatik music had begun to settle into a new home in the patnam, city—Madras. It was once a city of musical saloons, private concerts at the homes of the rich and famous or in old temples. All this changed in the first two decades of the twentieth century. The Music Academy, established in 1928, had quickly become the sanctum sanctorum of Karnatik music. Sabhas such as Parthasarathy Swami Sabha, Perambur Sangeetha Sabha and Jagannatha Bhakta Sabha were changing the nature of Karnatik music consumption. Ticket-paying public and membership-driven models became the accepted norm. This was enabled by brahmin families migrating from

Thanjavur, Tirunelveli and surrounding areas, the Chettiars from Karaikudi district and other high culture-seeking business communities, such as the Mudaliars.

With the power centre unambiguously shifting away from the agraharams of Thanjavur, Kumbakonam and smaller villages that dotted the district's rice bowl, musicians had to commit to becoming residents of the new cultural metropolis. Right through the late 1950s and early 1960s, the super-famous, the stars and those who aspired to stardom took the north-bound train to this coastal city. Naturally, the mrdangam makers of Thanjavur also made the move, following their customers and business to Madras. The first to make the move was Rajamanickam, soon to be followed by Selvaraj and Antony's sons. Antony himself kept travelling back and forth between Keethukara Street and Madras right up to the very end.

Madras was different and, at some level, cosmopolitanism forced changes on everyone—changes that some would celebrate and others would bemoan. It also opened a new chapter in the relationship between the maker and his clients.

2

THE MOVE TO MADRAS

'I don't remember if I passed or failed sixth class,' said Arulraj. Though the children of Shengol, Parlandu and Antony went to school, they rarely studied beyond class ten. Yet, Parlandu did not want his second son to enter this line of work. He hoped his older son, Selvaraj, would work as a maker, while the younger, Melgies, would study and get a steady, respectable job. Melgies even enrolled in an employment office but that went nowhere. Soon, he found himself in Madras, working as a mrdangam maker in the homes of artists.

Selvaraj and Melgies had an older sibling, F. Dominic, who had no interest whatsoever in the mrdangam. An athletic, strong-willed individual, he was the local tough guy. His own uncle Shengol was scared of him. 'You had to be careful with him,' affirmed Selvaraj. According to family lore, he died early because a black magic spell meant for his cousin Nurusami rebounded on him. Nurusami had fallen in love with a girl belonging to the higher nayakar caste and would not forsake her. The girl's family decided to get rid of him. Dominic accidentally stepped on an evil concoction of eggs placed on the street for Nurusami. Within six years, he had passed away.

Shengol's son Rajamanickam followed in his cousin Dominic's footsteps—he was the next family 'toughie'. Not much is known about Shengol or his work. He passed away sometime in the late 1950s, and was unable to do heavy work towards the end of his life. T.K. Murthy mentioned that Shengol developed a physical ailment that prevented him from working full time when he was older. He was not seen as being on par with his brothers, but he was always around, helping out and also catering to his limited clientele. Often, he supervised his nephews or assistants as they did the physically demanding jobs. Shengol could not have imagined that his son would go on to become a gifted mrdangam maker—some would say second only to Parlandu. In fact, Rajamanickam may just have been a wee bit better than his famous uncle in certain aspects.

We know, for instance, that he was a point of contention between Palghat Mani Iyer and Palani Subramania Pillai. Rajamanickam later said that he was too young to understand what was happening. But his relationship with Palani soured forever, never to be healed.

Rajamanickam was first among the Thanjavur makers to shift base to Madras, sometime in the early 1960s. He came in contact with mrdangam makers who lived in the city. Known for their 'Madras muttu' (muttu is the multilayered leather membrane on the two playing sides of the mrdangam), these makers were well established in mrdangist circles. Later, we will return to the Madras community, and to the fact that they influenced the Thanjavur makers—even if no member of the family readily agrees to that proposition.

Rajamanickam took great pride in his work, and possibly believed that it was a privilege for artists to have the opportunity to work with him. All this manifested in the way he organised his work. He had no fear of the social equations that dominated their lives; there was not a submissive bone in his body. A disciplined man, he had clear rules for how he worked. Work would begin in the morning, but breakfast and lunch needed to be provided on time. He insisted on an afternoon siesta, and was back in the saddle at 4 p.m., to stop only when he was satisfied. The family spoke of how he demanded specific menus for lunch from the boss's wife. Usually, artists got work out of the makers, but with Rajamanickam, the roles were reversed, they said with vicarious pleasure. While he was engrossed in his work, no one could talk to or disturb him. Unlike his first cousins, he studied until college, and played football at the district level and received many trophies. He had seen more of the world than any other resident of Keethukara Street, and from that came a confidence that the mrdangam artists had not seen before in the makers. The legend of Rajamanickam persists among the younger players. One told me, like it was a scandal, that he would eat seated at the dining table in artists' homes.

Palghat Mani Iyer is credited with changing the way mrdangam artists were treated. Creditable as that is, Iyer's caste advantage allowed him to push for such changes. That Rajamanickam made a dent on the psyche and behavioural patterns of brahmin musicians from his marginal caste position was an extraordinary achievement.

Compare this with Selvaraj's description of his loyalty to Mani Iyer: 'In the Mylapore house, sometimes I would be there at 6 a.m. with two idlis, one vada from Rayas Café, and the magazine *Kalki* or newspaper *Swadeshamitran* in hand. I would just keep it there. I also wanted him to see me first on 1 January. I would go and stand there at 5.15 a.m. and knock on the door.'

Selvaraj had a lot to say about his cousin—an amalgam of rivalry and admiration. 'When Mani Iyer gave me a mrdangam to be handed over to one of his students, I would keep the two-and-a-half annas meant for transportation and carry the instrument on my shoulder. That was our habit. Rajamanickam would not do this. He took it only by rickshaw.' Selvaraj and Rajamanickam were competing for Mani Iyer's attention, work and benevolence, and that led to squabbles. Selvaraj claims Rajamanickam lied to Iyer that he had stolen a mrdangam. At that time, Selvaraj was away in Delhi on work. On his return, he had to explain himself. And, like all makers, Rajamanickam was secretive about his craft. He would not let Selvaraj in on his methods. 'He would share a meal with me but I got nothing about work from him,' Selvaraj said.

Trichy Sankaran, professor of music at York University, Toronto, often invited Rajamanickam to work on his mrdangams and those at the department. During his 1991 visit, Sankaran videographed the entire process of mrdangam-making, with Rajamanickam explaining the nuances. The maker is wearing a white banian and green chequered lungi, and is seated in Sankaran's garage, surrounded by mrdangams. He talks minimally and only pauses work for Sankaran to get a better shot of something, or to respond to the professor's observations, make a brief remark and provide clarifications. Lean of build, he speaks with the self-assurance of someone in complete command of his craft.

Mrdangam players and those close to them describe Rajamanickam as a rebel of sorts, and saw in him 'attitude'. They described him as a difficult person, arrogant, with a sense of superiority, someone who took many liberties. He spoke too much, said some, and recalled his impertinence. Apparently, he had the 'gall' to ask Kitta Ayyar, who was also a school teacher besides being Mani Iyer's manager, to take tuition classes for his children, when the only children Kitta Ayyar had ever done that for were those of the master himself. And, of course, Rajamanickam did not come cheap. His nickname was 'Spencer', derived from the elite shopping mall on Mount Road. At times, he charged twice as much as the others did.

One interviewee blamed Umayalpuram Sivaraman, with whom he had a long association, for spoiling him and treating him like the boss. On his part, Sivaraman said that he took very good care of Rajamanickam, and paid him a monthly salary of Rs 1,000, not unsubstantial in those days, and allowed him to work for others for additional revenue. But Rajamanickam's break-up with Sivaraman is an interesting tale in itself, and one that has many storylines. Rajamanickam's cousins were by and large reluctant to talk about what transpired, or said that they were unaware of the details. It is obvious that something did go wrong. Sivaraman and Selvaraj gave me their accounts of the events.

Selvaraj said, 'There was an article in the paper, not sure if it was *The Hindu* or *Dinamalar*, saying that those who like Thanjavur work should go there and get the work done.'

Selvaraj did not remember the reason for this article, but said that Antony, Rajamanickam and he were mentioned in the piece as supporting this demand.

Sivaraman speaks of a letter rather than a newspaper article. 'Under the instigation of one person, one of ours (meaning brahmin)—I don't want to reveal his name—these people from Thanjavur formed an association and said that the Thanjavur muttu is great and that there is no other like it and no other nadam (tone) matches it. All artists are making lots of money by playing concerts, but what you're paying us is not enough. So you have to pay us more money, or else we will not work. They sent this notice to all the artists, except me. Rajamanickam was also party to this letter. When he came four days later, I asked him about everyone getting a notice. He told me that everyone had asked him to sign the letter, so he too signed it without understanding its contents. "Please don't get me wrong," he said. I said, "I have a proposal now. Let's see if you agree. You make a muttu, I'll pay you 2,000 rupees. But that should last for ten years. Apply sadam (the black paste applied on the dominant side). I'll give you 500 rupees. But it should last for two years. Tie the varu (the leather ropes that connect the membranes on the two sides together), I will give you 2,000 rupees, but it should last for fifteen years." He asked, "How is that possible?" I said, "You are demanding more money, aren't you?"'

Sivaraman said to Rajamanickam that a maker's work must be assessed by mrdangam artists and other people, not the makers themselves. He then informed Rajamanickam that he had a concert with Dr Balamuralikrishna in four days. He said sarcastically, 'You play for Dr Balamuralikrishna, I will apply sadam. You give me the money for the sadam and you take the money I would have got from the concert.' After recounting this incident, which ended with a severance of their association, Sivaraman said, 'That day I challenged myself: is the nadam in my hand or in theirs?'

Sivaraman first questioned the makers' right to determine what would be rightful payment for their work, and then demanded various assurances of longevity that he knew were not practicable. He went on to suggest a flipping of roles, plainly implying that, while anyone could do Rajamanickam's job, only Sivaraman can do what he does. It seems to me that even his final sign-off question is a declaration that the tone lies in his fingers and not in the hands of the makers. Yet, a player cannot replace the maker, not unless he trains seriously for it. Individual brilliance and artistry in making account for heightened perfection and tone—a fact that is freely acknowledged in the case of music-making. A mrdangam artist cannot create exquisite tone and resonance without a beautifully crafted mrdangam. The notion that the makers are dispensable while the player is not comes from an entrenched hierarchy of knowledge and skill that flows from India's caste system.

After this break-up, Rajamanickam continued to work for other artists, like Karaikudi R. Mani and Trichy Sankaran, until he passed away in 2004.

It is said that Palani used to jocularly call Rajamanickam 'papan' (Tamil slang for the male Tamil brahmin) because the maker was a vegetarian and Palani was not. Rajamanickam preferred the rasam–rice cooked by Sankaran's wife to hotel food, for instance. When Melgies was telling me about Rajamanickam's need for an afternoon nap, his wife Arogyamary blurted out, 'That is what all these Ayyars[3] do.' Some mrdangam artists have also spoken about how people like Rajamanickam became disciplined because they were trained in upper-caste environments.

Melgies, Soosainathan and I had a long conversation about this aspect of their lives: food. How much did their workplace, which was primarily the homes of brahmin mrdangam artists, affect the essence of their culture? The first thing I hear is that beef has now disappeared from their menu. Rasam (a thin tamarind-based soup) is a welcome addition, as is yoghurt, neither originally a part of their cuisine. His wife did not know how to ferment milk for yoghurt until she married him, Soosainathan said. Much to his irritation (Soosainathan belongs to the next generation), though, Melgies argues that non-vegetarian food makes people lethargic. Soosainathan counters that, despite everything, their heart is drawn towards non-vegetarian food.

What were their traditional meals, I enquired. Soosainathan described a typical day's menu. Breakfast was around 8.30 in the morning and consisted of kanji, that is, rice soaked in water and buttermilk to which onions and green chillies are added. This primary dish was sometimes eaten with masala-fried anchovies; outstanding, Soosainathan pronounced. Around 1 p.m. was sapadu, lunch, with rice as the staple and a fish or mutton kolumbu (a broth of tamarind and pulses), rasam and fish varuval (fish fry). Vegetables had a minimal role in their cuisine, except the drumsticks or tomato that were added

---

3. Brahmins are often referred to as Ayyars.

to the kolumbu. Dinner was more or less the same, usually leftovers from the afternoon. Of course, now dinner has also turned into a meal of 'tiffin items', as Soosainathan calls chapati, dosa and idli.

It is not just taste buds—the dialect too has changed. Listening to Rajamanickam in the video, it is clear that his expressions, intonations and accent are brahminical. In our conversations, Soosainathan used the brahmin term 'atthukari' to refer to his wife. When I mentioned this, he promptly responded that his brahmin dialect also changes, depending on the region that the mrdangam player came from. For example, he would slide into Palakkad brahmin lingo if he was in Palghat Raghu's house. All these influences were one-way: top-down from the player to maker, owner to worker, the brahmin to the dalit. Almost nothing flowed in the other direction. Selvaraj summed it up when he said that, while people are born into the brahmin caste, he grew up in a brahmin house. 'All my habits are brahmin. Even today, I eat lunch by 9.30 or 10 a.m.,' he said with pride. Making the oppressed complicit in their oppression is a particular ingenuity of the caste system; it allows Selvaraj and everyone else involved to turn a blind eye to caste inequality.

AS ARTISTS AND MAKERS MADE their way north to Madras, some changes were to follow.

By the early 1960s, the warp and weft of Tamil Nadu's social fabric had been redrawn. In the 1920s, E.V. Ramasamy— or Periyar, the father of the Dravidian political awakening— spearheaded the self-respect movement. He awakened Tamil people to the grotesqueness of caste and made a frontal attack on the brahminical nature of Tamil society. His arguments were cultural, educational, economic and personal, and through a series of public actions, he re-engineered the socio-political landscape of the state. Brahmins saw themselves as the targets of his actions, which at times they were. However, this socio-political revolution forced changes in their way of life, and that would not have happened without the Periyar-trigger. And so, unthinking, socially discriminative practices were redesigned or kept under wraps inside homes, and upper castes retained their ugly sense of purity mostly in private spaces. A senior mrdangam artist had this illuminating observation about caste: 'In general, caste I feel was for the welfare of human society. At that time, they did not think much of it, but nowadays it is blown out of proportion. If each person just continues doing what they do, then there is no problem.' Within the logic of the caste system, the maker knew this too—so if he was offered a place at the dining table, it was his duty to decline. These wordless caste-retaining negotiations would go through many more iterations as the times changed.

Beyond the larger political factors, there was one very specific shift that fundamentally altered the relationship between the maker and the artists, and that was a change in the workplace. Across Tamil Nadu, mrdangam makers were expected to present themselves at the artist's home to fine-tune, realign or adjust the instrument. All the work that preceded this—processing the skin and finishing all the heavy-duty labour on the wooden shell—was carried out in the maker's home. In Madras, however, things were different.

As the Thanjavurians entered this new urban space, they realised that the local makers had shops where artists gathered to get their work done. As one member of a mrdangam artist's family told me, 'It is their turf.' Yes, it was. But it took the Thanjavur makers three or four decades to understand the benefits of a dedicated workplace. In Madras, artists would go to the maker's shop, hand over the mrdangam and wait, or come back the next day to check, pay and collect. And this is something the old-timer musicians did not like. Many would still have the Thanjavur makers and their descendants come and cater to them personally. According to Melgies, 'We (Selvaraj and he) had opened a shop near Mundakanni Amman Kovil in Mylapore. Two months later, Mani Iyer asked him to shut shop. He needed my brother to go and work for him. So, Selvaraj could accept other work only after finishing Mani Iyer's.'

Initially, it helped that many of the mrdangam makers who made the move to Madras were bachelors. They lived in small rooms, at times sharing it with a cousin or brother, freelancing for artists at their homes. After marriage, the men either left their wives and children behind in Thanjavur or made do in the available space.

The houses of the artists in Madras too were nothing like those in the villages. As one young maker said, 'There are no houses with four entrances to say, "Ask him to come through this entrance and the other through a different one." I too entered that way in Nachiarkoil. There were houses with two entrances and there were rules about who got to use which one.' While a few musicians could afford larger homes, most lived in upper-caste, middle-class neighbourhoods such as Mylapore and Mambalam, where houses were just a few rooms with little or no compound space. Unavoidably, there was greater physical proximity between the maker and the artist. Most likely, the mrdangam was worked on in a hall right next to the dining area, the kitchen not too far. I am certain that some people laid down diktats about access to this space or that, but by and large, some caste rules were being silently reworked. In the villages, even in the changed environment, it was possible to hide the workings of the system. All you needed to do was devise alternatives out of plain sight, demarcate spaces and keep it under wraps. Everyone participated in the pretence. This was not possible in a middle-class urban home or flat. And, unlike domestic workers, the mrdangam makers had to work with the artists. When that happened in the middle of the house, it skewed the old dynamics.

Arulraj pointed to some of these spatial changes when he spoke of entering the home of a mrdangam artist that he knew right from his childhood, being offered coffee and eating in the house, at their dining table, off their plate. He was also comparing this to the experience of his family just one generation ago. He said, 'My father and his brothers were not like this; they would behave in a subservient manner within caste barriers.' He does not mention it, but this new 'privilege' was restricted to the mrdangam makers and not others of their caste group. In other words, it was not self-realisation but self-interest—and an acknowledgement of both the new environment and the complexity of their relationship—that led to the warping of space and access.

Mrdangam artists who wanted round-the-clock personal assistance in Madras had to find new ways of doing things. In Thanjavur, Mani Iyer had people working for him throughout the day, but they would go back to their own homes in the evening. In Madras, some artists decided to have a maker stay with them. Imagine this scenario in the residential topography of a nascent city. It is not very clear where in the house the makers slept, ate or bathed, but everything was definitely nearer than it had ever been. It would be fair to assume that the arrangement was similar to live-in house help.

Arulraj entered T.V. Gopalakrishnan's (TVG) household when he was around ten years old. Arulraj narrated, 'TVG told my father (Antony) that he would keep me at home to do all his work. I was with TVG for thirty-five years—staying with him. I was like a son in the house. I would buy the milk and provisions. When I went, he had just got married. He had no children. I was free there, and could not have been like that even with my own parents.' TVG said something very similar. 'He was with me from his ninth year. He was like my son. There was no jadi (caste), etc.' After he got married, Arulraj moved into his own house, but continued working exclusively with TVG. He wasn't paid a monthly salary. Instead, Arulraj maintained accounts of all the work he did and TVG settled that amount.

Once again we see the 'my son, his son' description. While it is clear that the relationship is not akin to that of blood, it is worth investigating why it is repeatedly expressed in those terms. For the maker, casting the equation in these terms provided emotional and social upliftment, while the mrdangam artist was able to present himself as a non-oppressive benefactor.

The uncomfortable truth that this paternalistic feudalism was a form of validation for the makers must not be brushed under the carpet. Being needed and valued by someone in a position of social power, and the dissolving of physical barriers and the stigma of caste, gave the maker a sense of equality. No one else on Keethukara Street was treated with this sort of attention by the brahmins, and so it was socially and culturally uplifting for the makers when they found themselves indispensable to a privileged community. The younger makers have also told me that they are recognised in their locality by the fact that they do mrdangam work, and that this differentiates them from the others. As the mrdangam becomes their instrument of social mobility, the discourse of discrimination takes a backseat, and as long as the casteism is not blatant, it goes unnoticed or unremarked. Or, indeed, explained away as the liberties taken by a father. Meanwhile, the relationship between maker and musician continues to work within set parameters, and both individuals function within the paradigm of caste, taking care not to breach unspoken boundaries.

The mrdangam player was in desperate need of someone to fulfil a certain need, a job they could not imagine doing themselves. When social changes exerted pressure on the existing ways of doing things, something had to give. Possibly, this also created a need for artists to present themselves as forward-thinking. It could be that the traditional father–son archetype also played its part: the distant, tough disciplinarian father and the respectful son. Johnson confirms, 'How we behave matters; we have to adjust. It is like how our parents beat us when we make a mistake.'

From stories narrated by the Thanjavur mrdangam makers, it is obvious that a few individuals, like mrdangam artists Thanjavur Upendran, Thanjavur Ramadas and the polyglot vina exponent S. Balachander, gave a generous helping hand to Antony, Selvaraj, Melgies and Rajamanickam as they made

Madras their home. They found the makers small rooms to rent and also recommended them to other mrdangam artists. Yet, they made no grand assertions of a family-like bond. Selvaraj's description of working at the homes of Thanjavur Upendran and S. Balachander was very different from anything he had said about other musicians. 'That was like our home. I would work inside or on the pavement outside Upendran's house, going in and out, it made no difference; the same with S. Balachander.'

To further elucidate the cruel effect that caste has on the relationship between these artists—the maker and the musician—I report a statement by Melgies's wife Arogyamary: 'Even a small help from them (brahmins) seemed big to me because they were Ayyars. My sister's husband works in Bombay. Whenever he comes, he gives my kids Rs 1,000 each and gives me Rs 2,000. Till date I do not see that as a big deal. But then an Ayyar comes and gives him (Melgies) 1,000 or 2,000 for his work, I keep that safe with a pride that an Ayyar has given us that money.' Social inequality gets embedded more deeply in the minds of the receiver, only to grant the giver even more power. This psychological condition—and the system that engenders it—needs to be understood if we truly want to listen to the voices of the makers or enter into the complexities of these relationships.

BY THE 1970s, KARNATIK MUSIC practice and learning had gone far beyond the closely held and protected gurukula system. Schools of music sprouted in various parts of the country. People from the brahmin community who were interested in

Karnatik music were sending their children to vocal, violin and mrdangam classes. This meant that the makers also had abundant work, available nationally. They were called to Bombay, Delhi, Bangalore and Calcutta, and would spend a month or more in those cities—a practice that continues to this day. All India Radio, government music colleges and large art institutions like Kalakshetra, the iconic Central government art institution, were also new places of work. All this expanded their area of operation and effectively their demand.

Palghat Mani Iyer was possibly the first mrdangam artist who needed a maker to assist him all the time. All of us who are insiders in the Karnatik circle have heard about Iyer getting his mrdangams ready in the first-class compartments of trains. But I rarely thought about the maker, the real person who was doing the work. Yes, Mani Iyer was particular, but he could not have approached the immaculateness he sought without the artistry of Parlandu, Rajamanickam or Selvaraj. Just imagine sitting in a moving train, making sure the artist has that perfect instrument. The makers had to compensate for the relentlessly rocking compartment and its moving floor with the steadiness of their hands, because when Iyer sat on the concert stage the following day and stroked that mrdangam, he needed to be inspired.

Rajaram describes the scene eloquently: 'My father would give instructions for work to be done on eight mrdangams. Kitta Ayyar or Rayar Babu had to take Parlandu and company to the Trichy junction with them. At the station, one person would take away the eight mrdangams already used. The train would stop only for ten minutes or so. Parlandu or Selvam (Selvaraj) would keep the box open, and as soon as the train arrived, load the eight refurbished instruments quickly into the first-class cabin, open the cover and show them to my father. My father would test the mrdangams in his cabin. After that, if there was some work left, then one of them had to go to the next station (an hour, perhaps more, away) with him. If that was the case, he would ask Babu or Kitta Ayyar to buy the tickets. There used to be many difficulties. For example, the ticket counter would be full, or the other person would have unloaded only half the mrdangams and, meanwhile, the train would have started moving. The first-class compartment was not like it is now. There used to be only four or six seats per compartment. So, if he (the maker) sat outside in the corridor of the compartment, he could work without any bother.' Usually, there was only fine-tuning required, but there were also occasions when physically demanding work had to be done.

Mani Iyer always demanded this kind of service. When he travelled for the Edinburgh International Festival in 1965, Iyer insisted on having a mrdangam maker travel with him. Selvaraj had agreed to accompany the master but backed out at the very last minute. Selvaraj explained that it was because his father wouldn't allow him to travel, but Rajamani said he had just made some excuse. Arulraj believes it was a financial issue. Mani Iyer—along with his son and Kitta Ayyar—visited TVG's home to ask Arulraj if he would travel with them instead. TVG himself was not at home then, so Arulraj simply said that he would come only if TVG, who had been his caretaker, gave permission. They came back the next day and Arulraj was seated outside the house, working on a mrdangam. TVG gave his approval and off went Arulraj to the UK. He was the first mrdangam maker to travel beyond Indian shores.

For Arulraj, the entire trip was a blur. Here was a young man who knew only his home town and a few roads in Madras. To travel all of a sudden to a faraway land in a machine that flew above the clouds and then to be shivering in the Scottish cold—it must have been a sensory overload. 'I didn't know anything. I was so young, only sixteen,' said Arulraj. 'At the airport, many people came, including T.K. Murthy. He garlanded me with the garland he had brought for Mani Iyer and told me to be confident.'

In so many stories that I heard from the mrdangam makers, Murthy appears to be the one senior mrdangam artist who developed a relationship with the makers that went beyond the compulsions of necessity. Many of the old-timer makers recognise this.

'The concerts were only half-hour each and there were so many other programmes, like Ravi Shankar on the sitar. It was so difficult to work in the cold. The black paste would not hold and I had to use the heater in the room to make it stick,' Arulraj said. Do you remember any incident from that trip, I enquired. 'When I went there, it was snowing and I developed a fever. Mani Iyer gave me brandy saying it was a "kashayam" (herbal medicine). He instructed me to sleep and said the fever would subside. That was my first drink.' His first drink from the one and only Palghat Mani Iyer? Not bad!

According to Rajamani, Arulraj was not a very useful addition to their retinue. 'Those days, he didn't know anything. He slept all the time, hardly did any work.' When Arulraj returned, he headed straight to TVG's house. There was to be no more international travel for him. He said, 'They took my passport and did not give it back, so it expired.'

Arulraj's younger brother Jesudass would travel to the United States much later, in 1982, after which their cousin Rajamanickam made multiple trips to Canada. As Karnatik music became an obsession for brahmins living in different corners of the world, the need for makers increased exponentially. Most of those who lived abroad managed some basic work on their own, but would haul their instruments back to Madras for a makeover. In some cases, it was easier to invite the maker to their country, so their work and those of other artists and students in the area could all be done during that one visit. But even now, not too many makers actually travel abroad.

In spite of these serious logistical issues, artists never try to make the instrument themselves! As someone said, 'We cannot do that work.'

ANTONY'S YOUNGEST SON, JOHNSON KENNEDY, made his way to Madras only after his father passed away. Antony kept shuttling between Thanjavur and Madras, but his home was always Thanjavur. Johnson was his parents' pet. When he refused to reappear for a subject he had failed in during his ninth-class exams, they allowed him to drop out of school. Johnson wanted to train in the family line, and his father ultimately relented. 'So I started gurukulavasam with my father. He was happy that I learnt very fast and was so interested. He trusted me fully. He taught me with greater freedom than any of my brothers,' Johnson said.

The training process involved observing, absorbing and practising. Each of the brothers had to assist and watch. Over time, they would be given more critical work. As Soosainathan said, 'Selvam (Selvaraj) told me, I will work, you watch and learn. It is just like learning music. Not everything is taught, is it?'

Soosainathan came to Madras with his paternal uncle Dorairaj, who made mrdangams for shops and companies. Then he moved in with his maternal uncles, who worked with professional musicians. He worked first with Melgies, then Arulraj and Jesudass before finally becoming Selvaraj's star disciple. Soosainathan went to senior mrdangam artist Palghat Raghu's house as Jesudass's assistant in 1987, and became Raghu's right-hand man after Jesudass's time. Soosainathan too was initiated into the profession by his maternal granduncle, Antony. 'When I was in first class, I joined Shetty in Thanjavur. I would come back from school at 4 p.m. He would come home and call me and ask me to pull the leather ropes. Every day, this was my job. My fingers had boils, so writing was difficult. If I did not write, the teacher would beat me. Slowly, I learnt other things. I studied only until eighth class.'

Antony's last student was his grandson, his daughter Salethmary's son A. Sowriar. 'I am the eldest grandson and also his last student. He taught his four sons and then me. At Thiruvaiyaru, where the Thyagaraja aradhana happens, after bathing in the Kaveri, we burnt camphor and prayed at the Hanuman temple. Then he took me to the green room where K.J. Yesudas (the Karnatik and film singer) and others were seated. It was there that he gave me the tools and blessed me.'

But learning was never easy, and many of the elders were tough tutors. Sowriar almost lost a finger while training with his grandfather. Impatient with his grandson's slowness, he grabbed the boy's hands and, instead of cutting the rope, cut his finger. Sowriar has a scar, a permanent memory of his grandfather and teacher. Like every student, he would travel with Antony to Thirunageswaram, Mannargudi, Kumbakonam and other towns on work. But soon Antony slowed down, and the onus fell on Johnson, Arulraj and Jesudass to take Sowriar under their wings. By the time Sowriar was eighteen, he too had embraced Madras. He would work with his uncles and be paid daily wages that depended on the work he did, taking home anything between Rs 200–300 a day, and on a very good day, Rs 500.

But how do youngsters find their own feet and become independent? All of them have a similar story. The father or an uncle will direct a few clients towards the next-generation maker and the baton is handed over. If there is more than one son, then the work is divided amongst them. It is up to the

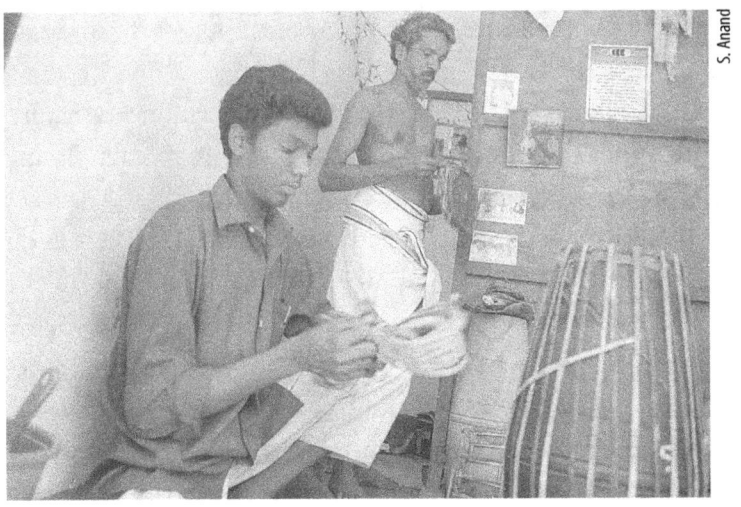

Jesudass with his son Edwin

young maker to then build and secure the relationship and make new ones. 'Johnson uncle told me to work for Thanjavur Subramaniam sir (mrdangam artist), and advised me to take whatever remuneration was given and to be obedient and honest. Till today, I am working for him,' said Sowriar. As for Johnson, he was always convinced that he could make it on his own. His skills and knowledge were put to the test by Thanjavur Upendran; passing that test set the ball rolling.

As Johnson put it, learning also meant understanding the artist's sense of 'sweetness in sound'. The more a maker works with an artist, the greater the synergy between them. This is not easy, because we are discussing a feeling, an abstract notion of an ideal that cannot be articulated in words. All the artist will say is that the mrdangam does not have the tone, tension, depth, roundedness, sharpness, feel or resonance that they are looking for. But what does this really mean? How does the maker translate that abstraction to a tangible sound? Over a period of time, the maker does indeed find a way to attain the perfection that the artist seeks. This is not a mind-reading game, but a matter of discovering the artist's emotional nature, the texture of his fingers, the strength of his strokes, playing style and his inherent musicality. To attain that tone, the maker will have to work minutely, and with scientific precision, on every aspect of the making process, from the selection of the skins to the final tuning touches.

'The happiness they get from a good instrument makes us happy. I don't stop until the mrdangam is a perfect fit for the artist's hands. And I make sure that they take delivery only when they are satisfied, even if it means another hour or two of work. They must exclaim with happiness, "Ahhh, this is good." But if they complain in disappointment, I feel terrible and cannot sleep. My mind will keep working on the problem,' said Arulraj.

Selvaraj described his joy at the sound of a particular mrdangam he had made for Karaikudi Mani. He called it stunning. Mani too spoke of how perfect that instrument was. However, he said that the instrument just *came together* perfectly. Though he mentioned Selvaraj as the maker, he did not directly credit him with creating the sound. All the elements fell into place, is what he said. It is true that, in every line of creative work, several things need to come together for that special perfection to happen. But nothing materialises without one extraordinary catalyst: the person who brings the known and unknown together in symphony.

In striking contrast, many mrdangam makers unabashedly acknowledge—often at the cost of being self-deprecating—how much they have picked up by watching and listening to the great artists.

Around 1991, one member of the Sevittian family set up a shop in Appar Swamy Koil Street, Mylapore—A. Gunaseelan, Antony's third son. By this time, mrdangam makers from Andhra and other Tamil communities had already organised their trade as a retail service outlet. Music shops were now more common and they needed mrdangams for sale and export. According to some members of the family, Gunaseelan was not a great mrdangam maker but had an eye for talent and also an entrepreneurial streak. He took on as his assistant Selvam, who was a superb mrdangam maker. Selvam did the majority of the work, while Gunaseelan took care of marketing, delivering and expanding the business. His timing was just perfect, and

A. Gunaseelan

he had a vision that no other maker in Madras did. The artists who came to him were highly sought after, which meant more concerts, and consequently more work for him. Guruvayur Dorai and the younger Thiruvarur Vaidyanathan were regulars. Teachers who had a large number of students, such as Kumbakonam Rajappa Iyer, also depended on him. Along with the teacher came all his students. Gunaseelan was also supplying mrdangams to music stores. This clever business management meant that as long as he lived—he passed away in 2002—Gunaseelan was making more money than anyone else in the family.

All this while, Parlandu's sons, Selvaraj and Melgies, were still going in and out of the homes of mrdangam artists, and Rajamanickam, until his demise in the early 2000s, also worked exclusively on personalised service. But as the new millennium dawned, younger members of the Antony family realised the benefits of separating their workplace from the homes of artists. In other words, this branch of the family slowly but steadily took over almost the entire business.

The old order of artists, consisting of people like Umayalpuram Sivaraman, Palghat Raghu, Karaikudi Mani and Trichy Sankaran, still got personal service. The makers were shrewd enough to realise that this would not change. An association with the old-timers also provided their work with a stamp of legitimacy among other mrdangam artists. It was a form of branding. When a young artist found out that a mrdangam used by his idol was made by Jesudass or Johnson, they would gravitate towards his shop and hope beyond hope to recreate that sound. This is perhaps an unconscious acceptance of the maker's brilliance. The establishment of shops also meant that, finally, the heavy leather work shifted from the maker's house to the kadai, or shop.

NORTH CHENNAI IS AN OLD neighbourhood consisting of suburbs such as Vyasarpadi, Korukkupet, Thiruvottriyur, Royapuram, Aynavaram, Tondiarpet and Ennore. It hosts a large dalit population, which largely makes a living as labourers, factory floor workers, fishers, auto drivers, daily-wage workers or scrap dealers. It is an area deeply scarred by negative stereotyping— dirty, uncouth, dangerous, a stay-away zone. A resident once told me that he never revealed where he lived when he went for a job interview. Culture is not a word commonly associated with north Chennai, simply because its culture is not that of the upper castes.

Mylapore is the very inverse of north Chennai. Almost every image of the city that is used by the government, travel houses and on television shows is Mylaporian in spirit. It is the centre of Chennai's brahmin sector, with any number of ancient temples and temple tanks, flower vendors and bangle sellers on the street, Hindu festivals, Karnatik music, Bharatanatyam, priests on scooters and the sea not too far away. As far as popular imagination goes, tradition, history and culture are all found in this tiny locality. But there are thousands who do not fit this pretty picture, living in tiny homes and housing-board flats abutting the polluted Buckingham Canal, which cuts through the heart of Mylapore—completely invisible in plain sight. It is easily forgotten that the beautiful Church of Our Lady of Light and the majestic San Thome Basilica are housed here too. The dominant image of Mylapore is one that obscures every non-brahmin tradition.

The Thanjavur makers did not visit this fort of the socio-cultural elite only to leave at sundown. There was no Keethukara Street beyond its gates. They lived in Mylapore and made it their territory, rubbing shoulders with their clients, who were mainly brahmin mrdangam artists. I asked many of the makers how they came to live here at the centre of brahminism. Their answer was simple: this is where the artists are, this where our work is and, hence, this is where we are. When Gunaseelan opened his shop in 1991, the city was still officially called Madras; by the time others from the family followed, it had been rechristened Chennai.

In fact, an entire area, stretching from Vivekananda College on the west up to Mundakanni Amman Koil Street on the east, has been the workplace of the Antony family and their relatives for nearly two decades. This area is home to a number of brahmin landmarks, including a lesser-known temple on the busy Royapettah High Road, the Appar Swamy Koil, which is where the nineteenth-century saint Appar Swamy is buried. It has no grand entrance, no tower marks its presence. In fact, the Hanuman temple diagonally opposite is far more popular. Behind the small temple runs Appar Swamy Koil Street, which is significant in Karnatik music history. On it was located the home of M.S. Gopalakrishnan, one of the greatest violinists India has ever produced. He was the son of Parur Sundaram

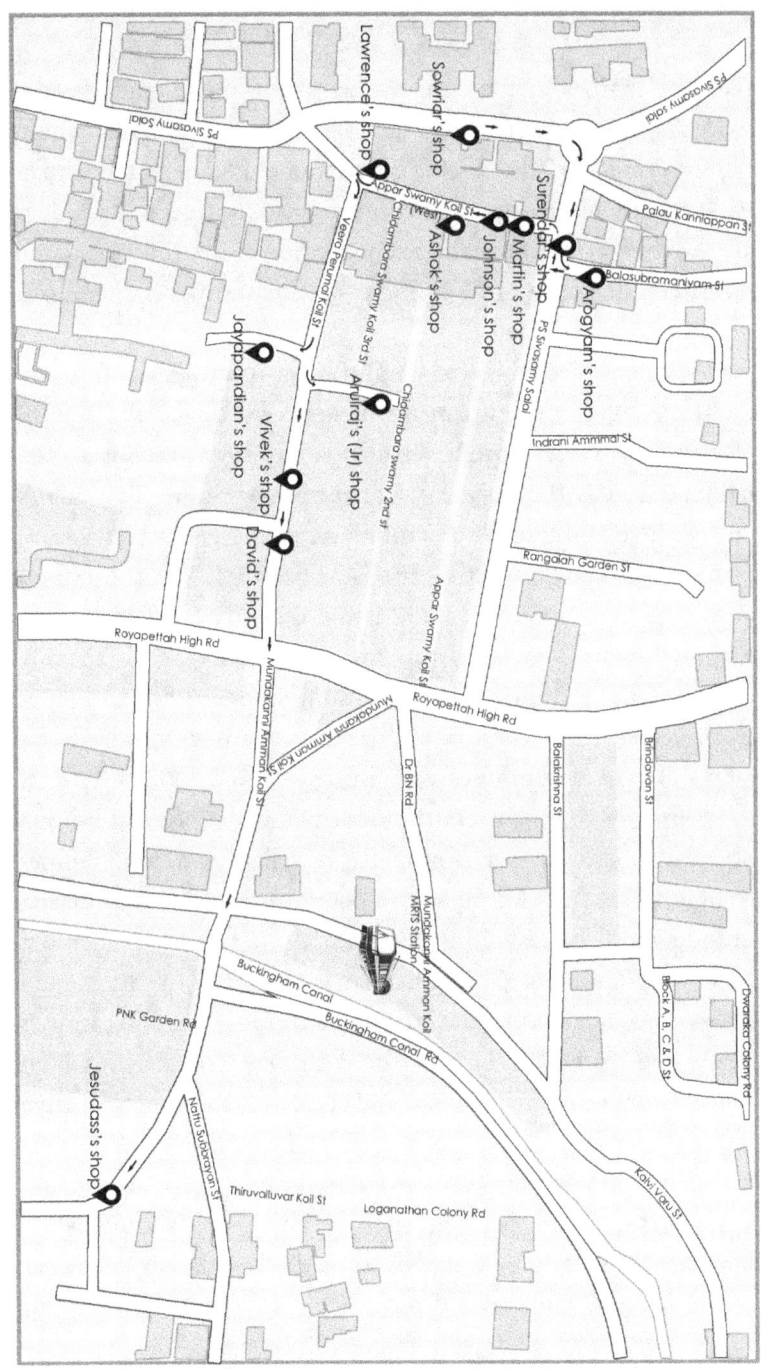

A map of the Thanjavur makers' neighbourhood in Chennai

Iyer, the man who took the violin to the north, and brother to M.S. Anantharaman, also a violin maestro, and the whole family lived on this street. Stories of M.S. Gopalakrishnan walking down the street and bargaining with vegetable vendors are part of Karnatik folklore. Unwritten in that history is the fact that the street is also home to the shops of mrdangam makers from Thanjavur.

A brief tour of this street and others around it, and a meet-and-greet with the mrdangam makers, will make the terrain clearer. Let us start from Vivekananda College, which is a local landmark, as is the adjacent Ramakrishna Home. This men's college boasts of illustrious alumni, including politicians, actors, businessmen and Karnatik musicians galore. It was the Hindu answer to Loyola College and Madras Christian College. When I studied there, it was sometimes teasingly called an 'agraharam' because of the high ratio of brahmin students. Sometimes it was referred to as 'laundry college' because just outside it was a dhobikhana, and clothes were hung out to dry on the street.

Opposite the main gate is a row of small houses and shops. Squeezed between tea shops, snacks sellers and little homes is Sowriar's shop. His in-the-process mrdangams are drying outside, and he is seated in a little room one step lower than the street—a common sight in Chennai, where layers of cement and tar have been added to the pavement and road, pushing houses below the road level. During the infamous Chennai floods of 2015, naturally, these dwellings and shops were flooded. As these thoughts cross my mind, a couple arrives on a scooter; they exchange a few words with Sowriar and carry away a mrdangam neatly cased in an army-green bag. There was a time when mrdangams were carried in canvas or cloth sacks on the backs of the makers. They would place a piece of cloth across their shoulders and lug one mrdangam on each shoulder all the way from their home to the artists' homes and back again.

About 50 metres north, at the roundtana (traffic island), there is a right turn. This street was once called Sullivan Garden Road but is now named after the legal luminary P.S. Sivaswamy Iyer. My parents lived there for a while, long before I came into the picture. A hundred feet down this road, down a small by-lane, is a blue grille, A. Arogyam's establishment. (A few months after the initial publication of this book in 2020, Arogyam passed away.) It is heaped with mrdangams, wooden frames,

Arogyam seated in his shop

ropes, cartons, skins cut into circles and water cans. Their home is above the kadai, and from the street, I can see the small veranda where Arogyam's father, Arulraj, and I conversed. Having spent his entire career in TVG's home, Arulraj had no ambitions of opening a shop, but Arogyam did and it has paid off. His unit is bustling with activity. This shop is larger than Sowriar's, and two of Arogyam's sons are seated on the floor, working on mrdangams: one is pulling at a rope to tighten it, while the other is checking the pitch of another instrument. A third person is fiddling with a cell phone, while his other hand is rubbing a large smooth pebble on the black spot of a mrdangam's dominant side. Watching over all of them are images of Jesus Christ and Mother Mary. There is another idol of a Christian saint whom I am unable to identify.

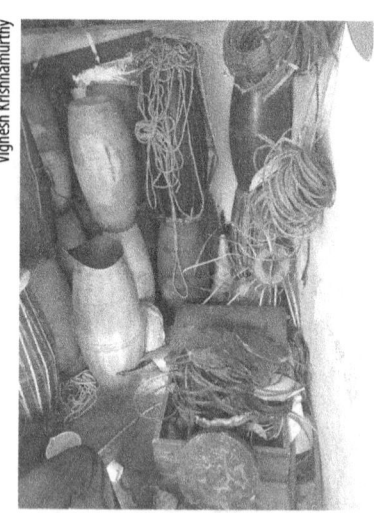
Vignesh Krishnamurthy

Surendar's road-facing space

From Arogyam's, we turn back towards the main road, fighting our way through the incessant traffic. There are horns sounding everywhere. Water tankers, the leaky road monsters that have come to symbolise Chennai, edge other vehicles off their path. On the other side of the road, I notice an orange tub, like the containers in which washed glasses are stored in hotel pantries. We peep in and find neatly cut skins arranged in sets. This is J. Surendarpeliks's workplace. Antony's grandson, a big-built, soft-spoken young man, is known to everyone as Surendar.

His shop has two spaces. The shopfront is a small opening, but just adjacent to it, set back a little from the road, is a typical Mylapore lower middle-class house that he has rented for Rs 15,000. Surendar has two or three people working with him. The room is full of mrdangams, about forty-five, on racks, on the floor, everywhere. A wooden mrdangam frame even serves as the stand for a water dispenser! I also spy a hair dryer, which is used to dry skin quickly, especially when the artists are in a hurry.

We leave the main road behind and enter the inner lanes. I almost miss a mrdangam shop on my left, at the corner of Appar Swamy Koil (West) Street and Appar Swamy Koil Street. (A fine example of how confusing street names are in India.) A massive poster of Liberation Tigers of Tamil Eelam chief Prabhakaran, issued by 'Association for Tamil Awakening', catches my attention. Hugging the poster is a blue-walled den with an odd inset slope, indicating a stairway to the first floor. This was Martin's outlet. Martin—Arogyamary's son, another of Antony's grandsons—trained under his uncle Johnson. He is not in but the shop is open; a couple of mrdangams rest on the floor and there seems to be no fear of theft. It could be that the man seated on the opposite side was watching the premises for him. These streets are lined with small provision stores, traders, tailoring shops, photocopying shops, single-room clinics, pharmacies, tea stalls and mobile repair shops. Much of the road itself has been eaten up by two-wheelers. Whether they belong to customers or the people who live on the floors above, we can't be sure.

A few steps more, and there's a shop on the left at an elevation from the road. Here, a man sits shaving a leather rope. This is Johnson, Antony's youngest son, the chellapillai, favoured child. You need to climb three steps to reach him. He looks like one of those moneylenders in Hindi films, seated behind a low accounts desk—a settu we would call him in Tamil. The shop is no more than 40 sq. ft and has mrdangams lined up almost to the ceiling on a metal rack. A few of his awards hang on the wall behind. Johnson is usually chewing betel nut or gutka and casually tapping on a mrdangam. He has moved shop in this area multiple times. Both Johnson and Martin pay about Rs 4,000 as monthly rent.

Johnson in his elevated shop

Just off Appar Swamy Koil Street and opposite Durgaiamman temple, is the new kid on the block: Surendar's youngest brother J. Ashok, who opened his own shop in early 2019. Ashok may be new but he is not jobless; in fact, he already has an assistant.

We are back on Appar Swamy Koil Street, heading south towards a minor three-way junction. In the 1990s, there used to be a shop at this junction. I remember that it used to display mrdangams practically on the pavement. Now I know that was Gunaseelan's shop. His son G. Lawrence moved across the road, right next to an auto stand behind Appa Stores. As we enter Lawrence's shop, we hear mrdangams of different pitches being simultaneously checked. He has his hands full, but still finds time to play with his little child. Lawrence remembers that his father had to pay only Rs 700 a month for the shop across the street, while he pays Rs 8,000 today. After Gunaseelan died, Selvam, his right-hand man, branched out on his own and so Lawrence had to begin afresh.

Next, we walk towards Royapettah High Road via Veera Perumal Koil Street. A few blocks down, there is a Vinayaka temple and a perpendicular lane where I remember meeting Jesudass. His shop used to be on this street, but has now moved. Jayapandian, Gunaseelan's wife's nephew, has set up his workshop there. Several people from Jesudass and Gunaseelan's extended family are also mrdangam makers now. There seems to be no way to enter Jayapandian's shop, though; plastic water cans block access. Interestingly, right in front of the shop is an unused hand pump. Jayapandian has painted his phone number on the blue wall along with the image of a mrdangam just above, and two butterflies below to add visual appeal. His shop is closed because he is also the on-campus mrdangam serviceman at Kalakshetra.

On the left side of Veera Perumal Koil Street is a small connecting road where R. Arulraj Jr, Jesudass's nephew through marriage, works. Dressed in a pink-and-black chequered shirt and purple lungi, Arulraj Jr is a minor maker in the professional circuit. But he reels out the names of music stores he supplies to: Lakshman Sruti, Saraswathi Musicals, Girish Musicals and Dawood Musicals. The demand is constant and the numbers add up.

Back on Veera Perumal Koil Street, there's a shop on every corner. Dressed like an IIT student, in a cream-brown shirt and worn-out jeans, J. Vivek is Surendar's younger brother. He is probably the first member of the Thanjavur family to open a music shop—Sahana Musicals on Sivaswamy Road—but he still has his mrdangam shop here. Trained under his uncle Johnson and cousin Arogyam, Vivek looks like a cool but serious young man. And this next-generation maker does mean serious business.

A little further down is the Selva Vinayaka temple, with its brightly painted idols on top and on its pillars. Right beside the main entrance is an independent room, almost like a shrine. This is Arulraj Jr's stepbrother David's shop. He has a large board right on top that says 'Kudanthai David, specialist mrdangam maker (sales and service)'. David and Arulraj Jr do not belong to Thanjavur; they come from Kumbakonam (Kudanthai is the old name for the town). Following Arulraj Jr and David, others from their neighbourhood in Ammangudi (near Kumbakonam), like Gopinath and Srikanth, have moved to Chennai and joined the mrdangam-making industry.

Wait a minute! I think I got that right. There might have been a plan for a Muruga shrine here originally. On top of David's board is a small statue of Muruga and his two consorts, Valli and Devayani. It appears that the plan was abandoned, and David makes mrdangams in the would-be sanctum. He

David's workplace within a Muruga shrine

caters primarily to Bharatanatyam mrdangam players, and so, although he is not known to Karnatik concert artists, he has enough work. David is young and casual, the local fun-loving lad. Arulraj Jr and David are the only ones who clearly state on a wall display that they also work on tabla and dholak. Others may also service these instruments, but their mainstay is the mrdangam and they do not want any other message to go out.

We are now at the end of Veera Perumal Koil Street and stepping on to Royapettah High Road, right in front of the

Hanuman temple. Across the road, we walk on to Mundakanni Amman Koil Street. Near this well-known Amman temple, deep inside a small corridor that says 'Mylai Laundry', is Jesudass's shop. His son Edwin works there in the evening after his day job as a health inspector with the Public Health Department. On the wall, 'They Make Mridangams Talk' says a *Deccan Chronicle* article, which also carries a picture of a middle-aged Jesudass. Right next to it is an award he received, instituted in the memory of Palghat Raghu with whom he had worked for many years. Lying on the floor are mrdangam bags, ropes, tools such as screwdrivers, cutting pliers, a drilling machine, spanners, metal hooks and nuts and bolts. Jesudass opened his first shop in 1999 and moved to many locations before settling down here. No one is at the shop when we arrive, but a man from the office opposite it gets chatting. He did not know that his neighbour was a member of the first family of mrdangam-making.

But what is with the blue? Many of the mrdangam shops are completely blue on the inside or outside, or have at least one wall painted an unmistakable bright blue. Is it colour vastu? Was it just the makers, or are people in Mylapore crazy about blue? Having spent so much time with many mrdangam makers, I would be utterly surprised if this was indeed the blue used as a symbol of dalit resistance.

In less than a kilometre, we visited twelve shops belonging to the same extended family. If I had been willing to take an auto and travel a little further south to Mandavali, I would have found two more makers connected to this family. Selvaraj is on his own there, and not far from him, Thanjavur Bhaskar, Sevittian's sister's great-grandson.

For the entire family, religion is a fluid idea, the temple and the church interchangeable. They are Christian without a doubt, in faith and in prayer, but not in socio-religious dogma. The pictures on their walls too reveal the ease with which they occupy two worlds: Mary, Jesus, a mrdangam-playing Nandi, Saraswati, Amman and Ganapati share space. And there is one image that brings all the sons and grandsons of Antony together—a framed copy of an article in *The Hindu* featuring

Antony with his wife, Ranjitham

the patriarch Antony. This one item finds a place somewhere in their shops: on the wall, in a corner or on a shelf. The Thanjavur tradition of mrdangam-making is now Antony's legacy.

But is the competition friendly between these brothers and cousins, I wondered.

'Our families all function independently. Work we may share, but the family units are all separate. We all come together at family functions and have a great time,' said Johnson. He suggests that, in the older days, they would be happy to help the client of a brother or cousin in an emergency but would never poach him. This professional code is missing today, he said, and then specified that there's no problem within the Antony family, only with other relatives he has trained. Arulraj emphatically states that there is no competition between any of them: 'We are all together.'

Presumably, there are professional rivalries within this family too, but what I gathered for sure is that the dominance of the Antony family has not gone down well with other members of the larger Sevittian clan. This may have caused family feuds off and on. Selvaraj had stories about Rajamanickam betraying him, and he complained about the jealousy he faced from his uncle's families and blamed them for the loss of work. Though they have trained each other's family members, the descendants of Shengol, Parlandu and Antony were and are competing for the same market. And each branch of the Sevittian family has maintained little inner-family clubs. Unfortunately, the sheer numbers of the Antony branch makes them more powerful than anyone else today. This is a mega shift from the days when Parlandu was the be-all and end-all of mrdangam-making. Simply put, Antony's family has dethroned the king.

3

THE MADRAS MAKERS

Old cinema aficionados reminisce wistfully about the lip-smacking peach melba at Elphinstone's Soda Fountain in the Madras of yore. In the days before multiplexes took over, Elphinstone was a popular cinema on Mount Road—the artery that cut across the city, and in and around which were all the major cinemas. In those days, theatres tended to be monolingual. So, Elphinstone, Odeon (Melody) and Midland screened English films, and Gaiety and Chitra Talkies Tamil films.

Situated just off Mount Road, in the multicultural suburb of Triplicane, was Star Theatre, the hub for Hindi films. The home of the Nawab of Arcot, the Wallajah mosque and the Parthasarathy temple, this area has been the symbol of an organic inter-religious living for a few centuries or more. But it has also been vulnerable to communal disturbances. An old resident recalls, 'Star Theatre was located in the Muslim-majority area of Triplicane. Some of my Sindhi friends also lived on Wallajah Road. The Hindu area was around Big Street, near the Parthasarathy temple. We had to navigate crowded roads in the area to reach the theatre on Triplicane High Road. It was surrounded by small eateries.' It is said that the film *Madhumati* ran in this theatre for more than fifty weeks. I remember that my father, who dabbled in films, was upset he could not acquire distribution rights for it.

These were my associations with the area—and then I discovered that, right opposite Star Theatre, Madras's most respected mrdangam maker had set up shop. Until I began asking questions about the Madras tradition of mrdangam-making, no one so much as mentioned his name. Everyone spoke of Parlandu and the Thanjavur family, who only came to Madras in the mid-twentieth century, and not of this man who lived and worked here well before any of them arrived. Perhaps the centrality of Thanjavur in the Karnatik mind had a role to play in this. This also meant that many of the musicians who lived in the city of Madras were forgotten. After all, mrdangam artists such as Venu Nayakar and Madras Kannan did not receive the recognition that was their due.

Although he is counted among the best mrdangam players of all time, Palani Subramania Pillai's ascent on the concert ladder may have been slower because he too was not based in Thanjavur. His isai vellalar caste was a big factor, of course. As was the fact that he was left-handed, which gave people an excuse for refusing to share the stage with him. The presence of a left-hander would require the violinist to switch positions with him. This is necessitated by the fact that the dominant side of the mrdangam needs to face the audience. Pillai's climb was slow and arduous, and not as fulfilling as a musician of his calibre deserved. C.S. Murugabhoopathy, a tough and reclusive artist who would not bow before anyone, paid a graver price. Belonging to the servai community of Tamil Nadu's Sivaganga region, he used to live further south before he made Madras his home. If Palani's dreams remained unfulfilled, Murugabhoopathy's were suppressed. He was undoubtedly a genius, yet he was never given the respect, encomiums or opportunities a brahmin in his place would have naturally received. Not only was Murugabhoopathy from outside the circle, he was also not subservient. When he died in 1998, many did not even know his name.

Until the mrdangam maker C. Varadan mentioned it to me, I did not know that Murugabhoopathy had married the politician Muthuramalinga Thevar's half-sister. In the past four decades, the thevar community has become one of the state's most powerful political castes, and Muthuramalinga Thevar's statue that guards Mount Road at the well-known Nandanam junction is a formidable symbol of that power. Thevars who belong to southern Tamil Nadu and the servais who belong to Sivaganga district occupy a similar social position and status in Tamil Nadu's caste structure. But all this made no difference in the brahminical circles. Political might does not translate to cultural prominence.

Unsurprisingly then, the already marginalised mrdangam maker is easily forgotten. Much like our mystery maker of Triplicane, Munusami. Before him, his uncle Chandrayya too worked out of Triplicane. Munusami trained under his uncle and, when he was ready, moved into a shop in the same area. He was the mainstay for mrdangam artists in Madras, and also helped those who visited from out of town for a concert. 'Dakshinamurthy Pillai (the legendary percussionist) used to get work done by Chandrayya. He worked on the terrace of a house in Triplicane, and Dakshinamurthy Pillai would sit there with him. For simple work, he would pay Chandrayya Rs 1 and gift him the angavastram or veshti he had received at the previous concert,' said Madras Kannan.

Kannan was the mrdangam artist on almost all Colombia 78rpm records, and was a staff artist at All India Radio. He did not belong to a family of musicians nor was he a brahmin. His father, Aadimulam Mudaliar, owned a textile shop in Madras. And for a brief period, in order to develop his business, Mudaliar moved to Burma with his family. But once he noticed musical flair in his son, he decided Madras had to be home. Kannan first came under the tutelage of Peethambara Desai, who lived in the ancient suburb of Triplicane in Madras, and later on learnt from Ramadas Rao in Thanjavur.

His mrdangam tone and style were hugely popular. People were in love with the timbre of his instrument—the credit for which must go to Munusami's workmanship. A busy man, Munusami had no time for personalised mrdangam care. So, when artists began moving to the metropolis, they had to change their ways. 'He was an extraordinary artisan. He worked for me from 1952 to '54. From Venu Nayakar to Madras Kannan, everyone used to go to him. He would say, "leave your instrument here and I will come to it later",' said T.V. Gopalakrishnan, who moved away from Munusami because he did not get the attention he sought.

But others accepted the maker's terms. Umayalpuram Sivaraman would take his mrdangams across on a cycle rickshaw.

By the time Guruvayur Dorai from Kerala met Munusami in 1949–50, the maker was already an old man. He would take a pinch of snuff now and then, and generously offer Dorai some too. Munusami had a discerning ear, and helped younger artists understand the nuances of the mrdangam's myriad tones as well as the tuning of the instrument with precision. Even with clients who were extremely fussy, Munusami would have the final word. 'Karaikudi Muthu Iyer used to sit with him from 10.30 in the morning until 4 p.m. Finally, Munusami would tell him that it was okay now, and would ask him to take the mrdangam as it was and play. Only when Munusami said okay would Karaikudi Muthu Iyer accept it,' Dorai recollects.

Karaikudi Mani, who rose to fame in the 1970s, called Munusami 'supremely intelligent'. 'Triplicane High Road was a noisy place, yet if you told him you needed an instrument at a certain pitch, he would deliver it perfectly tuned,' he said.

According to Sivaraman, Munusami's brother Keshavulu was a tambura artist at All India Radio. But Varadan said that the brother's name was Ethirajan, and he played the tambura at the Madras Music College and assisted his brother in the shop. As far as I could tell, Munusami was Telugu-speaking. The name could be Tamil or Telugu, but since his uncle and teacher was Chandrayya, it is likely that they were Telugu-speaking. Madras had a large Telugu population, many living in the northern parts of the city, while others, particularly the economically upwardly mobile, went on to occupy interior suburbs. Nothing more is known about Munusami or his brother. Nobody knows what happened to them, when he passed away, and what his children are doing. Unfortunately, there is nowhere to look, but it seems clear that no one in the next generation took to mrdangam-making.

Timelines are always difficult to fix in oral histories because people remember relationships and experiences rather than dates. When the memory is strong, the incident appears recent, but if the memory is inconsequential or needs to be forgotten, it is described as something that happened a long time ago. It is from these emotional imprints that we attempt to place people, movements and changes.

Towards the end of Munusami's raj in Madras, another maker walked into this Karnatik city. Hailing from the village of Pandur near Tiruvallur, Telugu-speaking K.M. Venkatesan might have learnt the craft from his grandfather. A man of multiple trades, he also played the mrdangam at the local terukkuttu (sacral/theatrical art form usually practised by castes at the lower end of the scale). Besides, he worked as a coal man in the railways, and taught at a school. I am not sure what he taught since Varadan does not mention his education. After living in towns like Kanchipuram and practising these various trades, he finally settled down in Madras and established himself as a mrdangam maker. His wife Lakshmi Ammal decided to bring along Varadan, her nephew (brother's son), to Madras and train him to assist her husband. Varadan, who lived in the village Kamarpandiyam near Tiruvallur, was around eleven years old when he was packed off to Ayanavaram in Madras to live with them. This must have been in the 1950s.

Varadan is named after the deity Varadaraja Perumal of Kanchipuram, and he said that they belong to the balija naidu caste. Balijas were traditionally traders, many of them involved in selling bangles, salt, etc. But they have also become involved

K.M. Venkatesan

in cultivation. There are many theories regarding their history, and since the caste hierarchies of India are so complex and location-specific, it is difficult to negotiate the maze of sub-castes. In the 1909 publication *Castes and Tribes of Southern India*, Edgar Thurston writes, 'Concerning the origin of this caste, several traditions exist, but the most probable is that which represents them as a recent offshoot of the kapu or reddi caste. The caste is rather a mixed one, for they will admit, without much scruple, persons who have been expelled from their proper caste or who are a result of irregular unions.' He goes on to mention the various occupations in which balija naidus engaged—hawkers, post runners, bakers, butlers, hotel keepers, head coolies and railway station masters. Thurston specifically noted that the balijas in Tirupati were involved in the red sanders woodcarving industry.

Varadan's village is about a hundred kilometres from Tirupati, but his family had no connection to woodcarving. He said their hereditary profession was agriculture. His father also climbed palm trees to collect leaves for thatching huts. He stresses that they were not toddy-tappers. There is some ambiguity, though, because Varadan said that his uncle learnt mrdangam-making from his own grandfather. It appears unlikely that a community would enter this hide-related profession unless there was a caste-occupation match. Of course, economic needs could have brought them into this fold.

'We lived in a hut on Ayanavaram Main Road and worked from there. We would get letters from artists like Madras Kannan, Palghat Kunjumani Iyer and C.S. Murugabhoopathy asking us to come and work, and we would go.' Venkatesan took his nephew everywhere, including the Boag Road home of Palani Subramania Pillai. Varadan said, 'Palani used to play well; good gumki,' referring to a specific stroke that was Palani's trademark. Venkatesan would have continued to work out of his home far away in Ayanavaram, if not for Murugabhoopathy's intervention. Bhoopathy, as he was referred to, helped Venkatesan start a shop in Maddala Narayanan Street in Mylapore—a permanent work space. This must have been in the late 1950s. A stone's throw from the Kapaleeswarar temple, on a street named after a suddha maddalam (a larger two-sided drum) artist, this shop still stands just as it did back then. The area abounded in musicians; Venkatesan could not have asked for a better spot. 'We had to pay a rent of

Rs 12 per month when we began, and now it has gone to thousand-something,' said Varadan. By the time the Thanjavur makers set foot in Madras, Venkatesan had already started operating from this address.

Every musician worth his salt has visited this shop. According to Varadan, even the great Mani Iyer would eat his tiffin at Rayar's Mess and then sit in their shop in Mylapore. Palghat Raghu too used to come, Varadan said. These must have been times when their regular Thanjavur makers were unavailable. The mainstays for Venkatesan were Murugabhoopathy and the stalwart Vellore Ramabhadran. Until his demise in 2012, Varadan did almost all of Ramabhadran's work. Sivaraman too worked for some time with Venkatesan, especially after his own fallout with Rajamanickam. 'That day I spent 10–12,000 rupees. I took all my mrdangams to Venkatesan's shop and told him to change the muttus,' Sivaraman said.

Dorai told me that Venkatesan had the unusual habit of tuning the mrdangam with his left hand, though he used his right for all other work. Not much more is known about Venkatesan. But he was in the business for long and is acknowledged as a very good maker. Varadan himself does not say much about his uncle except that everyone came looking for him. Venkatesan most likely passed away in the late 1960s, after which Varadan took over. Today, age has caught up with the nephew too, and not much work comes the way of this historic shop. Nevertheless, Varadan sets out every day from his Ayanavaram home and opens shop at around 10 a.m. and closes at 6 p.m. He also seems to have young boys to help. Varadan's son works in the Chennai Electricity Board and his daughters are married. He is the last mrdangam maker in this family—the only inheritor of his uncle and father-in-law K.M.Venkatesan's skill.

Having brought their nephew to Madras and taught him the work, Venkatesan and Lakshmi Ammal decided to marry their daughter to him. 'My aunt had a lot of affection for me and, since I had worked very hard for the house, they let me marry her.' This self-deprecation ran through our interview. Descriptions of meeting musicians or working with them were laced with expressions of gratitude. In every story he narrated, he was either being acknowledged by a musician, seeking something from them or being given a gift by them. His shop is filled with pictures of himself with various musicians and a few of his awards. A colleague of Varadan pointed to this as a sign of self-obsession, but I did not see it that way. My questions on the complexities of his life and relationships did not seem to

Vignesh Krishnamurthy

Varadan and his wall of awards

interest Varadan. He spoke with resignation, requesting support. Other makers told me that he does not know anything, is only an ordinary worker. I speculate that perhaps this affable man was not the best in the business and banked on his uncle's skills and reputation to come up in life, and an inferiority complex engulfs his psyche.

The most beautiful part of our conversation was the elegant simplicity with which he described the music of artists. 'M. Chandrasekhar (violinist) was set for Madurai Somu—romba super. At a concert in Mettur, people just lifted him up. He played so well.' Of Ramabhadran's playing technique, he said, 'He provided the groove so beautifully, it would come along like jilu, jilu, jilu.' That was his verbal approximation of the pleasantly sonorous gait that a well-tuned mrdangam has when its bell-like ring moves in tandem with the melody. This is a vivid description of Ramabhadran's style. He went on to tell me how Murugabhoopathy's wife would applaud her husband, especially when he used his unique left-hand fingering technique. 'Bale raja, bale raja,' she would say. In a world that typically speaks in a complicated, obfuscatory manner, here is a man who does not belong to its interiors but describes the music as it is felt and seen.

FOR FAMILIES WITH SOCIAL PRIVILEGE, tales of our forefathers are the background music to growing up. Their achievements, benevolence, struggles, courage and kindness are the family's storied past. With every generational telling, it swells and becomes reflex memory. We may never have met these great-grandfathers, but there is sense of pride in their illustriousness.

Even if we have never visited the village home of our forefathers, saying its name out loud gives us a sense of ownership. For many, an annual pilgrimage to worship their family deity is not just an occasion for prayer but also strengthens their notion of 'roots'. This entire celebration of the past and present, which is couched in belonging, comes from caste privilege. The privileged find ways of recording memories—through narrations, paintings, vessels, heirlooms, rituals, clothes and recipes. And within these carriers are transferred character sketches, jokes, smiles, disagreements and celebrations. The negative characters in our families too are given a role; their actions condemned, trivialised or jocularly set aside.

But for an individual from a marginalised caste, history is a burden of emotional, intellectual, aesthetic and economic denial and deprivation. Memory decides that forgetting is its job in the hope that the scars might disappear and explanations become unnecessary. Father and grandfather are remembered by name and function alone. Villages are not remembered, timelines erased and, often, names are blurred or altered. Even that which is recalled is not alive; it is just an event, something that happened. In a sense, this also defines how their present is viewed by society at large. These are people who have been barred from the memory of culture and society, looked at as tools, their entire intellectual and emotional being reduced to the service they provide. They too are socialised to believe in this contract.

It took me months to find G. Krishnamurthy; no one knew where he lived. I was told that he may be found in Arogyam's shop. He has become hard of hearing, they said. Finally I tracked him down through Sowriar. We were to meet in the afternoon, but Krishnamurthy and his wife had been waiting for me since morning. Dressed in an off-white shirt and white veshti, Krishnamurthy was all ready to speak. I did not know then that he was living in utter penury, on occasion sleeping on the pavement near Sowriar's shop, and suffering from asthma, which he said he developed only after he opened the mrdangam shop. 'It is only because of his wife that this man is even alive,' said Sowriar. Unlike the others in this profession, whose children were also mrdangam makers, Krishnamurthy's son was a dynamic percussionist. He was part of light music orchestras that travelled abroad for performances, and was on the verge of forming his own group. All of a sudden, he passed away. The loss of his son hit Krishnamurthy hard; he was broken. He shut his shop and the household collapsed. Until then, his shop was flourishing, and he had trained many makers—including the Thanjavur maker Gunaseelan (because his father Antony would not teach him). Sowriar too had learnt the nuances of tabla-making from him. Krishnamurthy now lives a hand-to-mouth existence, doing some work for Sowriar and Arogyam.

As always, I began the conversation by enquiring about Krishnamurthy's home town. Tirupati, he said. When I asked where exactly, all he would say was 'beyond Tirupati'. A little later, when I probed again, he reluctantly said, 'Tatiguntapalayam.'

'It's okay, it's not important. No one from the family lives there now.'

Were you born there, I asked.

Yes, he said, only to withdraw. 'I do not know.'

I don't know if his reluctance was because of something that had happened to his family there or because it somehow relates to his caste identity. A Google search told me that there are two villages near Tirupati with similar names: Tatiguntapalem and Tatiguntapalle. It is likely that he was referring to the former. His family was involved in some form of terukkuttu, he said. Krishnamurthy's father died when he was just ten, so it was his grandfather who told him that they danced, sang and also did mrdangam work. They travelled to many villages, enacting stories from the Mahabharata and Ramayana in their kuttu performances.

Krishnamurthy's grandmother worked as a maid at the General Hospital in Madras, while his uncles Chinnasami and Subramani lived in Guntur, making mrdangams and tablas. After learning the basics from his grandfather, fifteen-year-old Krishnamurthy was sent to Guntur to learn mrdangam- and tabla-making from Subramani. In 1960, Subramani received a letter from Madras saying that the reed used by Indian clarinet players was available for sale, and set out for the city with his young nephew. Unfortunately, when they arrived, it was no longer in stock. Subramani left for Guntur, leaving the boy behind with his grandmother. It is not clear what prompted Krishnamurthy to stay on in Madras. He explained that he later went to his village and brought his mother and older sister back with him. He had lost his two brothers by then.

Krishnamurthy's first job in Madras was at Venkatesan's shop in Maddala Narayanan Street. A few months later, he left. All Krishnamurthy said about it was, 'I didn't like working like a slave for someone.' As destiny would have it, he headed to Munusami's shop opposite Star Theatre. Munusami himself was no more, but Krishnamurthy worked out of that space, and this provided some sustenance to Munusami's wife. Later, he moved to another rented space in Appar Swamy Koil Street. He was the first mrdangam maker to open a shop in this area, way back in the late 1960s. It was only the third major mrdangam shop in Madras, after Munusami's and Venkatesan's. He no longer remembers the artists he worked for, but Madurai T. Srinivasan, who was *the* mrdangam artist in the Madras film industry, was his main customer. P. Ravikumar, his student, suggests that Krishnamurthy's work was geared towards the needs of the film world rather than the concert stage. (A fascinating discussion to which we will return later in the book.)

Courtesy: A. Sowriar

Krishnamurthy at work

As soon as he established a shop and work picked up, though, Krishnamurthy realised that he needed help. It is not clear when, but he brought his cousin Ramakrishnan from

Thimmasamudram (near Kalahasti, Andhra Pradesh) to Madras. Though Krishnamurthy says that Ramakrishnan was his aunt's son, the relationship may have actually been more complex. Krishnamurthy taught Ramakrishnan everything he knew, but did not foresee that his protégé would one day surpass him.

In 1977, the inevitable happened. Ramakrishnan opened his own store right next to Krishnamurthy's with help from Thanjavur Upendran—which might have added insult to injury for Krishnamurthy. Ramakrishnan became the man in demand. Karaikudi Mani, Thanjavur Upendran, Mannargudi Easwaran, Madrimangalam Swaminathan, Srimushnam Raja Rao, Tiruvarur Bhaktavatsalam and, occasionally, even the Antony-loyalist T.K. Murthy worked with him. When I asked Krishnamurthy whether the separation was bitter, he replied, 'No, no fights, nothing of that sort. How could I fight with him after having taught him all the work? His work was good. He was my student. Karaikudi Mani liked him a lot. I was working there first and then introduced him. They then stayed on because they could tell him to do anything and he would work relentlessly.'

Rajam, Krishnamurthy's wife, too painted a picture of cordiality. 'He left amicably and, since he had his own family, set up a separate shop. He died here only.' It might be true that, when he moved out, things were still relatively peaceful. After the move, though, the relationship soured. Ramakrishnan drew away Krishnamurthy's customers and this caused a lot of heartburn. One day, it is said, Krishnamurthy hurled his slippers at his cousin's shop. But Ramakrishnan's life soon descended into alcoholism, which his son M.R. Jyotiprakash attributed to the split. In spite of all the unpleasantness, however, Ravikumar—

who was Ramakrishnan's brother-in-law—was able to learn from both Krishnamurthy and Ramakrishnan. His basics came from Krishnamurthy, but he moved on to Ramakrishnan for advanced training. These were adjustments the cousins were willing to make, despite their professional rivalry.

Though Rajam said that they belong to the balija naidu community, other members of the family said that they were adi andhra or dravida. One member said he was kapu reddi on one side and chakkiliyar/adi andhra on the other. Another simply said SC, or Scheduled Caste. The other makers and mrdangam players say that Krishnamurthy belongs to the caste that makes shoes: chakkiliyar. For the Thanjavur makers, Christianity was an escape from caste nomenclature. At least to the outside world, they would just say, 'We are Christian.' The memory of their caste label was suppressed. This does not mean that their lives changed dramatically, or that caste dissolved, but they had the privilege of at least partial disconnection and that was empowering in some ways. One maker of Thanjavur descent told me that younger mrdangam artists today are surprised that they are Christan but never ask the makers about their caste. The makers from Andhra, however, are still mired in these associations, which explained their discomfort with, and fear of, discussing caste. I wondered whether balija naidu was their security vest against stigmatisation.

It was not my intention to root up the caste locations of makers, and I did not follow that line of enquiry further with them. But it is a fact that we need these specifics to understand the relationship between the castes involved in the work vis-à-vis the ones that need the work done. I must add that the line between understanding and insensitively prying is razor thin, especially when the interviewer comes from privilege, and I had to pause and check myself during these conversations.

Tondur Society in Tada is a government residential development that provided three acres of land and a plot for a house for those among the dalit community who had studied until class ten, Ravikumar informed me. He spent most of his childhood in Tondur but later moved to Kalahasti for his schooling. He lived there until he completed his ninth class. But right from when he was in class four, Ravikumar would visit his brother-in-law Ramakrishnan every summer, and help him with his work. He moved to Madras for his tenth class and enrolled in a matriculation school in T. Nagar. His uncle had other plans for the boy, and decided that he should learn to play the mrdangam rather than make it, and so Ravikumar registered at the Tamil Nadu Government Music College. This did not last long (with caste-based discrimination driving his decision to leave), and Ravikumar was soon a full-time mrdangam maker. He worked in Chennai for many years but eventually felt unable to keep up with the competition and pressure. Today, he is back in Tondur Society, waiting for his land to be bought by the government, who in turn sell it to private companies. The three-acre mango orchard has already been sold, and it is only a matter of time before they want his home. 'They are buying it, but many people have objected.' Where will you go, I asked. 'Either Chennai or Tirupati.' Ravikumar works for many mrdangam artists in the Tirupati belt, and also supplies to artists in Hyderabad. He has only a few clients in Chennai.

To round off the Ramakrishnan family, I spoke to his son Jyotiprakash, who was born only in 1983 and saw very little of his father. He learnt his trade from Krishnamurthy, before coming under the care of the Thanjavur maker Gunaseelan. Today, Jyotiprakash has his own shop in West Mambalam, Chennai. Another relative–student of Ramakrishnan, Radhakrishnan, works out of T. Nagar in Chennai and has the custom of artists such as Guruvayur Dorai. Unlike in the case of Venkatesan and Varadan, a few members of this family continue to be makers, but they are on the fringes now.

THE RELATIONSHIP BETWEEN THE KRISHNAMURTHY–Ramakrishnan family and the Thanjavur makers is difficult to describe. They each express mutual respect, affection, professional superiority over the other and sarcasm about the other's abilities. It is an uncomfortable and curious relationship, true, but there is a real bond between them too. They have learnt from and helped one another out. Ramakrishnan was possibly the only maker that the Thanjavur people thought of as their equal, making it difficult for them to ignore him. And there is no doubt that it was the Telugu-speaking cousins, Krishnamurthy and Ramakrishnan, who paved the way for Appar Swamy Koil Street to become Chennai's mrdangam-making hub.

The Thanjavurians do not easily acknowledge other makers. I would get responses such as 'I have not seen their work', 'we have to see it while they are working' and so on. Condescension dripped from their words. When asked if there was anything special about the Madras work, I got this response: 'I don't know. I go to work at 9 a.m. and return only at 9 p.m.'

As for the makers from Andhra, they make it a point to tell you that they were already trained when they came here. They don't want anyone to get the impression that they trained under the Thanjavur people. The Thanjavur people are boastful, they say, with evident rancour. One Telugu-speaking maker gently suggested that the customer should decide. 'This work is difficult, irrespective of who does it,' he said. Other than this, I just got contemptuous retorts like 'All of them are big people', or chuckles and diplomatic smiles. Later in a conversation, Sundar (name changed), a maker of Andhra origin, suggested a test: 'See, if you want to know quality, everyone should be given mrdangams to make and the maker's name must be kept secret. Top artists must play on these mrdangams without knowing who the makers are. Then you will know the quality automatically.' The laugh that followed said it all.

Venkatesan and Varadan seem to have kept their distance from the Thanjavur gang. Was this deliberate, I wonder. Were they differentiating themselves socially? My own conclusion is that Krishnamurthy's feeling that he was treated like a slave when he worked for Venkatesan came from their actual or cultivated caste differential. That might have extended to the Thanjavur community too. Selvaraj speaks about hanging out at Venkatesan's shop and occasionally helping with work, but there was nothing more there. Perhaps the social closeness of their castes played a role in keeping the Krishanmurthys and Ramakrishnans connected to the Thanjavur family.

There is no doubt that the present domination of the Thanjavur group is resented. One non-Thanjavur maker, who began as they all do, by saying that there were no problems or squabbles, said by the end of the interview: 'The whole town has descended on Mylapore. Father's older sister's son, father's younger sister's son, brother-in-law, maternal uncle's son, grandson and everyone else. They have packed this place.'

THE MRDANGAM MAKERS I SPOKE to were not only of different social backgrounds but also spanned generations. This diversity gave me another parameter to understand them. I must confess that it has been a complicated unravelling. There is so much embedded cultural history that it is hard to get a hold of what is really going on. Contradictions emerge and, if we are looking for clear right or wrong political positions to adopt, we may never get one.

For the older generation of makers from Thanjavur—who made the transition to Madras, and for whom the umbilical cord of the work is the personal relationship with the artist— change has been difficult to digest. They recognise that there is a measure of caste-based discrimination, yet miss something of the old feudal set-up, perhaps the strange intimacy of it. These makers seem to differentiate between the previous generation and themselves, and believe that their own relationships with artists evolved into a different connection. In the current relationship between the maker and the artist, they perceive a distancing: mere functionality, a job sans the personal touch. They position themselves as the mean between the ugly distant past and utilitarian present, and this is beautifully explained in something a maker said to me, 'Those days they kept us away and discriminated; today they keep us close and discriminate.' Their past and their present encapsulated in one line.

Describing what happens today, Peter (name changed) said, 'You come; we do our work with a great deal of love and affection. But you pay and go away, as though you have done your part.' He also gave me an analogy a little later. 'A person who works as a labourer in a construction site gets paid by the contractor, who then leaves. They should not reduce us to that.' He seems to be saying that something has changed from before. That their work has become contractual; therefore, the labourer–employer structure is more starkly visible. For him, the older model smothered this reality. When the maker had access to the player's personal spaces and life, and worked within that domain, there was the delusionary comfort of a personal bond that both masked the labour involved and allowed them to make excuses for casteist behaviour. Referring to the older relationship, Arulraj agreed that it is a labourer–employee relationship but added, 'At the same time there is affection, these old bonds have not been given up. This is affection that cannot be removed.' Johnson explicitly said that those days were better. 'In those days, it (discrimination) was far less, at least that's how I see it. People from our community had a lot of respect for them (brahmins). They would say, "We are going to ayya's house, he will definitely take care of me."' Another mrdangam maker too made a very similar statement. As did Johnson, who went on to enact a hypothetical conversation.

Maker: Ayya, I don't have money. (in a subservient tone)

Artist: What, da, you are coming and standing here? (with authority)

Maker: I don't have any work.

Artist: It's okay. Give him 200 rupees. (instructs someone)

This is internalised as personal affection. Even if the artist does not help, the lady of the house would do something for them, they say. Makers saw this as closeness, an atmosphere of working together, a fusing of sorts.

Another analogy further explains the problem with this notion. 'The relationship between the vidvan (an honorific often used for seasoned artists) and the worker is like that of a husband and wife. Only if there are arguments and disagreements between the husband and the wife will the family move ahead. If I am upset, I will not say much. They will notice that from my facial expression and introspect about how they spoke to me. It has been going on like this and it should hopefully continue.' This description uses an accepted social design—the inequality between a husband and wife—to explain the player–maker relationship. One maker also said, 'Even if we are disgusted, when they come, we will call them with love! That is how our grandfather and great-grandfather taught us and what we are now used to. How can we change suddenly? All said and done, a musician is a musician.'

When I commented that, if they were not mrdangam makers, musicians would observe all their usual caste and purity standards with them too, Peter acknowledged the truth of it: 'In our kind of society, they will just not care.' In the mix is also the knowledge that, if they are ostracised, they can survive, either by pulling a rickshaw or daily labour. As a maker said, 'I am ready to do the lowest work. But the mrdangam artist cannot—he will have to answer societal questions.' Implicit in this assertion about being willing to do the lowest of jobs is the claim of a higher status for his current work that caters to the brahmin's art world.

There is also the knowledge that the player is dependent on the maker. It lends a certain charge to their uneven relationship: the players have no choice, they cannot work with skin. There is a kind of helplessness associated with the artist's need, one that may even be internalised as power by the makers. The profession is then seen as a form of emancipation, which in turn keeps the makers deferential and compliant in a subordinate relationship.

There is an inherent non-combativeness in the older generation from Thanjavur. Their narrations show us the modulations and accommodations within which caste exists. They feel that, in the new professionalised space of mrdangam-making, there are no more conversations about personal lives or the sharing of private time—an intimacy that had smudged or masked caste discrepancy.

The unfortunate truth is that none of the older mrdangam players I interviewed spoke of affection, though there is an occasional reference to a maker as an almost-son. To them, the makers were always 'workers' even when they said 'he was like my son'. Right through my interviews, the term used to describe them was 'worker' or 'labourer'—not 'maker'. The other word artists used was 'repairer'. There was no exception, absolutely none. The instrument is made by the maker in its entirety, and later he helps in its maintenance, but he is never credited with the *creation* itself.

Even some mrdangam makers saw themselves as repairers, 'mere' mechanics. When I spoke of this injustice to a maker, he too argued that repair was a big part of what they do, and I had to point out that the manufacturing process is key to the whole thing before he realised the wrongness of it.

What happens when you label something as labour? It is characterised as a mechanical operation that lacks intellectual value or creative energies. The individuals engaged in that act are also reduced to just bodies and their work to supply. Social hierarchies like caste allow divisions to flourish with impunity, so everyone, even the oppressed, buys into it.

The English language does not possess the semantic flexibility to address an older person more respectfully than others—everyone is 'you'. However, almost every Indian language has these variations. In Tamil, for example, 'ni' is used to address a younger person or an individual of the same age as the speaker, whereas 'neenga' would refer to an older person. Many communities use 'neenga' for everyone, older or younger. Brahmins are notorious for using 'ni' abundantly, especially for individuals belonging to other castes, and for household help, office help or factory workers, unmindful of age. The rare exceptions are because of professional respect or public decorum. I have caught myself doing this with people in my own home. This behaviour was very much on display when I interviewed mrdangam artists. They would be respectful of any artist they mentioned, but the maker was always referred to by variations of 'ni'. It did not matter whether the maker was older, had passed on or belonged to their grandfather's generation. On the other hand, the makers never spoke of any artist in such a manner. In this simple act, artists were unconsciously establishing identity, superiority and caste privilege. Even the most obscure brahmin musician was spoken of with respect, but the master of masters, Parlandu, was always 'avan', 'ni', etc.

I wanted to understand how makers of earlier generations viewed discrimination. What I discovered was that, coming from the dalit community that had a rare direct link with brahmins because of an artistic necessity, they perceived discrimination only in terms of untouchability. In other words, the sharing of space, air, time, food and art was seen as castelessness. One maker was happy that an artist would put the money in his pocket instead of dropping it into his hands. Every time I asked about caste discrimination, the answer was, we have not faced anything like that. This was also how it worked for the older mrdangam artists. Hosting a maker in his house, talking to him, cracking a joke and demanding work with familiarity were seen as signs of an indifference to caste.

Paul (name changed) put it simply, thus, 'They have not treated me like an untouchable. All of them talk to me nicely and are close to me. The ladies, when they go shopping, call me to help them. So, they haven't behaved otherwise with me; I mean they have never doubted me.'

The word 'doubt' is important. Trust is closely associated with caste. Our levels of trust change with caste, region, language and gender, and when a person who is normally treated as untrustworthy is relied upon, that is experienced as a trans-caste event by the oppressed.

Members of the older generation spoke about the lack of recognition, financial security and public respect when asked about the discrimination they faced. And this they are vociferous about. They did not use the word 'caste', but they accused artists of being selfish and self-centred. In fact, Arulraj insisted that I write about this issue. 'Why do they not give us the respect and importance that we deserve?' he asked. The anger was palpable. 'If they do something, we will be happy and receive it; we will not ask. That is our nature.' Yes, there are the odd cash awards, like one given by the mrdangam artist Srimushnam Raja Rao, but a photograph I saw of that function is interesting in itself. All the five awardees (mrdangam makers), which includes the super-senior Selvaraj, are standing behind a seated row of mrdangam artists, a senior singer and an impresario. This is how it has always been, but it was a plain comment on the relationship between makers and players. In this context, it must be mentioned that a small, private organisation (Parivadini Charitable Trust) has instituted an annual award for instrument makers, and refreshingly, it is called the 'Parlandu award'. In the year 2013, Selvaraj was the first recipient of this award.

Having been to so many of their homes, it is abundantly clear that mrdangam makers still occupy the lower tiers, financially. To my astonishment, a senior mrdangam artist was actually uncomfortable that, during Chennai's December music season, makers could earn up to Rs 1 lakh. This was more than what many artists earned during that period, and thus was looked upon as wrong. Comparing the best, in-demand makers with non-established artists is illogical, to put it mildly. In other words, the maker must always remain at a lower financial level, dependent on favours from the players.

Makers wonder why musicians have not got together and recommended them for recognition from the government. The issue of pension is also repeatedly raised. None of the makers have any security once they grow old; usually, and they have not earned enough to depend on their own savings. As Varadan said, 'After you turn sixty, your body and muscles weaken. Then you will not have the physical power to do this work. Even if you somehow manage, the body will struggle.'

Due to the efforts of T.K. Murthy, Antony received a pension, but this was a one-off case. There needs to be a system in place, something the artists have never bothered about, leading to a feeling that the artists will take care of them only for as long as they are useful. Artists respond to these questions by asking the makers to bring their children into the business and promising them patronage. Deepavali incentives are cited as a way of doing something extra. This is exactly how they treat a domestic worker or a driver. And so I could not help but feel there has been an emotional misplacement on the part of makers. Their own social struggles have led them to believe that this rare trans-caste relationship is equitable. But equality needs no facades, and they do know that, even if they do not acknowledge it.

Hopefully, the grace of brahmin benefactors is not something future generations will yearn for. Tamil Nadu's vigorous social and equality movements, and the egalitarianism in its education policy, has influenced the next generation of mrdangam makers. There is a greater internalisation of equality as a right, not a favour. And the need to speak out is stronger. They still do not take on mrdangam artists directly, but they no longer evade difficult questions. Several younger makers I spoke to had no problem speaking about caste. At a professional level, one fundamental difference that I noticed was the makers' pride in their workplace—the shop. That formalisation of location has, without doubt, given them a purpose and ownership, even if it comes with its own set of challenges. Having artists come to them, rather than going to so many homes, is an inversion that most present-day makers have gladly embraced. But there are still complexities that play out, and of course, the 'next generation' is, in fact, a few generations, which adds to the multiplicity of viewpoints.

Interestingly, at the homes of many mrdangam makers, it was the wife who truly opened up the discussion with sharp interjections. They were not hesitant to problematise ideas. Even when they were not actively participating in our conversation, they would smile, chuckle from the kitchen, or peep in through a window and whisper words or exchange glances—all of which conveyed more meaning than the words I was recording. They are part of the inner lives of the mrdangam makers, but also observe their husband's work from the outside: a vantage point from which to view all that transpires.

Sowriar's wife, Sarada Sowriar, has an unusual lineage. Her grandfather, K.R. Vaidyanathan, was a brahmin Communist from Melakaveri in Thanjavur. When her grandfather passed away, all the shops around the bus stand in Mayavaram were closed as a mark of respect, she said. 'I remember being told that my grandfather used to wear the poonal (the sacred thread). He was very interested in public service and strived for equality. His brothers were not happy and wanted him to stop. In protest, he removed his poonal.' Vaidyanathan married a Sri Lankan Tamil lady and arranged for his daughter Seethalakshmi to be married to a dalit Christian. In a state where caste lines are rigid and honour killings always prevalent, this is uncommon indeed. Seethalakshmi was an equally unusual woman, and started a women's association in Thiruvidaimarudur. Her daughter Sarada thus grew up in a family alive with politics and social awareness. Naturally, she also heard stories of her grandfather's brave and revolutionary acts, and this has been an enduring influence in her life.

I asked Sarada if she was a practising Christian or Hindu, and she said neither. In her parents' home, religion was undivided. 'My mother was quite religious. She would go to

Amman temples and place mavilakku (lamp made of rice flour and jaggery) there, and also fast for forty days during Lent and wear white clothes. I used to ask her, how come she is praying to this god as well as that god. She used to say, they are all the same, we just need to believe and pray.' Deeply influenced by Periyar, Sarada has now moved away from religion.

She believes that the present generation of mrdangam artists has changed. But she opened with this rather uncomfortable statement: 'The fact that you are sitting with us, sipping tea, is a form of recognition. It is a big change that mrdangam makers are today invited into mrdangam players' pooja rooms.' She named one artist who does this. However, I have heard exactly the opposite from another maker who said that the mrdangam finds pride of place in the pooja room, but he cannot enter it. I argued with Sarada that, even if this were true, it could be the result of changing times and the shrinking spaces of urban India that have blurred caste rules. But she felt that modern-day artists care for the makers and enquire about their family and well-being. Though a Periyarist, she was not convinced that most changes are a result of the changing social and political scene. 'There are people who have genuinely changed,' she said, gently accusing me of being too cynical. Her point was that any change, however small, needs to be gracefully appreciated. 'Caste comes with birth. Brahmins have been a dominant caste for long. To me, that they have made these changes is a big leap forward for them. Everyone is equal in society today, and hence they are also changing.'

She felt that the makers have an inherent inferiority complex, a burden they carry from childhood. Michael (name changed), a maker, had said, 'The upper castes wear their caste with pride but we are not able to do that. They look down on us. That feeling remains within me.' Sarada argued that the onus is on the makers to break this cycle of oppression. 'More than the upper castes helping the lower castes to come up, people from the lower castes should make an effort to move up.' She went on to explain, 'When they are doing well, why would they want to move out of their comfort zone? We are suffering, and so we need to usher in the change.' Sarada's voice carried fight and rebelliousness, traces of her mother and grandfather perhaps. Passivity was entirely unacceptable to her; she wanted to take charge of the discourse rather than be the receiver of transformation. But eventually she did agree that none of this was as easy as her words suggested.

Peter was more pragmatic. Marginalisation is a reality in every sphere of work, he pointed out. 'The vina maker is unknown, so are all those working behind the scenes in the film industry. There is always someone below.' Another maker circled back to the lack of recognition and financial issues, and clearly stated that the changes in how the mrdangam players behave today is only because of social pressure. 'They also moved to the city. Earlier, if they were sitting in a bus, everyone else would stand. But in the city, everyone sat. So they had to change.' Neither of these makers believes that there has been a change of heart, a real understanding of caste or the creases in their relationships with artists. 'They are the artists and we are still the workers,' said one. 'In the earlier days, it was displayed openly,' said another. A colleague added, 'It was obvious in the earlier days. They would not allow us in, etc. Today, they talk, ask us to come in, give us water, but it is still there. It exists even if they deny it.'

A different manifestation of caste seems to be at work now. Paul speaks of how mrdangam artists are putting out videos on social media about the making of the instrument, thereby implying that they are doing and can do all the work involved, which is of course untrue. 'Can he work with the skin?' demands the maker. But since the artist is well known, everybody trusts his word. Right through the video, said a maker, the mrdangam artist referred to us as just workers, disrespectfully saying, 'That fellow would come, he would work.' By claiming knowledge of workmanship, artists are now infringing upon the maker's area of expertise, and the latter see it (quite rightly) as coming from a sense of caste and class superiority. I remembered that this ploy was not really new, it had happened earlier. Selvaraj had spoken of a senior mrdangam artist lecturing on the making of the mrdangam in Delhi back in the day. He was very angry, and said that the artist had no business speaking about something that was not his forte.

I was also curious about why very few from the family of mrdangam makers have learnt the art of playing the mrdangam. Many have self-learnt, and played the mrdangam for terukkuttu performances and tabla for light music and church music performances. Antony, Sowriar's cousin from his father's side, was a regular tabla player for the Islamic devotional singer Nagoor Hanifa. But no one has entered the Karnatik playing field. The instinctive answer when I posed this query was, 'We just do not have the time to learn; this work takes up all our time.' The work is a hindrance in other ways too. 'Initially, I was very interested in playing,' said one maker. 'But once we start working, we develop back problems and the hand itself becomes very hard. We also develop kidney stones because we are pulling at the leather straps, holding back our urine, and expending so much energy,' said a maker. The hand becoming hard was often mentioned as an occupational hazard.

Several makers also pointed out that mrdangam artists were unwilling to teach them. Today, some people show willingness, but it is too late for the makers I interviewed.

A few of the younger generation of makers have had opportunities to learn, though. Arogyam's son learnt the mrdangam from T.V. Gopalakrishnan for a while, and then joined Annamalai University to continue his education in music. Sowriar's brother Prakash has also been trained at the Tiruvaiyaru Music College, and Johnson's son Arunkumaresh has been learning from Umayalpuram Sivaraman for many years now. In fact, a Tamil film, *Sarvam Thaala Mayam*, was based on this premise: of a mrdangam maker's son learning to play the instrument. The movie failed to dig deeper into the relationship and the social nuances involved in this interaction, though. It was unwilling to peer into the dark spaces, listen to the unsaid words. Caste was presented as a concrete wall when it actually operates like a wicket gate.

In reality, all of those who learnt to play the instrument are now only in the business of making it. A Thanjavur family member made a pertinent observation about Sivaraman's disciple, Arunkumaresh: 'To be honest, if it was someone from the upper castes, he would have had his first performance by now.'

Artists expect that the sons of the makers will carry on the profession. When Ravikumar was a mrdangam student at the Government Music College, his teacher would pick him out from among all the students in the class to help with mrdangam work. And I infer that this happened on several occasions. His teacher told Ravikumar that he should not pursue learning the mrdangam, as it would take him ten years to become proficient and he would need to practice a lot; instead, he should learn mrdangam-making from his uncle. The teacher knew that Ravikumar was Ramakrishnan's brother-in-law, and one could make the argument that he called on the young man simply because he was actually skilled in the art of repairing and tuning the instrument. However, this isn't an easy argument to accept in the face of caste violence in educational institutions, where students are routinely picked out for tasks that are close to their 'hereditary' occupations. The fact that he dissuaded Ravikumar from becoming a mrdangam artist lays bare his caste prejudice. The twenty other boys in the class were neither asked to help with the instrument, nor were they told to give up their dreams.

When a mrdangam maker approached an artist for a job reference, the artist responded with an assurance to help him rise as a maker. When another argued over retirement benefits, the artist assured him that he would employ the maker's son too. The sons of these musicians are these days employed in the information technology industry, as chartered accountants or in the management sector in India or the US. I know for a fact that mrdangam players rarely encourage their sons to take up music as a profession, citing the financial hardships involved. These young boys have all learnt the art form on the side, alongside pursuing their real career goals. Yet, the players expect the sons of makers to be mrdangam makers. One artist said about next-generation mrdangam makers, 'There is money in this job, but the new generation would rather be employed as a peon in an office with an AC room.'

This put me in mind of an ill-advised education policy C. Rajagopalachari announced in 1953 when he was chief minister. It was actually implemented for a year. According to the scheme, elementary school children were to have a dual curriculum. One part of the day would be devoted to regular education, while in the second half, they would learn their hereditary work, meaning caste-based occupation. It would have been, without doubt, a system that perpetuated the caste system and trapped individuals from neglected sections of society within their caste-work stigma.

MRDANGAM ARTIST KALIDAS MADE A keen observation. He said that people from other communities entering the field of mrdangam-making is a very recent phenomenon. Need, he believed, drives them to these opportunities, but they are all exceptions to the rule. He was right; the presence of makers from non-dalit castes is still a rarity.

No Karnatik musician needs an introduction to the name Valangaiman Shanmugasundaram Pillai, a colossus who ruled the tavil for decades. As an artist and a performer, he was unrivalled. His son, S. Muruganandam, was worried that he would give his father a bad name if he tried his hand at tavil. Instead, he trained in the tavil's melodic partner, the nadasvaram, under Andavan Koil Selvaratnam and Valangaiman Soundarajan. Unfortunately, due to health reasons, he had to give up this dream. With both musical options out of the window, Muruganandam began taking care of the family farms. By the time he was forty-five, Muruganandam was unhappy about the direction his life had taken.

In 1985, he visited his brother-in-law Thanjavur Upendran's house in Madras. At that time, Ramakrishnan was doing all of Upendran's mrdangam work. Muruganandam would quietly watch and even help with small things, both when Ramakrishnan came home and at his shop. He observed how skin was bought, cut and processed. But a few of the maker's staff members, who were also his relatives, were not very happy with the situation. They advised their teacher not to mentor an outsider. So, the nurturing stopped. Muruganandam then shifted his training base next door to Krishnamurthy's. After spending some time there, he had gathered a fair bit of knowledge of the making. He also worked with and learnt from Jesudass.

Though he belonged to the isai vellalar caste, working with skins was not entirely new to him. 'At least in those days, unlike mrdangam players, tavil artists knew how to work on their instruments. Not everyone was a big name who could afford a maker; they earned a pittance and hence would do it themselves,' said Muruganandam. The tavil player, therefore, had to work with skin, and know the ins and outs of making his instrument. The process of making a tavil is divided among many people. Nevertheless, it appears that the procurement and initial work with the hide still remained with the dalit community.

Of course, these days, there are shops that sell the entire instrument. Britto, the mrdangam maker in Madurai, is now more involved with tavil-making, and finds it far more remunerative because of the international orders that come his way.

As we move down the pecking order of caste, the occupational divide between the artist and the maker shrinks.

So, those occupying the lowest rungs play a dual role: a dalit or tribal percussion artist is also the maker of the instrument he plays. N. Deepan, a Chennai-based parai artist, had told me that it was not enough for an artist to just know how to play, he is expected to master its making too. Similarly, drummers from the Koraga community in coastal Karnataka had shared with me their difficulties in getting cow skin for making their instruments. 'Even for us to get skin it's difficult. If we get it, some organisations come and protest.' They also help Yakshagana artists in the making of maddale (maddalam) and chande (chanda). In the words of one Koraga percussionist, 'Even now, after a season of Yakshagana performances, they come to us for the skin.'

In his early days as a maker, Muruganandam had gone to buy cow skin in Chromepet. After having bought the skin and opening it up, he was unable to figure out the skin that covered the animal's face. He had no clue that the cheeks of the cow also open up when the skin is spread out entirely. Watching him struggle, Gunaseelan and Johnson asked him to step aside and did what was needed. After relating stories about how he learnt various aspects of the making, Muruganandam stressed that he spent only a few days with other makers. According to him, it was just a few days here and there. In other words, it was his own observational skills, rather than specific lessons he received from these makers, that helped him learn. He was making the point that he was self-made. M. Navaneethakrishnan, his son, too spoke of this: 'My father had to learn the craft on his own. But it was easy for me to learn from him.' Interestingly, when Ramakrishnan died in 2001, Muruganandam took the initiative to conduct the ceremonies. Krishnamurthy would not do it, and Ramakrishnan's family had already left for the village. It could have been a soft acknowledgement of Ramakrishnan as his guru.

When Muruganandam was ready to start his own business, he requested a mechanic, who had a small place in the suburb of Mandavali in Madras, to help him locate a shop to rent. Instead, the mechanic suggested that they share his own space, and this marked Muruganandam's official entry into the mrdangam-making trade. By 1990, he had rented a shop of his own. Around this time, seventeen-year-old Navaneetham, who was living with his grandfather in Valangaiman village, moved to Madras and joined his father. Within the next four years, they moved into their own shop, buying it with the help of the mrdangam artist Srimushnam Raja Rao. They were becoming a professional threat to the Thanjavur makers, giving them a run for their money by taking over a large chunk of the market share. By the end of the 1990s, everybody knew his name and started connecting a good mrdangam tone with his workmanship. Muruganandam was only the fifth person after Munusami, Venkatesan, Krishnamurthy and Ramakrishnan to open a mrdangam shop. The Thanjavur makers were still going to the homes of artists across the city.

Muruganandam never did any work for his own brother-in-law, but Upendran's students were among those waiting for their instruments at his shop. The shop used to be abuzz with activity, and became a hub for mrdangam players to meet, exchange notes, discuss the previous day's concert and other community-related gossip. It has to be said that Muruganandam got a lot of support from the larger mrdangam community because of which he had a definite advantage over the other makers. And though he did not state it, he enjoyed the privileges of caste and his musical parentage. 'I have been treated with respect. They also know my family; they knew my father and that brought respect. Even Raghu sir (Palghat Raghu) gave me that respect,' Muruganandam said. Navaneetham added, 'Raghu sir would not usually speak unnecessarily. But when I went, he would always enquire about my grandfather and uncle and then about my father.' Sivaraman too would spend a lot of time with them. Unsurprising then that neither father nor son complained about lack of recognition or support from mrdangam artists. They are closer to the players in social

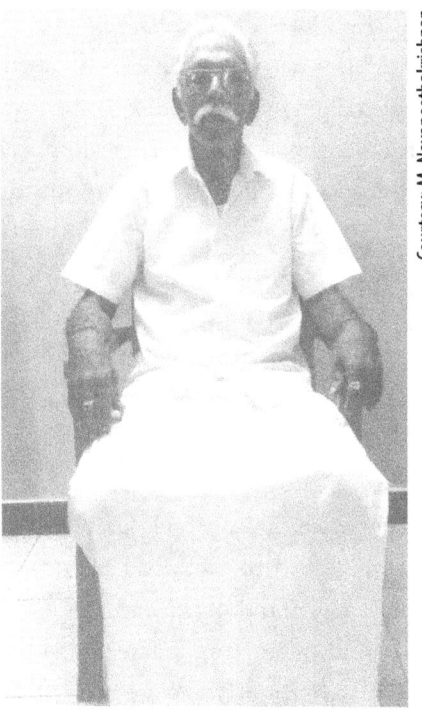

Courtesy: M. Navaneethakrishnan

Muruganandam at home

and artistic hierarchy, and found a natural connection. The Muruganandams were involved in an activity that was below their social rung, something that was held up as a thing to be admired. It was a baseline that was higher than that of the other mrdangam makers.

When it came to isai vellalar musicians, brahmin protectionism kicked in. Muruganandam's own brother-in-law, Thanjavur Upendran, who died at the age of fifty-eight, was unable to reach the heights that his brahmin counterparts did. But when an isai vellalar became a maker, there was greater comfort in the interaction. They were not competing for the same space as the brahmin mrdangam artist, but offering a service from a lower rank. Secondly, now the players did not need to associate only with the dalits for their mrdangam work. One Thanjavur maker subtly pointed to how caste affinity worked well for Muruganandam. After all, he was Upendran's relative and this gave him a headstart, the Thanjavur man insinuated.

Navaneetham now runs the shop, with help from his brother Dhanapal, a cousin and another boy close to the family. They are quite likely the first isai vellalar family in this business and, like the other makers, have kept the work within a close-knit family circle.

But the dominance of the Muruganandam family has diminished over time. They feel that the invasion from Thanjavur has affected work ethic and standards. The prevalent poaching of customers and deterioration in the quality of work comes from the new-generation Thanjavur people, they claim. At a personal level, there seems to be a negligible connection between the Muruganandam family and the extended

Thanjavur family. They maintain cordiality but there is no love lost. It was fairly evident that the Thanjavur makers thought very little of Muruganandam as a maker. They complimented Ramakrishnan, even Krishnamurthy, but Muruganandam got no mention when skill and craftsmanship were being discussed. I am certain the Muruganandams can feel their animosity. They react by claiming a higher standard of work, pricing and, crucially, of character. 'We do not compromise' seems to be their motto, implying that the Thanjavur people do. On multiple occasions during my interviews with them, there were insinuations about the nature and culture of the Thanjavur makers. Muruganandam's and Navaneetham's body language was pride-filled and forceful. They were an entirely different type of mrdangam maker.

MADRAS HAD ONE BRAHMIN MAKER—N.V.S. Mani, an Iyer, who had a shop near the Government Music College. For a while, on his way back from college, Ravikumar used to help him. Sivaraman did not think much of Mani's work and suggested that he was primarily a recycler of old muttus.

After Mani's demise, S. Balaguru is the only brahmin mrdangam maker in the city. He grew up in the suburb of West Mambalam and was working in the auto industry as a casual labourer when he injured his fingers in an accident. Balaguru's real passion was playing the dholki for Namasankirtanas and bhajan performances. He has been doing this from the time he was twelve years old, and has accompanied several household names in the Namasankirtana circuit. Later, he also began singing. The career shift to mrdangam-making happened by providence. 'In 1982, I had given my dholki for repair and that guy kept postponing the repairs. He was Arogyasami at Thousand Lights, a specialist at making dholki and tabla.' Britto had mentioned an Antony at Thousand Lights who was the mainstay for film and recording percussion artists. I think both of them are referring to the same man—perhaps his name was Antony Arogyasami?

Balaguru had a performance coming up at the Ramanavami festival in the village of Kettavarampalayam. Angry with Arogyasami's delaying tactics, Balaguru bought leather and got the dholki ready himself. And on that day, he decided never to depend on others for his instrument. Soon, with the encouragement of a West Mambalam-based musician, Sethalapathy Balu, and his two sons—both of whom are mrdangam artists—Balaguru made his foray into mrdangam-making.

As a brahmin, how did he feel about working with hide? 'It is wrong for me to do this. The people who should be playing the mrdangam after Nandikeshwara are the pillaimars (isai vellalars). You have Azhaganambi Pillai, Mamoondiya Pillai, Palani Subramania Pillai and the like. When it comes to singing, it was yadavas or odhuvars. Tavil and mrdangam were played by pillais. Brahmins were supposed to recite the Vedas, do their sandhya vandanam (a daily ritual performed only by brahmins), do unchavrithi (begging for alms) as a rule. Due to circumstances, these rules have changed. It is not practical for all brahmins to sit at home and recite the Vedas. That is my opinion. When you stop doing the sandhya vandanam three times a day, you have given up on your duties. In the last thirty-seven years, I have not stopped doing my sandhya vandanam thrice a day or reciting the Indraksheeyam. But you cannot stop anyone from doing whatever they want, is my opinion.' He also considered his work choice as a blessing from Jagadguru Shri Chandrasekharendra Saraswati, then the pontiff of the Kanchi Kamakoti mutt. 'I was telling him that whatever work I do I get injured here or there, what do I do. He said, stop going to work and let work come to you. Just work harder on what you are already doing, was his advice. So I started working with the instruments.'

But finding a bride was a challenge because of his line of work. 'I got married only when I was thirty-four. No one was ready to give their daughter in marriage to me because I was doing work with mrdangam and dholkis. There were twelve or thirteen proposals that got rejected this way. There were girls who liked me at bhajanais but their parents did not agree.' Balaguru finds himself in an awkward social position. He is committed to his work but feels that he is doing a job that only chakkiliyars ought to do. Circumstances have forced him to function far below his caste slab. Much like Muruganandam, but with even greater force, Balaguru said that he learnt everything himself. Gunaseelan had, in fact, offered to teach him but he did not take him up on the offer, Balaguru said. 'I am better than the ones who are traditionally in this field. I have not stood in front of anyone's shop. I have not learnt from anyone. I learnt it all myself.' This may or may not be true, but there is an evident and intense need to differentiate himself from the traditional makers. Balaguru is unable to reconcile the contradiction between his caste purity-related lifestyle and his work; perhaps placing that wedge between himself and the rest helps calm his disquiet somewhat.

Being a brahmin, Balaguru expected support from his own clan, the mrdangam artists. He was upset that this did not happen. Having made the socio-ritual 'sacrifice' of entering this line of work, he thought that many brahmins would come out to support him. His mrdangam clients are few; dholki-making and repairs form the majority of his workload.

Balaguru now wants more Namasankirtana performance opportunities as a dholki artist or lead singer. Namasankirtana is a highly brahminical art form, performed and received chiefly by the brahmin conservative. He truly belongs within that cluster. And perhaps hopes to become a regular there, his original home. He may not be able to earn enough to give up the dholki and mrdangam work, but the identity shift will certainly comfort him.

Balaguru as a Namasankirtana performer

Sivaraman also made it a point to mention the few brahmins who were or are involved in making mrdangams. Among 'our people', he specified, 'there was one person called Radhakrishnan working in Mylapore. Then, among brahmins, you know who did work for themselves, without going to any mrdangam repairer? Karaikudi Rangu Iyengar. Karaikudi Muthu Iyer told me this. After this, one great artist that I know is this Nellai Devaraja Iyer. There is also a student of mine, Ravindran, who does everything by himself.' He also mentioned Balaguru.

IF THERE IS ONE POINT on which almost all the makers agreed, it was the need for an association or a union that can represent their demands, address their needs, make changes to their working conditions and work out their retirement requirements. Some younger makers felt that such a body would give them the strength to face up to artists and set minimum prices for the various kinds of services they provide. Even caste-related discomforts could be collectively expressed without fear of backlash.

The lack of unity hurts no one but the makers themselves. There have been many attempts to form such a body but they have failed. One serious attempt that might have come close to fruition was in the 1990s. According to some, it failed because of egos and squabbling for posts. The makers met at Nageshwara Rao Park in Mylapore, but arguments broke out and that was the end of it. There are sporadic whispers and suddenly held meetings about restarting the sangam (union), but nothing has happened so far. Meanwhile, work continues, feelings quietly fester and relationships hang in limbo.

4

ARCHITECTS OF THE WOOD

I walked across to a small, nondescript photocopying shop on Chennai's East Coast Road. There were some field notes that needed copying. The man at the machine patiently allowed me to check each page for relevance before I handed it over to him. On a mat nearby was his son—eyes half closed, a milk bottle in his mouth—oblivious to all the noise. The shop owner sat at the computer, half-heartedly photoshopping an image.

'You should leave home by at least 3 a.m., only then can you get to Kanchipuram by 4.30. Then it will take you another couple of hours for the darshan,' said the boss. I was curious, what darshan? 'Don't you know? Atthi Varadar has risen after forty years,' he said. Momentarily, I thought of a Marvel movie superhero. But he was right; the lord had indeed risen.

The temple town of Kanchipuram is revered as one of seven places where a Hindu attains moksha. It is home to countless temples and deities—Ekambareshwarar, Kailasanathar, Kacchapeshwarar, Ulagalanda Perumal and others. Among them is the Varadaraja Perumal temple, home to the submerged lord, Atthi Varadar. Much like Bangaru Kamakshi of Thanjavur, he was also hidden inside the temple tank for his own safety. According to the website of the Sri Satyapoorna Math at Chinna Kancheepuram, the Atthi Varadar idol was immersed inside the temple tank secretively to save it from Muslim invasions.

Kamakshi of Kanchi has a particularly interesting tale. She is said to have been taken to Thanjavur centuries ago by Syama Sastri's ancestors who, again, wanted to protect her from Islamic invaders. Now she is Bangaru Kamakshi of Thanjavur to whom Syama Sastri, one of Karnatik music's father figures, addressed his musical pleas.

To return to Atthi Varadar, I learn that he is taken out once in forty years for forty-eight days. Unlike his previous sojourns out of his watery abode, this time, south India went into a tizzy—thanks to social media, of course. For residents of Kanchipuram, it was a nightmare. They couldn't come and go from their homes, had to cope with serpentine queues everywhere, and unknown people were requesting food or even a place to stay.

Atthi Varadar is no ordinary god—he is made of fig wood. Which means that whenever he is placed back in the water, he needs to be coated with various protective herbs and incenses to keep him safe until he makes his next appearance.

During the god's brief visit, Karnatik musicians made their way to Kanchipuram to sing his praises, and their melodies and rhythms rang across the temple. The beats that the fig-wood god heard came from jack wood—the holy grail of mrdangams. Its holiness is further enhanced if the jackfruit tree grows near a temple. The wood is then exposed to the sounds of temple bells and Vedic chants, and the resonance of an instrument made of such wood is, they say, unmatched. Artists like Mani Iyer would go to any lengths to acquire wood from an auspicious tree of this sort. While mrdangam artists believe Hindu temple bells and chants are the magic ingredient, the woodcrafter is more catholic in his search for these positive vibrations. 'There is a belief that trees near a church or a temple, or even a road where people walk and talk, or where bells toll, absorb the vibrations and produce good sound,' said Kuppusami Asari.

Though the jackfruit tree leads the way, monkey pod (kodukapuli) is not too far behind. Red sanders, Indian laburnum, copper pod, rosewood, coconut, neem, pithraj and ebony are all woods that the makers of mrdangam shells have tried. But eventually, for the best instruments, it has to be the time-tested jack wood.

Kuppusami Asari's family were carpenters and furniture makers until his father, Vadivelu Asari, met Somu Asari from Madras. Somu is a name that most senior mrdangam makers and artists recall. He was a colossus in the world of mrdangam shell-making. Although I had been following the story of mrdangam-making for a while, my imagination of it so far began and ended with leather work. But there is a stage before we even get to the leather—and that is selecting and seasoning the wood that forms the shell of the instrument. This is what the asaris traditionally do.

The asaris are members of the vishwakarma community. They are people of material art who work with metal, stone and wood. To them goes the credit for all the exquisite jewellery, carvings, sculptures and furniture that India flaunts as treasures and antiques in museums, and the rich and famous flaunt as part of their personal collections. Their craft requires an ability to measure and visualise by sight alone: that is, look at a piece of wood or metal and assess its length, breadth and even weight. This requires an extraordinary and complex arithmetic skill, and the asari community has devised its own ways of calculating, measuring and describing measurements. To the people engaged in the craft of woodwork, calculations are not a means to an end—inside these multiplications, subtractions and additions, the face of the figurine or the elegance of a table's legs come alive. There is an innate abstraction in their process of creation. Academicians may argue that they were craftsmen, not artists; and others disagree. But arguments of nomenclature aside, it is clear that these unremembered creators were possessed of an artistic imagination.

The mythological Vishwakarma holds an exalted position in the celestial universe. He is the architect for the most powerful; the maker of mansions that seat the Hindu pantheon of gods and goddesses. But his human counterparts have not fared well. Categorised as OBC (other backward castes) by the government of India, they occupy the lower rungs of the caste order. The ten million people who pushed and jostled to spend just a split second with Atthi Varadar would not have thought of the vishwakarmas to whom Varadar himself owes his temporal manifestation. Once designers of great temples and monuments, they are now invisible. Away from their creative pursuits, many people in the community have been reduced to labour activities that are adjacent to their traditional caste-based occupations. Those in the younger generation are also moving away to white-collar jobs. Their presence in Tamil Nadu's political or cultural landscape is minimal.

KUPPUSAMI'S FATHER VADIVELU TRAINED UNDER Somu Asari, and shifted from the furniture business to making wooden shells for mrdangams, tavils, pambai and other percussion instruments. The shell is referred to as the kattai—literally, wood, or a block of wood. But, in this context, it refers to a specially crafted hollow shell made for a specific percussive instrument, which could be a mrdangam or a tavil.

'Somu Asari was in Madras. He used to come here to buy jackfruit trees. That is how we were introduced to him. He stayed here and taught my father. We have been in this business for fifty or sixty years. Today, we make wooden shells for the mrdangam, tavil, tabla, udukkai, pambai, chenda and urmi,' said Kuppusami. While Somu's family no longer does woodwork, Kuppusami is ambivalent about the future of his own children. Though he says he is not sure about what they will do, I sense that he is not averse to them taking over his business.

Irrespective of whether they were from Thanjavur, Chennai, Peruvemba, Bangalore or someplace in Andhra Pradesh, the mrdangam makers took pride in their work, and were always ready to explain its technical and artistic niceties and nuances. The story with the woodcrafters was very different. They have no direct engagement with the actual sound that emanates from the mrdangam. The shell leaves their workshop, never to return, and they do not hear an artist test the instrument or even go to a concert. They never hear the first sound that rebounds through the shell they make, or experience the multitudes of tonalities that the artist produces via the resonating chamber they created. Perhaps it is because of this disconnect that they do not have the sense of participating in an artistic endeavour that the mrdangam maker does. If they had stayed on in the furniture business, the chair or cupboard would have been completed in their space; they could have seen it in its entirety, with those decorative curves and functional drawers. The mrdangam's wooden shell is an incomplete thing, the actuation of which happens later. Perhaps this is why they underplay their own work.

Kuppusami demonstrated the entire shell-making procedure in a matter-of-fact manner. At one point, he said it was simple work. Those who worked under him were also business-like about what they did. If I had not visited his workshop and seen it for myself, I would have believed them. It is nothing like the mechanical process they make it out to be.

Among the woodcrafters for whom making the mrdangam shell is a full-time profession, the earliest names we come across are Muthu Asari, Dakshinamurthy Asari and Subramania Asari. In the recording of an interview with T.R. Rajaram in 1984, Somu Asari said that Muthu Asari used to play the mrdangam in Pudukottai. Knowing that there have been no asaris who participated in the performance of Karnatik music, we could surmise that he may have accompanied terukkuttu or similar performances. All three of them were Somu's relatives, uncles through different parental connections. There was also a certain Narayana Asari who lived in Thanjavur, but I am not sure if he was a relative of Somu's.

Much like the techniques of mrdangam-making, the art of creating wooden shells was refined only in the early part of the twentieth century, at least as far as we can tell. With the Thanjavur makers, we are able to trace a history stretching back to the early twentieth century, but very little is known about the woodcrafters' work culture in the past. Somu Asari is pretty much our first point of reference.

We know little about his predecessor in Thanjavur, Subramania Asari. Mani Iyer's son Rajamani mentions that, while Subramania would take three or four days to make one wooden shell, Somu would get three or four ready in just a day's time. T.V. Gopalakrishnan had this to say: 'Subramania Asari was the best then. He made vinas, mrdangams and everything else. We couldn't provide specifications; we just had to take what he made.'

About Somu, we know that he started out in Pudukottai, and used to make wooden mrdangam shells for the grand old master, Dakshinamurthy Pillai. Somu Asari's fame grew because of his association with Palghat Mani Iyer. They first met when Iyer came to Pudukottai for Pillai's house-warming function.

I am going to pause here to address something that you, the reader, may or may not be wondering about, but is certainly bothering me. Why is it always Palghat Mani Iyer who crops up in these stories?

He could not have been the only individual who spent so much time on his instrument. I am certain that others too worked hard to achieve the acute precision he sought. But so strong has been the myth-building around Iyer that every mrdangam story has only him as the protagonist. There is no doubt that Mani Iyer was engrossed in his art, but he was not superhuman. Yet, within the Karnatik quadrant, it is near impossible to go beyond worshipping him. The upshot of all this is the disappearance of any alternative narrative, the invisibility of everyone else and the non-existence of stories with other heroes.

Astonishingly, even students of Palani Subramania Pillai, the only other contender for the top spot, do not recall folklore about their own guru. When they do, Mani Iyer makes an entry at some point to legitimise the story. The complete dominance of Karnatik music in the past three or four decades by Iyer's descendants and followers has only exacerbated the situation. He also mentored singers and violinists who later went on to become prominent musicians, and further perpetrated this one-sided commentary. Mani Iyer was an obsessive, tough go-getter who would stop at nothing to achieve his ends. This is how everyone in the fraternity, including his family, speaks of him. No one can deny the magnificence and majesty of Mani Iyer's art, but to be blind to the fact that his own unquantifiable self-assurance came also from hereditary caste privilege would be a travesty. All of these factors made him unchallengeable in his time and after.

For the marginalised communities that worked with brahmin mrdangam artists, being a part of Iyer's stories was an automatic stamp of excellence. Even in the thoughts of mrdangam makers, Palani always gets second place—an unfortunate mirror of how the Karnatik world treats his memory. And the third individual in the mrdangam's trinity of performers, C.S. Murugabhoopathy, is remembered only by Varadan, who owes his shop to the maestro.

Therefore, for Somu Asari, the turning point came when he made a few kattais for Mani Iyer after the latter's visit to Pudukottai. From then on, Somu was the only kattai maker that Iyer would work with. Somu may have shuttled between Thanjavur and Pudukottai for a while and then moved to Thanjavur. Later on, he shifted to Madras, timing his move close to that of his master. Apart from being a maker of mrdangam kattais for the who's who of the mrdangam-playing community, he was in demand with others, including those who were starting music schools and institutions. For instance, Professor P. Sambamoorthy—one of India's leading musicologists, and the man who published the original theoretical texts for students of Karnatik music—opened a centre for instruments. He tried reconstructing ancient, extinct instruments and also inventing new ones. Somu worked off and on for Sambamoorthy's Sangita Vadyalaya.

There was a time when Pattukottai had many jackfruit trees and the best jack wood was found in its groves. Pattukottai is more or less equidistant from Thanjavur and Pudukottai. T.K. Murthy told me that an entire tree from the area used to cost only Rs 15 or 20. But that source soon vanished, and Panruti took over as the Mecca for mrdangam kattais. Somu tells Rajaram, 'The best kattai was in Pattukottai, but after they built that new canal in Thanjavur, tree growth was affected.' Panruti, its replacement, is also well known for cashews. As we drive into the town, the road is lined with makeshift stalls selling cashews, vying for the attention of passers-by. Right behind them are strong cashew trees, thick and close-leaved.

Madras Kannan remembers the days when people from Thanjavur used to bring the kattai to Madras for sale. 'In the 1930s, when I was around ten, kattais were very cheap. They were just happy to get rid of the stock they had brought all the way and would not demand a big price. I would buy from them.'

Everyone makes a beeline for Panruti now. But what makes the jackfruit trees in Panruti special, I wondered. 'It is the red soil that is found in the fifty kilometres around Panruti. The soil retains moisture and helps the trees grow thick. But water should not be allowed to stagnate around the tree because it will cause the wood to split and crack,' Kuppusami explained.

Britto remembered the 1980s, when all communication was via inland postcards. 'We had to inform them that we need wood for so many mrdangams using fifteen-paisa inland cards. Once the kattais were ready, they would respond through a card. On receiving that news, we would travel either by overnight bus or train, and alight at Viluppuram.' From there, they would go on to Panruti.

The health of the tree, however, is only the first thing the woodcrafter looks at—there are several other requirements. 'There are twenty-two types of jackfruit trees in Panruti. When we look at a tree, we know how good it is. We do not consider trees that are light in colour.' Kattai makers and artists speak of the ideal wood being the colour of saffron, kumkum or honey, or reddish. As a tree grows, its girth increases in concentric circles. The newer layers are on the outer edge, closer to the bark and whitish in colour. As the tree ages, its inner wood becomes darker, from beaver brown to burnt umber and then chestnut brown. This is what the woodcrafters are looking for. The white immature wood found in the outer rings is called velladai and is to be avoided. Muruganandam had a Tanglish (an amalgam of Tamil and English) name for it: polish kattai, meaning kattai that looks like it has been artificially given a sheen. Navaneetham, his son, added that mature wood is closer to the base of the tree. This whitish wood is for beginners;

artists won't use it, he said. 'This wood splits when it is kept out in the sun; good wood will not,' Somu warns in his interview. Kattai that is a mix—older inside but younger on the outside—is not ideal either.

The best kattai comes from a jackfruit tree that is at least fifty years old, broad and not too tall. But that is not all. The woodcrafters also do not want any maru (scar), suzhi (a circular knotty formation that looks like an elephant's eye) or kanu (the joint in a trunk or branch where another branch had once grown). Finding a kattai that ticks every one of these boxes is a near impossibility, but they keep looking. There are many explanations for why these natural features detract from the quality of the wood. Here is one from Britto: 'They say, if there are swirls, the sound will be like an alarm in the night but not during the day. If there is a kanu, the asaris can stain it and give it to you, but over a period of time, that portion will pop out. And there should be no splits, for obvious reasons. And holes will allow insects in.' According to Britto, the best chance of finding the perfect wood is on the main trunk, not too close to the roots. It will have the most number of growth rings and not too many knots. Mani Iyer did not like it if his kattai had a single kanu; it had to be absolutely clean. He also liked the colour of the skin membrane to be white. Everything needed to be blemishless.

Not everyone felt like this. Dakshinamurthy Pillai had a very different perspective. Somu said, 'Dakshinamurthy Pillai used to say that every kanu has a sollu.' A stunning expression that has captivated me. 'Sollu' means 'to say' in colloquial usage, but the proper meaning of it is 'word'; here, it refers to a rhythmic stroke. Essentially, what he says is that each kanu is a percussive stroke embedded in the wood. In other words, the rhythm of the tree, markers of its time. A profound idea that spurred him to look for kattais with kanus.

The girth of a tree that is right for a kattai would be about fourteen inches. They would remove the bark and whatever velladai there might be, and bring it down to a wooden block about one foot wide. Somu Asari does not speak of measurements in feet. He uses 'suttu'. 'We can carve out a kattai only from a block of wood that has a girth of seven suttus.' It is a descriptive term of measure, not a mere quantifier: suttu means 'round', possibly referring to the tree's growth rings. Somu needs seven suttus from the mature wood closer to the pith of the trunk.

This changed the way I thought of the wood. It was no longer only a resonating chamber, but an entity that was capable of coming alive with sound, and with colour, rings and various marks on its body. Thinking of kattais in this manner shifts our engagement as a listener.

Mani Iyer believed that reducing the width from two feet to the eventual one foot should not be done with a saw. He insisted that they cut it with an axe, and believed that the sound of the axe would enter the wood. Here are two different belief systems. Dakshinamurthy Pillai feels that Nature gifts us life's rhythms through its marks, while Iyer wants the woodcrafter to physically exert himself, and through his labour enhance the sound of the kattai.

The two apertures of the hollow kattai are covered with membranes made of animal hide. The dominant end has a smaller aperture, and this is what faces the audience in a typical performance. This is called the valandalai, the right-side head. The larger aperture on the other side has a characteristic bass tone and is called the toppi, which comes from 'topi', cap, a Hindustani word that is now part of the Tamil lexicon.

The kattai is not cylindrical. The diameter increases as we move towards the centre but is at its maximum a little off-centre, closer to the toppi; here, the circumference is anywhere between thirty-three and thirty-six inches.

Karaikudi Mani told me that the kattai cut from the lower section of the trunk should be shaped so that the wider aperture, the toppi, is closer to what was the base. If this is inverted, it would spell doom for the artist, he said. 'The shastras say that a person playing on such a mrdangam will not be hale and hearty; he will not do well.' While I am quite certain there is no shastra written specifically on this subject, Karaikudi Mani is convinced about it, and has convinced Kuppusami of the same.

These so-called shastras drove Mani Iyer to bend over backwards in his search for sandalwood kattai because that wood is considered sacred. He tried using the offices of Karnataka's leading violinist Mysore Chowdiah to acquire such a specimen. However, sandalwood of that size was very hard to find, and while money was never the impediment, all efforts failed. His next experiment followed the semantic trail: mrdangam came from 'mrth' (clay) and angam (part, limb). So it must have been made of mud at some point in time, he thought. He got this done, but then realised that it was not operational because if they tried to fix leather membranes on it, the mud kattai would crack. So this kattai remained a showpiece in his house.

FROM A SIX-FOOT LONG BLOCK, Kuppusami is able to craft three kattais. But first he allows the cut trunk to lie outside the workshop for three months. 'Then we make a small rough hole of about four inches through the wood, apply cow dung on both sides and let the kattai be for another two months. The cow dung is replaced after a month, though. All this helps in the sound that you finally get from the kattai and gives it longevity,' Kuppusami Asari told me later over the telephone.

When I visited Kuppusami in Panruti, the frontage of his workshop was packed with wooden blocks of different sizes, colours and ages. They had been cut at different times, some drier than others. One man was cutting out the bark from a smaller two-foot piece, obviously a kattai in the making, with an axe. Kuppusami had about four people working for him; each one taking care of different aspects of his small industry. He said there were at least a couple of other woodcrafters in town who specialised in kattai-making, and they were all his pupils. Kuppusami's own family members are not into instrument-related work. His brothers are all furniture makers, and he is a little sad that the people he trains are not from the vishwakarma community. 'They are vanniyars. Very few asaris take up this work,' he said.

After the cow dung-pasted kattais have sat out for two months, the crafter begins shaping it to the required size, shape and weight, conforming to multiple dimensional specifications.

In the interview with Rajaram, Somu Asari described the process as it was in his day: 'After cutting the wood from the tree, we would apply cow dung on both sides of the chopped trunk and leave it. This was done because sometimes a woodcutter was not available. It was kept in such a manner that air does not enter the uterus of the trunk.' Somu meant the pith of the trunk here because he went on to say: 'The uterus takes in all the water and nutrition that triggers the growth of leaves and flowers, enabling the plant to become a tree.' According to Somu, it was important to keep the wood dry and not allow any moisture to enter through fissures in the wood.

He also reported something Mani Iyer had told him: apparently, the wood used to be placed in a paddy field for about ten days. It would inevitably attract insects there, and the quality of the wood could be ascertained based on whether the insects affected the wood or not. An older gentleman, whose muffled voice was heard in the recording of Somu's interview, added, 'Mani Iyer told someone to place the kattai in paddy. That fellow did not know how to go about this treatment. He would leave it there for three months. When it was taken out, it would look like sandalwood.'

Karaikudi Mani and Guruvayur Dorai and some others also spoke of soaking the wood in water for a period of time. Karaikudi Mani gave me the details of this lengthy seasoning method. 'We have to soak the block of wood in water, then bury it in lake sand for a month or so. After which we should let it dry in the shade. Only then can we find out if the wood cracks or not.' Kuppusami Asari was even more specific about what used to be done. 'My father told me that, in those days, they would dump about ten kattais in a tank of salt water for about ten days. This would brighten the colour of the kattai and stop cracks from appearing.'

After Mani Iyer had bought the kattais, a hole just big enough for a hand to go through would be made in each of them, and they would be transferred to his house. There is one statement that Somu made during his video interview that went by so fast, I did not even notice it in the first hearing. He says, 'Ayya will take the kattais in the car to his house, irrespective of where he was. He will send one or two kattais every couple of months. He was scared we would steal and sell them.' He says this flatly, no emotion in his voice. Rajaram too had described this wood transfer routine to me: 'The other thing is that you cannot store the wood in Somu's house. He will sell it!' It is clear there's a trust deficit from Mani Iyer's side, but Somu's acceptance of it is unusual. We do have to take into account the fact that he was speaking to Iyer's son in that interview. It was nonetheless a distressing statement to process, especially because Iyer was Somu's main patron. The enormous imbalance in power and social capital made it possible for Iyer to disregard Somu's feelings, secure in the knowledge that the woodcrafter wouldn't leave him. He had to be bound to Mani Iyer; there was no other choice in his caste-bound society or his economic circumstances. Perhaps he thought to himself, 'So what if he does not trust me as a person. He still needs me for his mrdangams.'

But this should not have surprised me because many mrdangam artists said the same thing about the Thanjavur makers, pointing to their dishonesty and duplicity. When non-dalit makers speak of the Thanjavur family, they accuse them of using substandard material or lying to artists about its source (e.g. they use skin bought in Chennai but inform their clients that it was directly sourced from Thanjavur). At some point, almost everyone makes some 'adjustments' in their work, so it is not entirely unlikely that some of them do this. What matters here is not the truth or untruth of these accusations, but the fact that they are made only against makers of certain castes.

SIZE MATTERS. OR SO SOME mrdangam artists believe. I would like to explore the truth of this idea in the case of the mrdangam.

The Indian system of music is based on the foundational idea of a fixed tonic that is determined by the vocal range of each singer or the tonal range of the lead instrument. Because the speaking voices of men and women have different vocal bandwidths, the fixed fundamental tonic is automatically different for those two genders. The average male voice's tonic, designated as the first svara (note) in an octave, Sa, is between the pitches C and D. The average female voice bases its tonic Sa between the pitches G and A. This means that the mrdangam valandalai, the narrower aperture, must be tuned to these pitches, depending on the individual artist it is meant for. The valandalai is the harmonic side of the mrdangam, and the toppi provides a variety of bass sounds as contrast. The question that I am asking is: does the pitch affect the size and construction of the kattai? But let us first answer that racy question, does size matter?

In the pre-microphone era, men did not sing at a range anywhere close to their speaking voice. In fact, their tonic was the same as that of women because they wanted their voices to reach audiences. Higher pitch means higher frequencies, thus more decibels and consequently a larger reach. This was especially necessary for open-air concerts, such as in temples.

Madras Kannan said, 'Those days, the mrdangam was only 22 inches long. The size had to be increased only when musicians like Poochi Srinivasa Iyengar, Vedanta Bhagavatar and Ariyakudi Ramanuja Iyengar reduced their sruti (tonic).' Perhaps Kannan made a mistake in the measurement value; the older mrdangam would have been 18 inches, not 22. Several musicians corroborated this. So, the first increase in size likely happened very early in the twentieth century. With that generation of singers bringing down their tonic, the mrdangam size grew from 18 to 22 inches.

It was probably in the early 1950s, when some Karnatik singers of repute dropped the tonic even more, that the size went up further. Rajamani had mentioned that this trend was started by my guru Semmangudi Srinivasier, and that others like Madurai Mani Iyer followed suit.

T.K. Murthy asserted that it was Dakshinamurthy Pillai who engineered this larger kattai. But Pillai too appears to have used the 18-inch mrdangam. 'I have seen a mrdangam that was used by Dakshinamurthy Pillai at a Murugan temple in Pudukottai. It was about 18 or 19 inches. It looked like the mrdangam we give a seven- or eight-year-old beginner today,' said Kalidas.

These 18-inch mrdangams also had no body curvature (a necessary condition for the modern mrdangam), and the apertures of the kattai were quite large, given the small size of the instrument itself. Kannan said, tongue-in-cheek, 'Those days the mrdangam was comfortable to play with, and its size remained within the extent of the hands in its natural stance.' He was hinting at the fact that the mrdangams in use nowadays are unnecessarily large. Back then, the mrdangams were also so light that artists could hang it around their neck with a cloth and play, standing or walking. Selvaraj pointed out that even Mani Iyer had played with a small-sized mrdangam.

But both Palghat Mani Iyer and Palani Subramania Pillai soon went on an enlarging spree, 24, 25, 26 … until Mani Iyer had a 28-inch mrdangam constructed, and finally a 30-inch one. There is no clarity about whether this truly augmented the aural palette of the instrument. Kalidas believes it did. 'The larger the volume of air that is trapped inside,' he said, 'the more weighty the sound will be.' He added that if the artist needed larger apertures, the kattai itself must be bigger so that the slope is gradual. But was such a slope needed in the first place? We do not know for sure that the slope of the mrdangam kattai has any role to play in its sound quality. The older mrdangams, even though they were tuned to a higher pitch, did not have it. As far as I can tell, the jury is still out on this explanation.

But there is no doubt that these endless attempts to increase the size—and, importantly, weight of the mrdangam—impacted the instrument's expression. The transitioning playing style of the era too shows this. A careful listening to some of the older artists—predating the Mani Iyers and Palanis—gives us a glimpse into the role and intentionality of the mrdangam artist. There was a time when its rhythm was interwoven with the melody of the voice and the violin or vina. Its role was subdued and had a flowing gait to it. This changed dramatically with the Mani Iyer–Palani generation. There was a greater frontal display of individuality, an emphasis on the rhythmic aspects of every composition and of the mrdangam artist's own presence on stage. Listen to any recording of Mani Iyer or Palani, and you are immediately struck by their obvious boldness. The mrdangam artist's search for a more aggressive musical expression drove many of the instrument's physical and aesthetic changes. It was an exploration driven by the artists' desire for attention and for a greater focus on the mrdangam artist during a concert. This required structural changes to the form, presentation and appearance of the performative act. All of which have entirely succeeded in changing the music and position of the mrdangam.

Another aspect that drove mrdangam artists of that time would have been a desire to assert a more muscular musicality. Mani Iyer was the brahmin mrdangam artist who took on and vanquished the isai vellalars, who had dominated the instrument thus far. Perhaps then, the tavil, which was played only by isai vellalars, could have been an unconscious instigator of change too. The playing and display of the tavil has always been regarded as a raw display of male power because of its sheer tonal explosiveness and the visible physicality that goes into its playing. The mrdangam artists were also looking to present a similar mien both in stage presence and style. To my mind, at least part of this need for a larger mrdangam was driven by male testosterone. The early mrdangam was barely more than the seated width of the artist himself. Now it was heavy and solid—burly, you could say. When Mani Iyer arrived with two or three mrdangams, all carried by his students, there was a grandeur to it, an unbridled display of power. During a concert, he would signal, and his students would frantically hand over the second mrdangam, while the first one was checked by the mrdangam maker seated in a corner of the stage. The whole thing was a show of dominance—including the instrument itself.

We know from Somu Asari that Mani Iyer often used a 25-inch mrdangam. But Kalidas—irritated that these changes are associated only with the legend of Iyer—said, 'You can make up a story and give it names. I have seen a 26-inch mrdangam in my guru Palani's house. And he played for M.D. Ramanathan, Semmangudi Srinivasier with it. He also played for G.N. Balasubramaniam with a 25-inch mrdangam. He would say his chest ached when he played these bigger mrdangams.'

Eventually, Mani Iyer too found that it was not possible to indulge his fantasies beyond a point. There is one picture of Mani Iyer with the 30-inch mrdangam that never found a place on the performing stage; it was physically impossible to play.

KUPPUSAMI ASARI'S ENTIRE WORKSHOP WAS strewn with sawdust; I could barely find the ground beneath. Kattais of different sizes and hues were strewn about. On my left was a lathe machine that could hold a block of wood and rotate it. The woodcrafter placed a kattai that had been seasoned under the sun and with cow dung on a wood-working lathe.

The kattai was held by a 'chuck' on one end and supported by a 'tail stock' on the other, but was free to rotate. When the belt-driven lathe machine was switched on, it turned the block of wood at a very high rpm. The woodcrafter, standing parallel to the machine, used a hand-held chisel and began shaping the outer surface of the wood.

Slowly, a mild arc emerged on what was a jagged, unsymmetrical block, then tentative slopes formed, angling down towards both ends. With the approximate shaping done, the woodcrafter made a clear indentation that defined the point where the kattai is at its broadest—an elegant depression

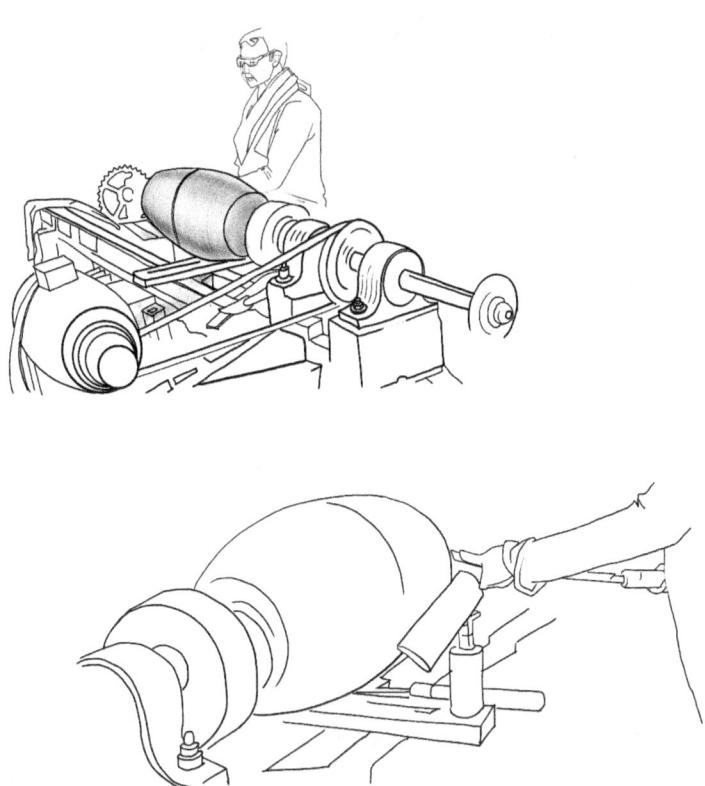

that went right around the kattai. This cleft line is, as I have mentioned, closer to the larger aperture, toppi. With the wood turning at such a high speed and the chisel moving on it, I could see vertical and horizontal motion lines. The shape appeared almost miraculously. The woodcrafter barely caressed the surface, but the wood visibly responded to the touch. As he moved the chisel up and down, left and right, it seemed as if liquid wood was flowing in both directions. A few more decorative and symmetrical line-rings were drawn on both sides of the main indentation.

The mrdangam-shell that I watched being crafted was for an adult male voice. Over the years, in consultation with artists, woodcrafters have put in place some tonic-dependent standardisations. The kattais are usually 22 inches in length for female tonics and 24 inches for male tonics. The standard measurements of the aperture for kattais made for female voices are 6¼ inches on the valandalai side and 7¼ inches for the toppi. Here is the general range for the size of the two apertures, end to end, including the wooden frame:

For tonics between F and A
Valandalai diameter: 6¼ to 6½
Toppi diameter: 7¼ to 7½
For tonics between C and E
Valandalai diameter: 6¾ to 7
Toppi diameter: 7¾ to 8

There are no absolutes, though, and many mrdangam artists and woodcrafters have made small variations to accepted norms, sometimes going up to 7 and 8 inches (valandalai and toppi, respectively) for lower male pitches.

Woodcrafters also have some superstitions associated with these values. Apparently, the valandalai diameter of a 24-inch kattai made for tonics between C and E should not be exactly 6¾. And the mystical number reasoning attached to this is 6¾ + ½ + ¼ = 7½. When Rajamani explained this to me, he confessed that he too did not understand the logic. At any rate, the actual diameter is always a little less or more by just that wee bit. This is shastram is what they say.

When Somu was at the zenith of his craftsmanship, everything was done by hand. They had a wheel that needed to be worked physically. But in order to get enough revolutions on the wood, I presume there would have been a sort of lever system to attain high speed. When I asked Kuppusami Asari if the mechanisation had helped, he was categorical. 'The sound is better with the machine-made instruments. We used to work with our hands as no machines were available then.'

The chiselling of the mrdangam as it rotates is still done entirely by sight and feel. Hence, the degree of the two slopes towards either aperture are variable. Each mrdangam has its own gradient value. Due to this individuality, the playing membranes cannot be removed from one kattai and fitted on to another. Each playing membrane, be it the valandalai or toppi, is seated and fixed on one specific kattai. This is because each kattai is inimitable, the slope and exact shape of the aperture varying a little between each kattai.

But people agree that Somu's kattais were the exception. He was such a master that you could detach the membranes from one kattai and attach them to any other as long as the diameter of the apertures was the same. He achieved uniformity in the angle of the slope without any specialised measuring tools. Selvaraj said: 'Somu Asari, the master craftsman, used to give us a 20-inch kattai on which we would fix the playing membranes. After it was ready, we would just transfer them to the actual concert kattai. His brilliance lay in how perfectly they fitted on another kattai. Today, this is not possible because the curvature towards the openings varies with every kattai. Not so with Somu Asari.'

Back in Kuppusami's workshop, once the outside surface of the kattai had been shaped as needed, it was moved to a larger wood-working lathe. Here, the mrdangam was held in the chuck and supported a few inches from the other end in a steady rest which had a rotating bush.

More specifically, the toppi side was held in the chuck, which was connected to the belt system. All these lathes have been modified to suit the needs of mrdangam-making. For boring the kattai, a custom-made drilling rod—slightly curved but straightening towards its sharp end—is fixed on to the tool post. The tool post has rotating wheels, allowing for the drilling rod's traverse and longitudinal movement. This allows the machine operator to move the drill deeper into the kattai, then retreat and enlarge the circumference by moving the drill in the parallel direction.

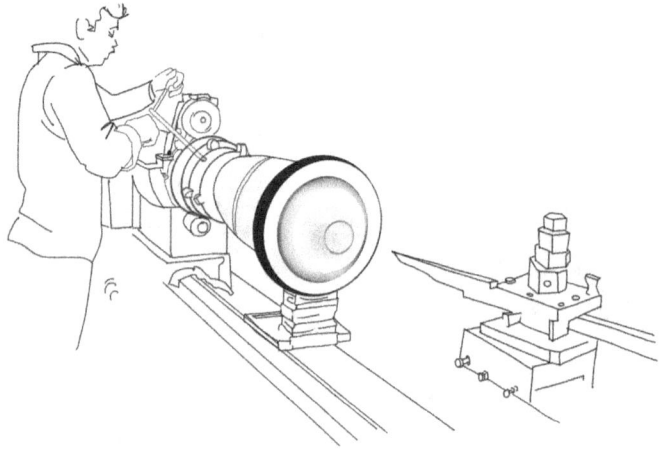

The woodcrafter stood parallel to the lathe, controlling the two movements with rotating wheels: one towards and away from the kattai and the other towards and away from him. He decides the exact angle of the drilling rod, tightens it and begins drilling from the centre of the valandalai. There is one more specification he has to keep in mind. As he is hollowing the wood, he must make sure that the final diameter of the frame—that is the thickness of the frame on the valandalai and toppi—is ¾ inches. As he goes deeper into the kattai, the thickness increases and there is specificity to that too. At its thickest point, which is where the circumference is the largest, the kattai is approximately 1¾ or 2 inches thick. The outer diameter at that point is about 11.5 inches, and the inner diameter of the hollow, 9.5 inches. All this is achieved by controlling just two rotating handles; there is no other tool.

Kuppusami's assistant was laughing as he explained all these details, moving the drill accurately all the while, not in the least worried that he may end up chipping off just a bit more than needed. 'We do this by experience,' he said. Much like a foosball player, he had one hand on the handle that moves the drill in and out, and another to adjust the point of entry. With utmost steadiness, he handled the machine, transforming the wooden block to a hollow kattai. When he reached the thickest point in the kattai, he turned the mrdangam around and started from the toppi side. When he finished drilling from that end too, the entire kattai was finally hollow. I thought of tunnels being drilled from both ends, meeting somewhere in between. When I put my hand into the kattai, it was rough and uneven; at its densest point, the thickness was more than 2 inches. 'Wait, now we will make it okay,' he said.

To achieve smoothness and to refine measurements, another kind of drilling rod was brought out. The rod itself is perpendicular to the kattai, but its short, sharp head is parallel to the wooden shell. As the woodcrafter moved the rod into the hollow, this blade faced the inner walls and shaved it clean.

The machine operator made sure that the sharp head was only just skimming the surface of the inner walls. The inner wall started becoming, like the outside, soft and silken. Once again, the kattai was turned around and the clean-up was done from the other end as well.

There is one more danger in all this: that, at the end of this process, the frame shape of the valandalai or toppi becomes elliptical, a serious error. Not something that would ever happen with Somu Asari's work, of course. At the end of this lathe work, the kattai is cleaned and polished with wax or castor oil. Makers and artists are sometimes tricked by crafters who colour the wood with varnish, making it seem like good inner wood when it actually has a large velladai section. Mrdangam makers often speak about the need to be careful. 'If there is a crack in the wood, the kattai makers will stick it with gum, apply a powder and cover it. That is how they work nowadays,' Guruvayur Dorai had also said.

In the course of the interview, Somu Asari often spoke of his own ignorance. He made it a point to attribute everything to the genius of Mani Iyer. He spoke of himself as if he were just another lathe machine. Rajaram, too, wanted only to know more and more about his father's ideas, knowledge and creativity. Though he mentioned the need to document Somu's techniques, the interview was focused on what Somu knew about Iyer's ideas. Somu himself was unseen—there was very little interest in his life, or the changes he had personally made to the mrdangam kattai. Much like court musicians who surrendered their very selves to the king, Mani Iyer was Somu's lord. There was a sense of ownership in the relationship that is difficult to put into words. So strong was Iyer's hold on Somu's mind that the woodcrafter was convinced his own imagination was really Mani Iyer's. On his part, Iyer might have been convinced that it was only his thoughts that Somu had absorbed and was implementing. Somu says at one point, 'He (Mani Iyer) told me about this; that's how I know. What do I know on my own? In this world, no one has done anything like Palghat Mani Iyer has for the mrdangam.' He also tacitly devalued Palani by saying, 'He (Palani) said, "do whatever you do for Ayya".'

The only stories that Rajaram could share about Somu Asari were about his alcoholism and Iyer's struggles to ensure he was sober enough to do his job. 'By 6–6.30 in the morning, Somu would be drunk, even though those were times of prohibition. The previous night he would have come, taken money and got drunk. Even in that state, he would mention the dimensions of the mrdangam perfectly. My father would ask for them and he would say, "Ayya, I will surely do it in the morning." But at 7 a.m., he would be near the sewers, drunk. So Surendran (Palghat Mani Iyer's student) would go at 5 a.m. and sit at Somu Asari's house. Even then he would slip away. But after two or three days, if you caught him, he would finish what people take five days to do in three-fourths of a day itself.'

This is a repeated theme, of a drunk Somu, a drunk Parlandu. Even makers of non-dalit castes spoke of the drunkenness of the Thanjavur family. Kalidas suggested that alcoholism was rampant among dalits. 'They were all good but had this one drawback—drunkenness. Starting from Parlandu to Gunaseelan. I think the youngsters today are better. It had nothing to do with the mrdangam or anything. It was more due to their community and caste. Even today, alcoholism is more prevalent among the dalits. The lower you go on the financial scale, you find more alcoholism and a lack of willingness to work hard. It is the women of the house who do all the work. I am not casting any aspersions; I am just making an observation.'

Interestingly, the drunkard-genius is a valorised trope when the imbiber of spirits is from among the upper castes. T.R. Mahalingam, the flautist, is a classic example of someone who was an alcoholic but whose drunkenness is spoken of with much affection. His genius eclipsed everything else, they would say. But Somu, the undisputed champion among woodcrafters, would never be given that leeway—his drunkenness is a defect born of his caste. This hypocrisy of the upper castes, and those aspiring to be like them, is insufferable.

Arulraj from the Thanjavur family had a different interpretation. 'If they (his father and uncles) had extra money, they would head straight to the liquor store. Immediately, their mood would change.' He was speaking in the context of how the older generation unquestioningly accepted their social status and the way they were treated. Alcoholism could also have been an escape from reality.

5

THE DEPTH OF SKIN

My co-musicians had just arrived in Sydney, one of them a mrdangam artist. They had filled out the immigration and customs form unthinkingly—a uniform 'no' to every question, just as they did in the US form. Karnatik musicians travel to the US frequently, which is what led to the reflexive box-ticking.

Unfortunately, the Australian immigration and customs form is a rather different beast, and asks some very crucial questions. The mrdangam artist had just woken from a long nap, and having cleared immigration, he placed his bags into the scanner. And he was promptly stopped. The mrdangam bag was opened. There was no need to inform the officer that it was made of leather and wood; it was only too obvious. My colleague went into panic mode, unable to string even a few words together. The violinist standing beside him was told to stay out of it by a gruff-voiced customs official. Our concert was the very next day, and I was arriving in a few hours. There was no way he could afford to lose the mrdangam.

Australia, you see, has very strict fumigation rules. If you are bringing into the country anything made of leather, wood or similar material, whether for import or personal use, it has to be sent ahead. The authorities will fumigate it in order to ensure that the item carries no disease that might ruin their agricultural economy. I understand that they are conscientious about intra-country travel too.

The artist was asked about the mrdangam, its construction, material and age. On the wall behind the officer was the poster of a dholak, a similarly built percussion instrument—clearly, he was familiar with Indian instruments. Now, this mrdangam artist is practically incapable of lying; he blurted out that the instrument was new, just a month old. Later, he said, 'You could still smell the skin; it was fresh. How could I lie?' Everyone could smell it: this was a brand new mrdangam, only just delivered by the maker.

My friend had hoped to use it for a few concerts in Australia and then sell it to an aspiring learner on his way out. This is standard operating procedure for mrdangam artists: buy new instruments and sell them at a premium outside the country. Their old, precious, heirloom mrdangams rarely board an international flight. Mrdangam makers often complain about how artists make a killing on these sales but just pocket the proceeds, never sharing a part of the profit. Anyway, at that moment, the customs section of the Sydney Kingsford Smith Airport smelt of cow, buffalo and goat hide. Even though they had all been cleaned and fitted, the place still smelt like an abattoir.

More than a decade later, I tried to persuade Soosainathan to let me accompany him to the abattoir. He vehemently dissuaded me. 'It will be horrible and scary. Nothing like anything you would have seen; brahmins cannot handle it.' When I interviewed Ravikumar, he too had said, 'Some people said they will come, I refused to take them. What if they faint there?' I persisted, and eventually Soosainathan relented. 'Leave at around 5 a.m. and pick me up near the Central Station,' he said.

The Chennai Central Station, which is now the rather cumbersomely named Puratchi Thalaivar Dr M.G. Ramachandran Central Railway Station, is a familiar location for me, even more so a few decades ago, when the airfares were too high for most of us musicians to afford. I drove to the main road in front of the station, where Soosainathan was waiting. My student who was to accompany me had chickened out at the last moment. So, Soosainathan and I set off alone; Melgies would join us later. We turned right at Chennai's iconic Ripon Building and then I lost my bearings entirely. These were parts of the city I had never visited—too north-Chennai for a southerner like me. After more turns and curves than I could keep track of, Soosainathan directed me towards what looked like the entrance to a market area.

It was a Sunday morning. As I drove in, there were small stalls with low plywood tables on the side of the road. Early risers were negotiating the prices of beef, blood jelly and boty. Soosainathan pointed to the blood and said that it is used in sambar. My eyes popped; I had always thought of sambar as quintessentially brahmin. The very name oozed vegetarianism to me—kolambu might have signalled a non-vegetarian possibility, but never sambar! At the time I went on this field trip, I was quasi-vegetarian. I had progressed to seafood, a transition in which the lack of blood helped.

'Do you see that?' asked Soosainathan, pointing at an awkward-looking blob of meat. 'That is boty.' For the next five minutes, he attempted to explain what a many-splendoured thing it was. Boty is the intestines of the goat, and according to Soosainathan, has medicinal properties and is very good for health. I was suddenly terrified about what was in store.

On my left was the slaughterhouse, and opposite it goats awaiting their turn watched the proceedings. All the goats had numbers written on them—their Aadhaar number! The slaughterhouse itself was owned by the government of Tamil Nadu, and individuals were allowed to use the facilities for a charge. I was told that most people in the business were Muslims, while the workers were mostly dalit. We parked the car a little further inside, and walked on, turning right at the bend. Here, cows and buffaloes hung upside down on sharp hooks. The carcasses were half-skinned or being skinned. Soosainathan informed me that I had missed the actual slaughtering. 'Today is Sunday, so the demand is much higher; everything begins early.' I looked down and realised that there was blood all around me. That's when the smell really hit me. How do I describe it? It was not a stench, not repulsive and it did not make me queasy, but it was all-consuming. Like a low, heavy cloud, you could actually feel it on your skin.

But something unexpected happened to me within minutes of reaching this place. All around me were men dressed in banians and lungis, their clothes and bodies stained with blood, walking around, laughing, bargaining, making small talk as they worked, and sipping from a tea cup with their bloody hands ... This was their workplace, I realised; their everyday, their normal. Nothing here was unnatural. The killing of animals was their living, an accepted and necessary fact of life. And somehow, as I watched them and all the buzz and activity, I eased into the place.

Kali was our contact person. After introductions and explanations about what a 'Peter' (Chennai slang for an upper-class, English-speaking dude) was doing here, he asked me why I did not bring a camera. Not long ago, the Bombay High Court had upheld the ban on cow slaughter in Maharashtra. And since 2014, when India elected Narendra Modi as prime minister, giving the Bharatiya Janata Party a majority in the lower house of Parliament, there have been numerous attacks on dalits and Muslims who traded in beef. Of course, this is a state subject, and cow slaughter is legal in Tamil Nadu. All the same, I was worried that a camera would make people uncomfortable. Now I saw that no one here really cared.

We followed Kali through the effluence of the abattoir, body liquids mixed with water, across channels meant for the liquids to drain. Kali pointed to a small heap and said, 'Check this.' It looked like a dirty jute sack, but it was buffalo skin. Soosainathan asked me to touch it and make a judgement. 'How is it?' he asked. I had no clue what it was supposed to be like. The skin felt both hairy and gooey. Then I was asked to touch another skin, which I obediently did. All the while, Kali looked at me with curiosity and a little irritation. My presence was delaying the transaction. Soosainathan said, 'We'll take this one.' He explained that it was thicker and hence better.

Buffalo skin makes up two layers used for the toppi, goat skin being the third. After an initial quote of Rs 1,500 for the chosen skin, they mutually agreed on Rs 1,300. The skin now had to be hauled out of the slaughter shed. With Kali's help, we put it on a three-wheeled cart and had it brought to an open area nearby. As we walked, Soosainathan said, 'Nothing goes waste here. Every part of the animal is used for something or the other: food, leather, medicines.'

Mrdangam artists often say that no animals are killed specifically for the instrument. In an interview to S. Anand in *Outlook* magazine in 2003, Sivaraman had this to say: 'Cows are not killed to make mrdangams. They are slaughtered anyway and we merely use the hide.' In that same article,

Rajamanickam at work in Trichy Sankaran's home in Toronto in 1991

Rajamanickam had responded with: 'Have these people ever been to a slaughterhouse to see what we do? We examine cows and choose the healthy ones that have good, lustrous, soft skin. The cow should have given birth at least a couple of times but shouldn't be too old.' This holds true for the buffalo or goat as well.

For the mrdangam, it is always the skin of the female animal that is used. The logic is that the skin of a female that has delivered at least twice is more stretchy. For another instrument, called the suddha maddalam, they use the bull, since that requires a thick, tight membrane.

When Soosainathan needs skin, Kali chooses a buffalo specifically for this purpose from the lot that has made it to the slaughterhouse. When an animal chosen for the mrdangam is skinned, he has to make sure that the knife does not leave too many marks. These marks on the skin are called 'katthi adi', literally, injuries caused by the knife. So, the mrdangam skin comes from a buffalo or cow specially chosen for its skin qualities, and then skinned in a specific manner.

Another lie perpetrated by some artists is that only the skin of animals that die naturally is used. John Britto explained why such skin will not work. 'When they slaughter the animal, the neck is slashed. This ensures that all the blood is pumped out and the veins below the skin are drained of blood. This gives the skin elasticity. In an animal that dies a natural death, the blood clots, and the skin becomes like cardboard. If we were to soak it in water and try to stretch it, the leather would break.' Sometimes sellers try to cheat gullible mrdangam makers by applying salt on an old animal's skin to keep it free from infection. To check for this trickery, makers lick the skin and test for salt.

We waited for about forty-five minutes in the rising heat before Melgies made his entrance. On another day, Soosainathan had teased Melgies about his sense of time and commitment: 'If I ask you to come on the day someone dies, you will arrive for the tenth-day ceremonies.' Melgies finally arrived and brought with him long iron nails that he dumped on the dusty ground. The shirt was removed and the veshti folded and tied at the waist, and he was ready to start working. Lying in a heap in front of us was the skin. But, as soon as Melgies and Soosainathan opened it up, it was an entirely different object. The skin was still moist, the hairy outer surface sticky because of the blood that had oozed, and the inside dark pink, cream and dirty brown, with dust and sand sticking to it. The buffalo had been slit from her abdomen, which meant the skin opened up inside-out, like a bedspread. It was first laid out in the sun with the inner fleshy side facing up. You could actually see the veins under the flesh and stains of blood all over. The odour was still powerful. Ravikumar had referred to this smell as the smell of 'kari'—the smell of red meat.

Soosainathan and Melgies began stretching the skin and nailing it to the ground. As they tugged at it, adjusted and nailed it at the edges, I could make out the shape of the animal. The face was split into two parts, with the ears closer together. It seemed as if the buffalo had shed its skin, as a snake does. The front legs looked like hands and the hind ones appeared elongated. The hairy tail was intact. The nailing had made the skin taut and raised it a little above the ground. Melgies produced a sharp blade, and Soosainathan announced, 'Now we need to take the javvu out.' What is javvu? Is it fat, I asked. No, it is the flesh below the skin. With utmost care and patience, they began removing the javvu. Much like the chefs on TV shows who peel an apple with such finesse that the entire skin comes out as one continuous swirl, Melgies and Soosainathan removed the thin layer of flesh with surgical precision. It came off like dried Fevicol would from your hands.

I couldn't resist giving it a shot. It looked easy enough. But the flesh was really stuck to the skin. I needed to cut with precision while simultaneously pulling the flesh off—and this had to be managed so that the knife would leave no marks on the skin. After about fifteen minutes and many tattered pieces of flesh, I gave up. Once the flesh was cleaned, the inside of the skin looked absolutely white; I mean bright white. All this took about an hour. Now, we had to wait. The sun was bright in the cloudless sky. Melgies said the skin would take about two hours to dry. As we headed to the tea shop around the corner, our bodies exuded the smell of fresh meat.

After a long chat about politics, mrdangam-making and other things, we returned to ground zero and waited for another hour under the hot sun. Soosainathan then took out a piece of chalk and drew a line down the centre of the skin, head to tail. Then he began drawing circles in free hand on the parts of the skin that would have covered the stomach. These circled pieces of skin are called thattu, literally, 'plate'. The process itself is called thattu podradu, or making the plates. The non-thattu part—skin from the back and sides—was first cut out. Following this, the thattus were carved out very carefully with a sharp knife. As you might have guessed, these thattus will be used for the two buffalo membranes of the toppi. He cut out nineteen thattus from that one buffalo skin.

'There is very little room to do all this work nowadays,' said Melgies. Earlier, they used a private piece of land on the other side of the road. They would tip the security guard a little and also get some tokens from the people in charge. I don't know if the tokens had any validity; more likely, it was just a payoff. Now there are buildings on that property, which means all the work needs to be done on a narrow stretch of land within the grounds of the slaughterhouse.

Later, Muruganandam told me about another place nearby. 'Near Choolai, where you went, there is not much place to nail the skin. So, we would do that closer to the railroad. As we did our work, someone could be defecating next to us.'

The place where makers dry the skin, in and around Choolai, is also a meeting point, a place for private conversation. An old lady wandered in and was warmly greeted by my friends. Her husband, Arikutti, used to supply skin. Now he was gone, and his wife had no home or work. The makers gave her some money and she returned the favour by getting them some water to drink. Soosainathan told me that he had not seen her for a while.

Close to us, a rookie arrived and stretched a buffalo skin. 'He bought the skin we rejected,' whispered Soosainathan. The newcomer had a compass and a few other instruments to get the work done. Melgies and Soosainathan had never seen him before, and wondered whose shop he worked at. There was amusement in their eyes as they saw him struggle with the skin and the gadgets. They gently offered help, but he was not interested. Like any young adult, the newcomer just wanted these two know-it-all oldies out of his way. 'We do not use a compass and measure the size of the thattu exactly because some extra is always better. We cannot be sure about the size of the mouth of the frame, you see, and need some room to manoeuvre. This guy does not know that,' muttered Soosainathan.

My work was done, but my two companions had more to do. They would take the thattus and the rest of the skin home and dry them under a fan. The whole house would be fogged with the strong smell of the hide, Soosainathan said. I believe him; it took a couple of days and a wash for my car to be rid of that redolence. Late at night on the same day, Soosainathan would soak the remaining skin, and leave it overnight. The next day, it would be cut into long strands called 'varu', or thongs made of buffalo leather. These are used to tie the membranes on either side of the mrdangam together. Over the years, the varu has been replaced with kayaru, or rope. T.V. Gopalakrishnan experimented with many different materials and finally settled on Teflon ropes. Others use polyethylene ropes, parachute ropes made of nylon kernmantle, or even flat nylon webbing used for climbing. These are more durable and easier to work with. But some traditionalists still insist on the varu.

It was time to leave, and all of us got into the car, exhausted, dying for a cold beer. We headed to a TASMAC shop, waited until noon for it to open, and got ourselves some beers. It had never tasted this good before. There was the heat of the day, of course, but also the overwhelming nature of the job: life and death, the smells and textures. This was an overbearing physical and emotional alternate reality for me. Perhaps even for those who inhabit this space on an everyday basis, the polarity between this world and the one beyond the slaughterhouse gates would be hard to reconcile.

I know non-vegetarians who have told me that they gave up eating meat for a month after witnessing the actual killing of the animal. And it struck me that my experience at the slaughterhouse shared nothing in common with them. I am struggling with words here, but this much I know: I did not feel sorry for the animals or repulsed by the fact that they would be killed. I realised that I had been bracing for the possibility of both feelings. Instead, the experience rearranged and problematised my notions of rightness. The makers kept telling me that artists refuse to understand what their work really means. They are troubled by the lack of empathy towards the hardships of it.

WE MET AGAIN A FEW days later to get the toppi muttu ready. Soosainathan had soaked the thattus in water overnight. Buffalo skin, being thicker than cow and goat skin, needs to soak longer before it is soft enough to work with. The hair was still on the skin. Soosainathan said it would be removed later and was easy to do. Unlike the cow, buffalo hair has more gaps between the follicles, he said. A little more cleaning and removing of javvu, and the thattus were ready.

Melgies took four varus that were knotted at the very end on one side, and using a screwdriver, pushed them into four holes on the circular leather frame of a discarded toppi muttu. The playing surface on that old muttu, made up of buffalo and goat skin, had been removed; what remained was only its outer leather ring. The discarded toppi muttu now has a new name: it is called a 'kavanai' and plays a very essential supportive role. Because it was once a toppi muttu, the kavanai already has holes on the rim. Into four of these were inserted four varus, which divided the ring into equal quadrants. With the four varus hanging freely from it, the kavanai was placed on the floor. The wooden mrdangam shell was then positioned vertically inside the kavanai in such a manner that the toppi-side opening was above.

We were now ready to place the skins on top of the toppi-side opening. Do you remember learning to cut a hole in the centre of a circular piece of paper? You fold it twice into a triangular shape and just chop off the pointed end. When it's opened up, there will be a perfectly circular hole right in the middle. Melgies did exactly that with two buffalo thattus.

There is an interesting expression that the makers use to refer to skin from the lower part of the animal, be it buffalo, goat or cow. As one moves away from the vertebrae, the skin thins. Hence, the thattus are sometimes thick on one side and thin on the other. They call this mottha–melisu (thick and thin). The closer the skin is to the vertebrae, the less the chances of this happening. In the case of a buffalo, however, the skin covering the back and upper stomach is used for varu. This means that buffalo thattus are cut from areas where the probability of mottha–melisu is high. In order to adjust for this natural anomaly, makers combine two thattus that will offset each other's thickness and thinness; i.e. the thick side of one will cover for the thin side of the other, and vice versa.

Melgies placed two buffalo thattus one on top of the other so that the hairy sides were on the outside. He made four holes through the thattus, aligned to the holes in the kavanai where the four varus were fixed, and then used the varus to fasten the thattus to the kavanai.

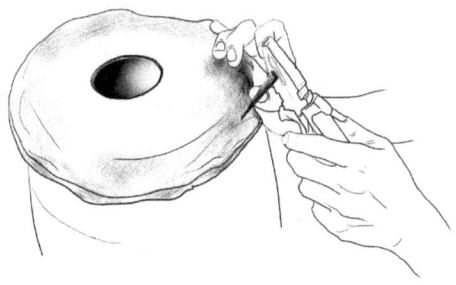

The four support varus that are threaded through the kavanai hold the skin during this initial stage of thattu-making: these are called thanguvarus or thangukayarus, depending on whether leather thongs or ropes are used. 'Thangu' means weight-bearing—and also used in the context of a friend whose shoulder is available to lean on.

The extra skin on the toppi's rim was cut out. 'Watch carefully now,' Melgies said. 'I will make two new holes between each of the four holes that hold the thanguvaru.' Using a short metal piece with a sharp end, he hammered in these holes on the skin.

The Tamil word for hole is usually tholai or ottai, but the makers use the word 'kannu', which means 'eye'. I wondered why. Author and poet Perumal Murugan gave me a possible explanation. There is a tradition in Tamil where words that are considered inauspicious are sometimes substituted with others. It is possible that 'tholai' is perceived as destructive and has been replaced with 'kannu', which is auspicious. For instance, the last thing that is done after sculpting a deity for worship and placing it in the sanctum sanctorum, is the opening of its eyes—an auspicious act. There were now twelve equidistant kannus just below the rim of the kattai.

Melgies then took out a long varu from a bundle of thongs. He began tying the two thattus to the kavanai below. As he moved around the mrdangam, stringing the varu through one kannu after another, he cut off any extra skin on the sides and also removed the four thanguvarus, looping this long varu through those holes. When one varu length ended, he took another piece of varu, knotted it to the one he was using and continued. Every time he put the varu through the two-layered membrane and the kavanai, he dipped the tip of the screwdriver in castor oil to enlarge the kannu and make it easier to pull the varu through. Finally, when he had completed the entire circle and looped the varu through all twelve kannus and twelve aligned holes in the kavanai, Melgies kept the varu end hanging but unyielding. Varu used like this is known as 'poivaru'. Poi means a lie—you will know soon why.

The Thanjavur makers used leather thongs in the past, but Madras makers have always used some sort of rope. Sivaraman had said 'Madrasule kayaru'; in Madras, it was rope. 'Yes, it used to be thick and come in six-piece rolls. It was like the rope used in dholkis,' affirmed Melgies. Now, everyone is using rope. The more I followed this story, the greater my conviction that the Thanjavur makers have actually learnt a lot from the makers of Madras, so much so that their distinct identities have dissolved.

Pulling at each varu loop, while resting both his feet on the mrdangam to create force and counterforce, Melgies began tightening it. In one hand was a metal hook to tug at the varu; in the other, a folded piece of cloth to ensure that the varu did not injure him when he grabbed at it. Pulling with the hook, pushing with his feet, grabbing the varu with the other hand, while the hook moves to the next thong ...

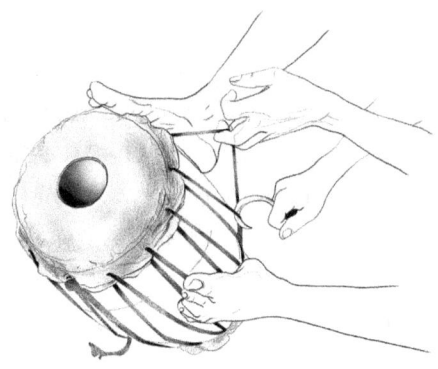

The mrdangam had begun its time-keeping.
pull-push-grab-pull
pull-push-grab-pull
pull-push-grab-pull
pull-push-grab-pull

As he went round and round, the membrane got further stretched, and the varu pulled the wood closer into a tight embrace. After every round, Melgies would do a final tightening by pulling at the varu at the very end where it was untied. Because this varu is rough and there is friction, the tension holds even though the end is not tied. The varu never slipped or loosened. On the third round, I could hear the skin crackling under the tension. Melgies gently knocked on the thattu, and a 'dup' sound emanated. This 'pulling' part of the work is called poivaru pidi, that is, the holding or pulling of the false varu.

Now, Soosainathan was ready to take over. 'Give me the wooden plank to sit on,' he demanded of Melgies, who responded with: 'This guy orders me around a lot. Okay, do the work, Superstar.' Soosainathan looked at me and said: 'Do you know, Selvam (Selvaraj) would sit on the floor for hours without a plank and just keep working.' There was admiration in his voice.

The best buffalo skins are from nattu buffaloes, the local ones, he declared. 'Delhi buffaloes and those with twisted horns do not give us the tone we need. Their skin is slimy like a seal, and does not have strength. Once, without knowing, I used the Delhi buffalo skin and the toppi muttu just tore. The nattu buffalo looks bony but the skin is strong and weighty.'

Soosainathan took out a blade and removed the hair from the edge of the skin, right at the outer rim of the wooden frame. He then took out an odd-looking circular rubber piece and placed it on top of the thattu. This was a simple modern innovation that allowed the maker to mark new points for kannus with precision. You see, the twelve kannus Melgies had made were only to hold the thattus together and were made towards the edge of the skins. They fall on the fold over the edge of the wooden shell. The kannus that Soosainathan was now making would be used to braid the skins together, and hence are made exactly at the outer edge of the shell's frame. Soosainathan made sixteen points on the edge, using the marking contraption, and another sixteen between those in free hand—a total of thirty-two kannus.

So far, I have referred to the skin membranes as thattu, not muttu, and there is a reason. The word 'muttu' denotes stitching. In fact, when the edges of a lungi are stitched together, it is referred to as muttu adikardu, or stitching it together. Soosainathan is actually going to do that now, and so I will switch to using 'muttu'.

Another fascinating aspect of the Thanjavur makers' vocabulary is the contextualisation. The same material is referred to with different names depending on what it is used for. You've already heard two words for the leather thong:

thanguvaru and poivaru. The poivaru is temporary because its job is only to hold the skins together in high tension so that the thattus can be braided together.

'Give me that ul sattai,' Soosainathan told Melgies—a new term again for the varu. This thong is smaller in length, and Soosainathan checks if it is long enough to go around the circumference of the toppi, then thins it a little with a blade. 'Ul' means 'inside' in Tamil; we'll soon see why this short length is called that.

All this while, in a bucket next to him was a bundled varu dipped in water. But it was placed so that the ends were above the surface of the water. He took it out now and sharpened the ends. Of this, he said he needs two lengths, each measuring one bagam. What is one bagam? It is the length of one end of your hand to the other when both hands are stretched out sideways in line with the body. This varu is the pinnrasattai: pinnal is braiding, and sattai, usually meaning a whip, is in this context understood to be a long cord.

Varu in water, with the ends above the water level, awaits Martin's attention

Now began the most visually aesthetic part of this entire process. The two bagam-long varus were put through two kannus each. They looked like four creeper strands on a circular wall.

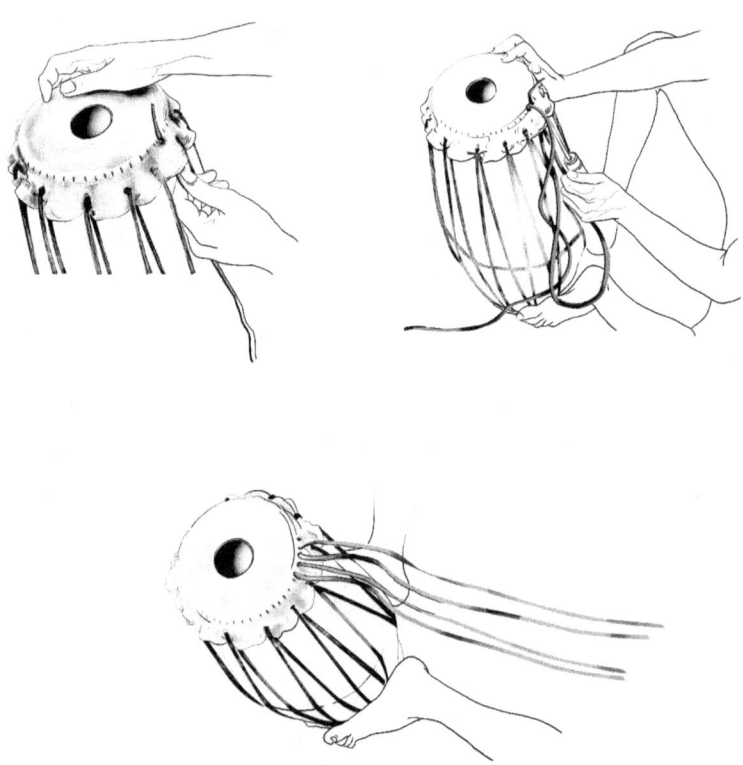

Braiding, say of hair, usually requires three strands and is typically a vertical line. Here, the braid was horizontal, going around the rim of the wooden frame, and used four pinnrasattai strands. Suppose we numbered the four strands from left to right?

Soosainathan put One into the fourth kannu from the left, inserting it from above.

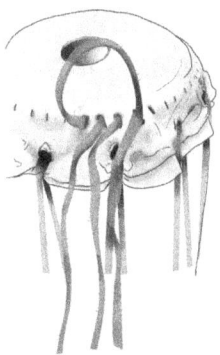

He then took it out from below and pushed it through the next hole from below, pulled it out from above and left it to hang.

Then, Two was pushed in from above into the kannu where one had been pulled out from and then pushed through the next kannu from below, pulled out from above and left to hang.

Next, Three was pushed in from above into the kannu where two had been pulled out from and the process was repeated.

After which, Four was pushed in from above into the kannu where three had been pulled out from and the process was repeated.

He had now completed one cycle.

Soosainathan kept dipping the screwdriver in castor oil, opening up the size of the kannu and pushing through the pinnrasattai. After one round of this braiding process, he used the screwdriver and opened up a tunnel-like gap within the braid. And through that he pushed the ul sattai—the sattai that is pushed inside the pinnal. This helps lift the braid a little above the wooden rim and holds it tightly in place and shape. Soosainathan then tightened the pinnrasattai by pulling at all the four sattai strands. The braid now held the ul sattai in a tight grip. Soosainathan continued braiding, making sure that every braid went over the ul sattai.

We now have four different names for the buffalo-skin thong: thanguvaru, poivaru, pinnrasattai and ul sattai.

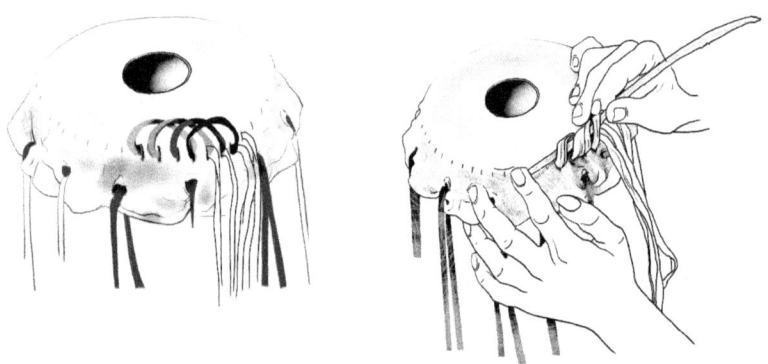

Soosainathan braided all the way around the circumference of the toppi and was back where he began. Finally, he dexterously made a hole on two of the four pinnrasattai strands, inserting the other two through them and twisting them into a bind. They now looked like mating snakes. This was essentially a locking system. This muttu had to dry for a day or two, after which there would be more work to do.

BIRYANIS ARE AT THE HEART of the most heated epicurean battles in India. So many towns and cities are synonymous with the biryani they serve. Hyderabadi, north Malabar, Lucknow,

Calcutta … But there is a town on National Highway 48, which connects Chennai to Bangalore, that biryani connoisseurs outside of Tamil Nadu (and perhaps Karnataka) may not know of. Situated about fifty kilometres from Vellore, the town of Ambur is, however, known to every non-vegetarian Tamil. It had a population of just over a lakh (according to the 2011 census), and is a Muslim-majority settlement known as much for its flourishing leather business as for the lip-smacking biryani. My brother and nephew make it a point to stop there every chance they get.

But I turn to Ambur now because, when leather is the prime mover, makers of percussion instruments and suppliers of skin cannot be far.

Soosainathan and I took the popular Chennai–Bangalore Brindavan Express that leaves at 6.30 a.m. On the way to Ambur, he told me that, for a long time, goat skin was also sourced in Choolai, Chennai. But now goat-skin purchases have shifted to Ambur. We were to meet S. Kumar, who had emerged as the main skin supplier to the mrdangam makers of Chennai, Bangalore and many other cities in the past few decades. There are others, naturally, but he is the big daddy of the trade. In fact, Kumar now not only supplied skin but also made some instruments. His shop was much like that of the mrdangam makers in Mylapore. There were skins rolled and stored all over, as well as wooden shells of many kinds of instruments, a gas cylinder, rings of some kind and even a television set. I also noticed some work-in-progress mrdangams on the floor. Kumar was in his late forties or early fifties. Tough, quick and sharp in his responses, there was no beating around the bush with him.

'My father was from Salem. My maternal grandfather had been in this industry for fifty years. Then my mom took over. She used to make tavil thattus, tabla kattai, mrdangam kattai, urumbi, pambai, udukai and thappu,' he said. They were not just in the business of skin but also wooden frames for a variety of wood-and-skin percussion instruments. 'We also deal with just leather: goat, cow and buffalo. We get the goats from Andhra and they are skinned in the Hosur–Krishnagiri area. We get the buffalo skin locally and do all the work here ourselves.'

In quieter tones, he said, 'My father was from Rasipuram and was in agriculture. He was a gounder, but I don't know my mother's caste.' When Soosainathan prompted him to be open, he retorted, 'If I declare that my father is a gounder, wouldn't I be open about my mother's caste? But I don't know. My mom says naidu, I just accept it. As if that is going to come and feed us. They just learnt this job and did it generation after generation.' At any rate, it was his mother's side of the family that had been in this line of work. 'They even made new harmoniums and shruti boxes. I am the only one to have a shop. I even export and the sales are good. But my main customers are companies in Mylapore and T. Nagar in Chennai and in Bangalore. We also supply leather, mainly goat and cow skin, to people who do this job.' That is, mrdangam, tavil and tabla makers.

'The skin supply was done by my mother and grandfather, and without that, how can we survive?' he asked. 'My elder son Naveenkumar has also joined this business. My brother-in-law is also here. His name is Vimal. His father, Raja, is my uncle; I learnt the trade from him. He is my guru.'

Kumar used to work out of a shed on the side of the main road, his workplace practically on the road. But he wanted a better place once his son began working too. Naveen had also trained in mrdangam-making under Arogyam for seven or eight years, which explained the half-made mrdangams I saw in the store. Now he was spreading his wings, even travelling to Delhi for mrdangam work. Will he soon emerge as a threat to those in Chennai? Only time can tell.

But how did you end up here in Ambur, I enquired. 'This has turned out to be our destiny. Earlier, there was not much work, very difficult, very small market. We did work for people who did bhajanai (Namasankirtana) in villages around Thiruppattur and in the hill villages. If we stayed there for three months, we would earn 500–600 rupees. Now, just our monthly expenses are over 1,000 rupees. They would ask us to stay in a thatched shed outside the village, and give us food in a leaf and pour water onto our palms to drink. They wouldn't let us inside the house or even in the village. This was about twenty-five or thirty years ago. They were very conscious of caste. These days, things are not that bad. They need us for the job, so they make a lot of adjustments. Otherwise, we will tell them to do it themselves. Don't give it to us if you can't respect us.' Kumar said with some surprise that even Ayyars now tell Arogyam that the skin sourced from him is good. 'They even smell the skin, that is an improvement!'

Music shops and companies have given Kumar's business a boost, though now there are many others competing for a market share. Kumar travels to Chennai six to seven times a month to deliver up to seventy goat skins and twenty cow skins to mrdangam makers. Earlier, all the makers would assemble at one place and share in the bounty, but now, with larger requirements and so many more makers, this is impossible. Kumar has to physically go to each maker's shop and show his wares. 'People like Soosainathan come to Ambur and select the skin personally because they get a better choice. When I bring a set to Chennai, he is limited by what is in hand, which is not the case when he comes here.'

The time had now come for Soosainathan to take his pick from the bundles of goat skins in Kumar's shop. Kumar began unbundling and rolling out the skins. I had no idea that goat skin was so large. I thought of the goat as a small or medium-sized animal, and the sight of such a large surface area was difficult to square with the image in my head. The skins still had hair on them: jet black, black with white patches, brown on the back and slowly fading to cream down the sides, and an alluring golden brown. All of these were from mountain goats from Kadappa and Guntur in Andhra Pradesh. The environment and what the goat consumes deeply influences the nature of the skin, several makers told me. 'Around Madurai, the fat content in the leather is higher because the goats drink more fresh water. Whereas, in Madras, the salt in the water is higher, and when the goat drinks that, the fat content comes down. The leather is much thinner there,' Britto said. Makers look for thin goat skin.

Like with buffaloes, these skins were also from female goats. 'Male goats have too much fat,' Soosainathan told me later. The Tamil word for fat is kozhuppu, also used to mean an individual who is egotistical and arrogant. I guess it is no surprise that female goats are more grounded!

Soosainathan was specifically looking for two-colour skins with spots, something that is rare to find. And he said, 'I use such skin only for the toppi and valandalai muttus I make for professionals.' T.V. Gopalakrishnan had mentioned: 'When it comes to goat skin, they want black goats. There should be spots on the skin, specifically for toppi skin. The hair should be soft on those spots, as that provides better resonance. There is logic in everything.' Soosainathan picked six or seven goat skins.

The skin closer to the central vertebrae, coming down the shoulders and up to the stomach, is used for the valandalai, the narrow aperture of the mrdangam. The indentation near the hind legs, the flank, is called the allu, and the skin covering it is allu thol (thol means skin). Allu itself seems to be an expression from a regional dialect, Thanjavur perhaps. This skin is said to be soft and thin, and ideal for the toppi. They also take the skin from behind the forelegs, below the ribs. Though this area is known in Tamil as 'vila', some makers also call the skin from here as allu thol.

The mrdangam makers have a delightful tendency to point to parts of their own body while trying to explain which part of the animal the skin comes from. For instance, Sowriar pointed to his abdomen area while speaking about the allu and his own throat when referring to the cow's throat. This instinctive action caused me to wonder if, in some incorporeal sense, the skin had become part of their being and the mrdangam an extension of their self. It is the tendency of artistic processes to embed themselves in the artist.

From one goat skin, a maker can get a maximum of four toppi thattus and six valandalai thattus; eight if he is very lucky. Selvaraj had told me that, in the 1970s, one goat skin was about Rs 50; today, it is anything between Rs 400 and 550.

Sitting in Kumar's shop, Soosainathan drew circles on the goat skin he had chosen specifically for the valandalai; he did not bother about the allu section of this skin. He handed the chalk-marked skin to Naveen, who began cutting them neatly. As work progressed, I turned to observe the street. A bullock cart passed by on the well-laid tar road, which was lined with small houses and stores and an MGR poster a couple of doors away. Young men, presumably friends of Kumar or Naveen, were seriously observing the skin work here. Perhaps my camera was an attraction too.

Suddenly, Kumar expressed anguish at not being told that Selvaraj had passed away. He died a week ago and no one bothered to tell me, Kumar complained. Selvaraj was one of the masters, but when he passed on, very few noticed. Imagine the number of WhatsApp messages, Facebook posts and newspaper articles that would have appeared if he had been a great mrdangam artist. None of us bothered; even I did nothing about it. I also heard that no mrdangam artist was present to send off this great maker.

BACK IN CHENNAI, THE BRAIDED toppi muttu had dried over a few days, and was now ready to be fitted with the goat skin. Drying is crucial to the process. The hole in the centre of the toppi muttu allows air to pass through the mrdangam shell, allowing it to dry fast. But if the muttu does not dry uniformly or retains any moisture, it will not be able to hug the wooden frame evenly. Worse still, the ul sattai could get twisted inside. This will result in non-uniform sound.

It was time to complete the job, and so I met Soosainathan again. Now that the muttu was ready, the role of the poivaru was over. Soosainathan removed the poivaru and took the muttu out. It looked like a designer doughnut, with embroidery on the side and a small hole in the centre. Soosainathan turned it over so that the outward-facing side was flat on the ground. He had already removed the hair from the thin allu skin of the goat with a blade and soaked it in water. This one he had bought on another trip to Ambur. He took the skin out, squeezed it as hard as he could and dropped it back in the water, and then repeated the process. It was like he was washing clothes. I was concerned that the skin would tear but nothing of the sort happened. Soosainathan explained that this process would help the skin soften and become pliable. When he was finished, it looked as soft as a chapatti.

After the goat thattus are cut out for the toppi and the valandalai, a thin strip is cut out and immersed in water, and the remaining skin is put aside.

Soosainathan placed the allu skin on the inside of the toppi muttu such that it covered the muttu completely all around the perimeter. There was a gap between the goat skin in the rear and the buffalo skin in the front of the muttu. The goat skin was delicately tied to the muttu with twelve small pieces of the goat-skin strips using the holes made for the poivaru. The hairy side of the skin faced the outside of the muttu. Soosainathan made sure there were no wrinkles in the allu skin as he tied it. The muttu was now visibly three-dimensional because of the gap between the buffalo thattus and the allu thattu.

The toppi mechanism is a thing of beauty. Two membranes made of buffalo skin are braided together, rock solid, while the third layer of thin goat skin is simply tied on the inside and is flexible. These variations offer the artist two different surfaces, tensions, strengths and tonalities. But the goat skin needs to be closer to the buffalo-skin membranes so that there is no gap on the surface while playing. This is achieved in a stunningly simple manner.

The toppi muttu is placed on the floor inside out, the goat skin facing up, and the maker neatly places the toppi side of the shell on top of it. The pressure of the shell automatically forces the goat skin to move and close the gap between the two membranes. But the goat skin can still move a little when the mrdangam is played, adding to its sonic diversity, thus allowing the creation of more strokes. Which came first is anybody's guess, but there is no doubt that these innovations in the making extended the possibilities of the mrdangam.

In the final stages of getting the two muttus ready, the top two layers of the buffalo skin will be cut open even more at the centre, giving the goat skin thattu a larger open playing surface. I will describe this in detail later on.

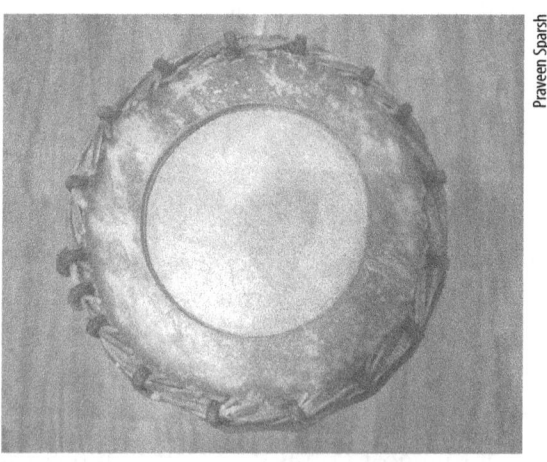

The toppi muttu mounted on a mrdangam; this is the view after the buffalo skin has been cut further, exposing more of the goat skin

The goat skin is easily removable too. If it is eaten by insects or small holes appear on it due to wear and tear, the maker only needs to remove the toppi muttu, untie the goat skin and replace it. Only if the buffalo-skin layer ages or is damaged does the toppi muttu need to be entirely replaced. The next step in the making is preparing the valandalai muttu, which is fixed to the other side of the shell. Now that the toppi is braided and fits to a tee, it will play the role of the kavanai—the support ring.

PALGHAT MANI IYER WAS OBSESSED with the toppi, and tried everything in his power to bring it under his control. It was not just about attaining perfection; he wanted the toppi to be obedient and respond to his whims and fancies. If he tried adjusting it, which is usually done with a large, smooth pebble, it must respond in a jiffy. With one knock, he wanted to be able to bring the tone down or raise it. He would spend hours with the makers in the hope that he could make the toppi respond as he wished. When Rajamani returned from office, a triumphant Mani Iyer would sometimes be waiting for him. With childlike impatience, he would immediately summon his son. One hit on the pinnal from above and the frequency would go up; one hit from below, the frequency would drop. Proud and satisfied, he would feel like he had conquered the toppi. But by the evening or the next day, the toppi would have developed a mind of its own, and the battle would resume.

Iyer's obsession with the toppi may also have had something to do with his colleague, friend and bête noire, Palani Subramania Pillai, who was known for the most elegant toppi sound. The toppi is the bass side of the mrdangam and its resonances are in the lower registers. Palani's toppi sound was deep, sustained, moving, reverberating, which gave his mrdangam a distinctive tonal equilibrium. His valandalai's tonality was tight and gripping, while his toppi was a languorous drawl—a sonic tension that remains unmatched. Guruvayur Dorai, his student, told me, 'He would keep tapping on it and look for a uniform tone. If it is a little off, he will ask the maker to start all over again. The toppi should sound like the tambura. Rom rom not dhom dhom. It is a balance.'

Though the toppi side is not tuned to any pitch, Palani had an aural image of its sound in his mind. When he tapped gently at its central region, he needed to hear that open baritone. And when he tested the stunning circular stoke called the gumki, it had to result in a prolonged deep sound that had its own exquisite tonal curvature. If he did not feel these sounds, Palani would reject the muttu.

Mani Iyer missed this in his own mrdangam. Besides, the fact that Palani's toppi was always spoken about made him desperate. Once, Parlandu went to Trichy for a few days to work with Palani. When he returned, Iyer was fuming. In the words of Rajaram, the other son of Mani Iyer: 'As soon as Parlandu came home, my father asked him why he hadn't come to work for so many days. Parlandu said Palani was in Trichy and had asked him to do some work on his mrdangams. My dad dropped it for that moment, but he could not keep quiet. After an hour, he went up to the mrdangam room and asked Parlandu what work he did for Palani. Parlandu said that he worked on the toppi muttu of about four mrdangams. So my father further queried, so what is his mrdangam size? What muttu does he put? How does he select the skin? Parlandu answered each question. But my father persisted, and asked how Parlandu selected the skin for the toppi muttu. Parlandu said that the work was similar to what he did for my father. My father didn't believe him and said that he was unable to get that toppi sugam (contentment and comfort in sound and playing). What is it that you do differently there? Do the same for me. Because my father insisted, Parlandu said, if we used thinner skin (goat), we will get that sound quality. So my father asked him to do the same with his mrdangams also. After a month, when the mrdangam was ready, my father tested it and said, no, it is still not like his. These trials happened two or three times. At home, we began calling that muttu "Palani muttu". Parlandu tried many things, but my father was still not satisfied. One day, just before he left for Bombay, he shouted at Parlandu, asking how he could be considered a good mrdangam maker if he could not get this done. So, Parlandu told him that, by the time he came back, the new muttu would be ready, because he was getting some very good skin. When my father returned from Bombay, Parlandu had kept the mrdangam ready along with five–six others. Whenever my father came back from his trips, there would be four or five mrdangams ready, which had been worked on. He checked all of them and asked for the one with the Palani muttu. He checked it and said that it was still not like Palani's. Parlandu gave him a very sharp response. With his hands over his mouth, he said, "Ayya, I will say something, but you should not get upset. That is in his hands."'

Mani Iyer's search for the elusive flawless toppi also led him to try deer and monitor lizard skin. All these attempts failed.

6

THE BEAT'S HIDE

There is a general belief across the globe, and even among many Indians, that Hindus do not eat beef. Yet, there is evidence that there was considerable beef-eating in the Vedic period and later, including among brahmins. Many Hindus continue to eat beef, especially among the dalit communities but not restricted to them. Besides, India is among the world's top five beef exporters. That the cow is an unslayable holy animal is a modern brahminical concept, not one necessarily shared by the larger population. But the brahmin castes, who have had an outsized impact on policy and in constructing cultural norms when compared to their size in the population, have established this untruth as a sacred universal, so much so that it found a place in the Constitution of India. Although this provision is only in the Directive Principles, which means it is not enforceable by any court, the cow still finds special mention. And, over the years, many state governments have brought in laws that banned or regulated cow slaughter.

Article 48 of the Constitution reads, 'The State shall endeavour to organise agriculture and animal husbandry on modern and scientific lines and shall, in particular, take steps for preserving and improving the breeds, and prohibiting the slaughter, of cows and calves and other milch and draught cattle.'

Born in a traditional Palakkad brahmin family, Palghat Mani Iyer went through a period of battling a contradiction: an instrument that necessitated taking the life of three animals—most crucially, of the holy cow—was his very life. Although Iyer believed that the mrdangam was a veda vadyam (a Vedic instrument), he asked himself whether it was right to kill a cow to construct it. Isn't it a sin, he wondered. In search of self-reconciliation, he decided to approach the Shankaracharya of Kanchi Mutt, whom every devotee addressed as maha periyava (the great elder). But Iyer hesitated: was it not inappropriate to pose such a question to the pontiff? Unsure, he resolved to instead speak to C. Rajagopalachari, whom Mahatma Gandhi called his conscience-keeper. Through friends, he reached Rajagopalachari and asked him this question.

Rajaji, as he was known, gave him a pragmatic answer by quoting a proverb: 'Don't look for the source of a river or the antecedents of a saint'. In other words, he asked Mani Iyer not to seek difficult answers. How convenient! It is the maker who plays the role of an intermediary for the artist, veiling the origins and allowing the latter to seek comfort in such a proverb.

The cow is removed from the artist's sight. Since the killing and skinning happen beyond his circle of existence, he can act as if it does not happen. The maker stands at the threshold, keeping the cow and the brahmin apart, helping the latter maintain his 'purity'. So, the maker is vital for the player, yet his role also keeps the maker 'polluted' and unequal. Once the blood is removed, the skin is cleaned and cut in shape, then dried and finally brought to the artist, it has been transformed through the labour of the makers into a resource, a lifeless ingredient. I have overheard mrdangam artists justify this need for cow skin by saying that the animal itself prays that its skin be used for this blessed instrument. To Ravikumar, the maker, the skin itself has life; one to which no negativity is attached because it comes alive through shruti. But he either did not acknowledge, or did not see fit to speak the hard truth: that it is the maker—he, and others like him—who give the skin life after death. I had to intervene and remind him.

Ravikumar

At any rate, the irony does not escape the makers, even if the players fail to see it. As a maker told me, 'We talk about goats and cows. Most artists are brahmins. They don't like the smell and don't know anything about how we process the skin. But the instrument will be in their pooja room. The makers are not given that respect.' Another said, 'When I work on the mrdangam, I use my legs to hold it. But you take the same mrdangam inside your room and worship it.' (The legs and feet are, of course, another source of ritual pollution in the brahminical worldview.)

To maintain an unblemished image, artists need to distance themselves and their audience from these realities. The conservative audience of the sabhas must not get so much as a whiff of the abattoir.

In these short excerpts from my conversations with the maker Sundar (name changed), the revulsion and fear they witness are starkly evident.

> **Sundar:** The makers' job is risky work. What will they (the artists) say? Will they tell people that we work in blood and muck? How can they say such things in a sabha? That will cause people to fear the mrdangam and tabla. They will feel horrible that artists are playing these instruments.
>
> **Krishna:** Why will they be scared?
>
> **S:** People fear it. For death rituals, there is molam (percussion ensemble), right? People see this with that view and there is bias against any skin instrument.
>
> [...]
>
> **TMK:** Like you said, on stage, we can't say that this has come from blood.
>
> **S:** (gesturing) You cannot!

TMK: So that has to be hidden?

S: Yes.

TMK: So, you have to be in hiding?

S: (laughs; makes a gesture of helplessness)

TMK: You can't come out.

S: Yes, sir. That it has come from blood. That we did this. They do not need to know we nailed the skin here and did all this. The audience doesn't need it. People don't need it. Because it's readymade and they see it.

TMK: Like it's magic?

[…]

S: People don't see the paddy crop at all. They only see the final rice that comes home. This is similar.

TMK: Sabhash! You put it beautifully. Very beautifully. But the difference is that, with your job, they have a dirty image of it.

S: Correct. Not just dirty, they also have fear … Everything here in the final product is sanitised and clean. But they still have a fear about that … that blood.

When I asked Mohan (name changed) whether all this will change, he said, 'If it had to change, the people of those days, the first ones—Mani sir, Murthy sir and all of them—should have changed things. The artists of today won't change it, and whether the next generation will ever do anything to bring in change is doubtful.'

There might have been a trigger to the existential crisis that Mani Iyer confronted. Alkattan, Parlandu's cousin, was considered an expert at choosing skins and made very good varus. I have not been able to ascertain how exactly Alkattan is related to Parlandu. In such situations, the English generality 'cousin' always comes to the rescue. Iyer gave Alkattan a job. He said he wanted top-draw cow skin, no compromises and the cost did not matter. Alkattan said it would cost Rs 100. Iyer gave him that amount immediately, in advance, and headed out to a restaurant around 3 or 4 p.m. When he returned, he found Alkattan standing outside his house, cow in tow. Iyer was startled, to say the least. Alkattan informed him that this cow had great skin, but the seller wanted Rs 120, and so he wanted to check with Iyer before completing the transaction. Iyer was shocked. Almost certainly, this would have been the first time he had to make a decision on the slaughtering itself, and take responsibility for something that was thus far hidden. He just shooed Alkattan away, and demanded that he take the cow with him. This incident from Iyer's life is a universal condition—I am certain that no mrdangam artist would like to be placed in a similar situation. Skin just drops down from the heavens, as far as they are concerned.

Selvaraj had told me that Mani Iyer could look at a cow and tell whether its skin would work. Cows would be brought to the front of his house; Iyer would look through the first-floor window and later negotiate a price or gently ask the seller to leave, depending on the quality he saw. Rajamani refuted this story, saying that the only occasion when Iyer was placed in such a predicament was when Alkattan landed up at their doorstep with a cow! Nevertheless, it is clear that Iyer was very interested in learning about skin, its nature and quality. And, according to Selvaraj, it was cow skin that he was most serious about. He also had a thing about the colour of the skin, especially cow skin. Mani Iyer liked it to be white, said Selvaraj.

It is clear, though, that both Mani Iyer and Palani really tried understanding how skins are chosen by the makers. They would still only look at skin that had been sanitised by the maker, but they had started buying larger quantities of processed skin for storage in their mrdangam rooms. Needless to say, all of this was purely born out of the need for a special and specific sound—an obsession with the instrument.

The mrdangam artists, however, deny that Mani Iyer or Palani knew or learnt skin selection. As Dorai said, 'Only the maker knows what kind of skin to pick. When and where, only the maker knows, artists do not. They can immediately tell us whether it can be used for the valandalai or toppi. Munusami and Venkatesan were experts at it.' Sankaran was unequivocal when asked if Palani selected the skin. 'That we cannot do. But they (Palani, etc.) knew from experience which skin will work and would suggest that to some extent. Thanjavur people (makers) were knowledgeable about this.'

S. GABRIEL, SOOSAINATHAN'S FATHER, TOOK ME to the place where cows are slaughtered in Thanjavur. Driving past the CRC shed, a bus depot, we slowly moved away from the more densely populated areas. A smaller road led to even smaller roads, then houses transformed to hutments, and paddy fields surrounded us and then gave way to open lands and the invasive seemai karuvelam (*Prosopis juliflora*) trees.

Soosainathan does not usually make this trip himself. His father does all the required work: cleaning, cutting and drying, and finally cleaning the hair by applying ash on it and shaving it off with a blade. He sends Soosainathan readymade cow thattus. There are many others in this part of the business, mostly relatives of the Thanjavur makers, who ship ready-to-use skin to Chennai. One good cow skin costs approximately Rs 3,000, but the rate is variable and changes according to the season. It is much harder to get skin during the rains.

'Turn here,' Gabriel shouted. We seemed to have missed the spot. All I saw was a nondescript asbestos shed on the other side of the road. Not even a shed, just a roof on four bamboo poles. Inside was a wooden cutting table, some ropes hanging from the ceiling and nothing else. 'Tomorrow is Sunday, right?' Gabriel asked. 'They will cut tomorrow; they do this every Sunday. I come and buy carefully because we need thin skin. I buy whenever Soosainathan informs me of a need.'

Soosainathan added, 'My father dries the skin and brings it home at 1 or 2 p.m. to cut thattus. When they get home, he will apply vibhuthi (ash) on the skin and remove the hair. After that, they cut out the thicker thattus, medium thattus, mottha–melisu, etc. and send them to me.'

Thanjavur makers swear by the quality of the cow skin in their district. They refuse to buy from anywhere else, claiming that it is superior to other skin and ideal for the mrdangam. Other makers, like Muruganandam or Balaguru, scoff at this premium placed on Thanjavur cow skin. While Muruganandam buys his skin from Ambur, Balaguru buys from Gumudipoondi, north of Chennai, close to the Andhra border. Ravikumar, who lives not too far from Gumudipoondi, however, buys his skins from Naidupettai and Kalahasti. His buffalo skin comes from Tirupati, Renigunta or Choolai.

There was one universal complaint about the quality of skin, both from the makers and the players. They all spoke about the deteriorating health of cows today. They eat plastic and all kinds of rubbish, and that is affecting the health of their skin, they complained. Karaikudi Mani said, 'Since these animals eat only posters, the skin and the mrdangam do not have life.' It's hard to miss the irony in that statement.

It is difficult to say what is truly unique about the cows of Thanjavur, but the belief in the excellence of their skin among the makers from the area and the players who work with them is very strong. Masters like Rajamanickam were very specific about the skin they chose. If something did not come up to his expectations, he would dispose of it outright. There was no question of recalibrating his work to suit average skin quality.

Bangalore-based P. Krishnakumar, a mrdangam maker who belongs to the Peruvemba family of makers from Palakkad

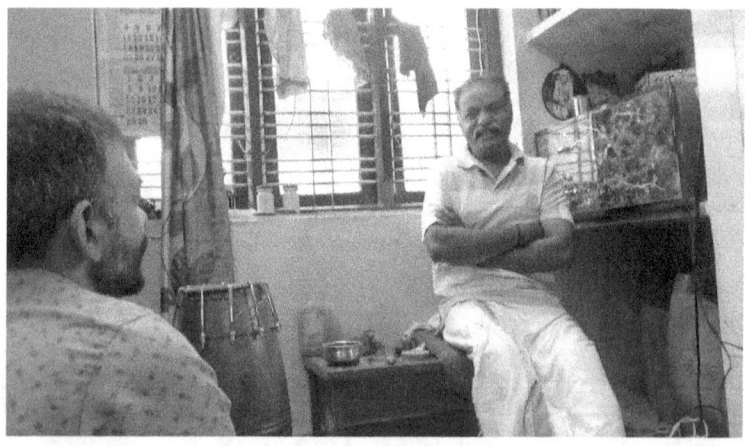

Krishnakumar in conversation with the author

district, had another take on this matter: 'There is a difference in the skin of cows in Kerala and Tamil Nadu. The cow skin in Thanjavur is heavy. In Kerala, they just let the cow graze in the harsh sunlight; so fat in the skin is less.'

This is a territorial battle and each maker has his own reasoning for why a particular source is the best. Mrdangam makers in Bangalore get their skins from Tamil Nadu, Kerala or Andhra Pradesh. When asked why not Karnataka, they said that the cows from the other regions were healthier because they had more grazing lands. Another practical issue was the lack of a convenient place to dry skin in Bangalore. Therefore, people like Kumar make regular trips to the city with loads of skin. 'At one time, goat skin (which they call meke charma in Kannada) was available in Yeshwantpur, Bangalore, where there was also room to spread the skin, nail it and do the needful. Not anymore, though,' said Srinivas Anantharamaiah, another mrdangam maker from Bangalore.

THE VALANDALAI IS THE PREDOMINANT, assertive side of the instrument. The toppi lends support, much like the dagga for the tabla. It is the valandalai that is tuned to the tonic of the singer or instrumentalist whom the mrdangam artist is accompanying, or, in the case of a mrdangam solo, to a specific tonic of the mrdangam artist's own choosing. Therefore, the making of the valandalai involves paying attention to minute specifics, being systematic in the preparation, and a great deal of intricate work, careful listening and physical effort. If even one thing goes wrong, the muttu will have to be simply discarded.

This right head of the mrdangam has three layers of skin, each with a different utility. The bottom-most one is usually cow skin and is known as the okkarara thattu, which means 'that which it sits on'. This layer sits on the wood, and the two musically functional thattus sit on it. The role of the okkarara thattu is to be a cushion between the wooden frame and the other thattus; it has no tonal role. 'For that, we can use anything. We could use two layers of goat skin or one layer of cow skin. We can use buffalo too. It only needs to be smooth and soft,' Navaneetham said.

The middle layer is goat skin. This is called kottu thattu. Kottu means 'to knock' (like rapping someone on the head), but also refers to stroking a percussive instrument. In this context, the word probably also indicates the sound that comes from playing a specific kind of stroke with the forefinger on the centre of the thattu. I can only describe it as a blunt, firm 'tok' sound, similar to the knock on a wooden door.

As we saw in Ambur, this skin is cut out from either side of the goat's vertebrae—an area that is not likely to yield mottha–melisu skin. The makers call it sama thattu, meaning its gauge is equal all over. For the valandalai, the thattu has to be sama thattu, because any variation in gauge will affect the tuning of it to a designated pitch. In other words, every part of the muttu must align at one perfect pitch. For exactly the same reason, the cow-skin membrane right on top must also be a sama thattu. When the tone is higher than the desired tonic on some part of the valandalai muttu, it is called ecchu; when it is lower, it is known as taggu. This 'ecchu–taggu' is something the maker watches for at every stage of the process. This last cow skin layer, right on top, is called the vettu thattu. Vettu means 'to cut', and that is exactly what is done: it is an annular layer. A circle is cut in the centre of this thattu in such a manner that the kottu thattu below is exposed.

One cow skin gives a maker about twenty sama thattus—ten thick ones and ten of medium thickness—if the skin is large and of good quality. The second set would need to be cut slightly away from the vertebrae, and will thus be of only medium thickness. All of these thattus can be used for the valandalai. The maker will be able to cut out another twenty thattus from other parts of the cow, which will most likely be mottha–melisu. These he will use for the okkarara thattu. Sometimes he will use two layers for the okkarara thattu to compensate for the inconsistent thickness. The mottha–melisu skin is also used as vettu thattu on mrdangams made for students, mrdangam schools and shops, since these clients are not particular about tuning the instrument's pitch to minute correctness.

Some makers claim that the best thattu in a cow comes from the skin that hangs off the throat. Each school of mrdangam-making has its own judgement of where the ideal thattu is found on an animal's skin. There is no universally accepted theory. Krishnakumar was specific that in the selection of skin used for higher tonics (female voices), the thattu must be cut out of the neck section, but for mrdangams of lower tonics, the higher back and shoulder area is better. The only point on which there is no disagreement is on the goat allu thol used in the toppi muttu.

An important point in the selection of skins is that until the maker removes the hair from it, he cannot be sure about quality, even though he has made a fair estimate. Sometimes, the skin turns out to be too thin once the hair is shaved off. The skin is chosen by sight and feel. Even mottha–melisu is figured out by touch alone. Mrdangam artists have no clue about this process or the sensory sharpness needed to differentiate between identical-seeming skins. This is an ability that comes only with experience and training, and watching the stalwarts at work.

Soosainathan had already soaked the goat and cow thattus in a bucket of water for about an hour, and the mrdangam in front of him was comfortably seated on its toppi muttu. He then hooked the poivaru, or the false varu, to the part of the toppi muttu that hangs off below the pinnal on the side of the wooden frame. Soosainathan made a small circular opening on the vettu thattu just as he had done with the buffalo skins in the toppi muttu. Then he placed the three membranes—cow (okkarara thattu), goat (kottu thattu) and cow (vettu thattu)—on the valandalai side of the wooden shell. He took a cutting plier and pulled at the three thattus so that they stretched. Holding them at that tensity, he put in four kannus and tied the thanguvaru exactly as he did with the toppi muttu. Then eight more kannus for poivaru were added.

Since this is the valandalai side of the mrdangam, the maker is extra careful about maintaining equal tension all around the muttu, and takes care to pull the membranes with equal strength. If he does not, ecchu–taggu issues may creep in.

Soosainathan strung the poivaru and removed the thanguvaru. Now, we come across a fifth expression for these leather thongs: malkuvaru. Since cow and goat skins are softer and thinner and the poivaru pidi is very tight, it is essential that the valandalai skin gets lateral support to avoid tearing.

The poivarus are looped vertically, which means that, if there is too much pull, the skin will rip. Therefore, a varu is also added horizontally, woven in and out of the poivaru kannus, to be the weight-bearing varu that absorbs and bears the pressure being exerted vertically.

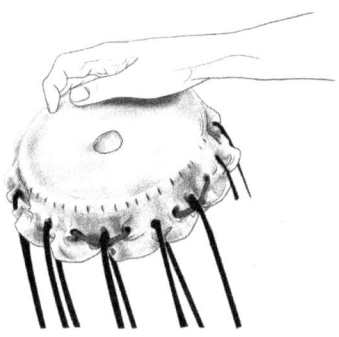

The most strenuous part of mrdangam-making is poivaru pidi for the valandalai. Before beginning, Soosainathan checked the toppi to make sure that it is well-seated on the frame and had not moved as he worked on the other side. He knocked on the edges of the muttu to make sure he could hear the sound of the wood, which comforted him that the muttu was in its required position. The poivaru pidi for the toppi was just two rounds, because there was no checking of pitch. With a small hook in his hand, Soosainathan began yanking at the varu, pushing at the mrdangam with his legs and then moving to the next varu.

pull–push–grab–pull
pull–push–grab–pull
pull–push–grab–pull
pull–push–grab–pull

Each time Soosainathan pulled at the varu coming out of one kannu, an assistant tapped at the kannu directly opposite it to check the pitch. Doing this by himself would have been so much more difficult.

Opposite kannus respond to each other. The tension on one kannu is equal to the tension at its opposite counterpart because the varu-looping is such that the skin stretches in a linear direction. Soosainathan kept moving from kannu to kannu, while the other person continuously tapped at the mrdangam. They made sure that the pitch at each of the twelve kannus was more or less equal. As Soosainathan kept going, I could see his muscles tighten, his breathing getting heavier and the strain on his face. After each cycle, the frequency emanating from the membranes was also increasing exponentially. After two such rounds, he took a break. During the break, he took the pinnal sattai out of the water and sharpened its corners. Then the poivaru pidi resumed, and went on for another four rounds. At this point, the frequency of the muttu was much higher than any Karnatik female singer (between G and A). When I checked the pitch of the sound from the muttu at the end of the poivaru pidi stage, it was at the higher octave of D—a range I am not sure even sopranos sing at. You may wonder why the tension needs to be so high; this will become clearer in the next chapter. The varu was by now stiff as a metal rod, and Soosainathan was using every ounce of strength in him to continue pulling it. He had to use a screwdriver to even get a grip on the varu. And he was exhausted.

Antony, they say, was a master of the poivaru pidi. He was a strong man. Sowriar, his grandson, elaborated, 'Not even a small stick could go in the gap between the wood and the varu.

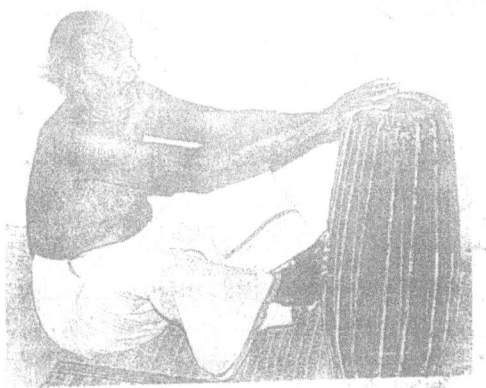

Sebastian Anthony tuning the mridengam.

A newspaper article about Antony

His hands were strong. Even at eighty-five, when he held my hand, I couldn't get out of his grip.' Selvaraj, Antony's nephew, too had very high praise for his poivaru pidi, though he did not think much of the rest of his work.

Poivaru pidi done, Soosainathan took out his rubber marker and accurately marked positions for sixteen kannus. Instead of adding one kannu marking between each one of the sixteen as he had done for the toppi, he added two, the measuring done visually as before. So, the valandalai has forty-eight kannus for the pinnal, while the toppi has thirty-two. Soosainathan proceeded to make forty-eight kannus. Everything about the pinnal process was the same as for the toppi muttu. Some makers might use two ul sattais on the valandalai side, though. As the muttu ages, the pinnal tends to slide off the sides and fall off the frame. It is said that two ul sattais stop that to some extent, giving it a stronger hold and keeping it upright for longer.

The valandalai muttu usually takes longer to dry. This is because both sides of the wooden shell are now closed. With very little air circulation going through, drying is slower, especially around the pinnal area, where many strips of buffalo skin have been braided together.

There used to be another technique of braiding that no one uses anymore. Earlier, the braiding or pinnal for the valandalai was done with cow skin, not buffalo skin. At that time, especially in the Peruvemba school of making, there was a 'madakku sattai' process. Since cow skin is softer and more supple, the maker would take a broader strip of varu, fold it lengthwise into two so that the softer inner side was on the outside. This made the varu smoother and easier to braid through the kannus. When the buffalo sattai goes through the kannu, one side of it is rough and the other soft. This means that it sometimes gets stuck and needs to be pulled out with a cutting plier. This would not happen with the madakku sattai. However, holding the fold down was hard; it kept opening. The maker had to constantly wet the sattai and fold it, over and over again. It was more laborious, and so the makers dropped it. Makers from Kerala say that there was a visual beauty to the madakku sattai that the single sattai just cannot match. Johnson also indicated that this technique was once in vogue in Thanjavur.

Makers could be pranksters too. Selvaraj once decided to use pig skin instead of goat skin for the kottu thattu and did not tell Mani Iyer. He knew fully well that Iyer would not approve. When Mani Iyer tested the mrdangam, he found the sound strange and was unable to understand why. When he checked carefully, he realised that the skin looked odd. It was then that Selvaraj told him with a wicked smile that it was pig skin. I have also heard that other makers and artists collaborated to experiment with snake and cat skin!

BEING IN THE BUSINESS OF skin is not easy. Everything goes against the makers: their caste, economic standing and social location. People do not like that their area is being downgraded because of the skin and leather strewn around. Complaining about the dirtiness of the work indirectly and derogatorily points at the makers' caste. Sowriar's wife, Sarada, told me that most brahmin mrdangam artists from Mylapore have no issues with their presence. It is the non-brahmin Hindu middle class that gives them a hard time. This could also be because the makers' homes and shops are usually cheek-by-jowl with the properties owned by people belonging to socially mid-level non-brahmin castes. They share small square feet areas with the makers, and are uncomfortable with the scent of freshly peeled skin. If the makers are shunted out, these complainers have nothing to lose. For the mrdangam artists, though, the makers are indispensable and their proximity is a necessary condition.

Peter (name changed) expressed anguish that society still discriminates against them and that they find it difficult to rent places. Landlords are not comfortable with hide-work being done on their premises. Often, the owners are renting out multiple small homes or shops, tightly packed together, and they do not want to take a chance.

In the past, though, makers managed well enough, even in the cities. Near Varadan's house in Ayanavaram was a small partially fenced open space. The roads were narrow, and I parked my car with great difficulty, making sure my vehicle hugged the wall. 'You know, where you parked your car now, we used to nail goat skin there. But those days are gone. That compound used to be a big pond. We used to soak the skin in its waters and leave it there through the night. We even made buffalo skin varus and cut the thattus on our laps and hung it to dry. I have made complete mrdangams there,' Varadan recalled.

In the early days, some mrdangam artists who had slightly larger homes in Madras provided space to get the job done. In the garden behind Madras Kannan's house, for instance, Venkatesan used to dry the skin. 'I would give him food three times a day,' Kannan said.

Madras Kannan was not a brahmin. The few brahmins who accommodated the skin work in their homes too got used to the sights and smells of it. Melgies got married in 1978 and wanted to move to Madras. Krishnamurthy Iyer, who was a music teacher in T. Nagar's Krishna Gana Sabha, lived in West Mambalam. He had put up the bachelor mrdangam artist Thanjavur Ramdas in his house. Melgies used to go to Krishnamurthy Iyer's house and work on Ramdas's mrdangams. Since Ramdas knew Melgies from his Thanjavur days, they let him live in the house for a few months until he found his own space. During this period and later, when Melgies moved to his own rented house just a stone's throw away, he helped by being a kind of security guard for the Krishnamurthys. Often, he would stay at their house until late at night and use the premises for goat skin-related work. Was Krishnamurthy Iyer okay with the smell? 'In the beginning, he used to have an issue, but since we were working there regularly, he got used to it,' Melgies said. 'We would also work keeping that in mind. We dried and cured the skin in Choolai and then brought it here. We would only cut the thattus and all that over here. But once, we nailed the skin here, and even Ramdas tried his hand at it. At that time we knew many people on Baroda Street. They came asking what was going on.' Krishnamurthy and Ramdas were those rare brahmins who were not worried about what neighbours might say. For mrdangam artists like Ramdas, there were the competing issues of limited space and the need for high-quality work. This conundrum allowed for caste transgressions.

Arogyamary recalled, 'As long as we lived in a rented house, it was always difficult. Cleaning the skin and drying it in the

Melgies with his wife, Arogyamary, who passed away in 2021

sun. Once we buy the material, we had to worry about the sun and rains. And if it rained, the skin would become wet and go to waste. You know how much he has suffered; he never talks about all that.' Melgies added, 'We don't buy new skin when it rains.' His wife continued, 'Even if they reduce the price, we do not buy it.' Melgies wanted to soft-pedal his difficulties, taking pains to explain that he always told his landlord in advance about the work. But Arogyamary would not let it go. 'We also had to take care that dogs don't carry away the skin when we put them out to dry. Do you understand?'

Then there is Britto, who works in the backstreets of Madurai, and has been raided by authorities on the suspicion that he was dealing in deer and tiger skin. 'I have had issues because of complaints made by people who don't like me. They complained that I am engaged in smuggling deer and tiger skin. My shop was raided by forest officials. I showed them everything I had, and asked them to take a video of everything here and at home. My wife was so scared when the police officials came home. I even showed them the skins that I had been soaking. The officials could not take the smell and had to smoke a cigarette to mask it. They asked me how I was able to work in such conditions. I told them I was used to it. But they could not get over it so easily. It was they who insisted that I display all my awards and press coverage in the shop. *The Hindu* newspaper did an article on the things Madurai is famous for, and along with the jasmine flowers and jallikattu, my shop was also chosen as a landmark. I had asked the Kalai Panpattu Thurai (the Tamil Nadu government's Department of Culture) for a certificate since I was often the target of such raids. They told me to go to the police station and ask for it. I asked them, "How would the police know about this craft? You are more aware of what I am doing. If you inspect and certify my shop, that would help. Often, my shipment of leather is stopped and taken for inspection. They give it back once they inspect it, but this is unnecessary trouble and your certification would help." I told them this, but they didn't care. If you go there, only the performers are recognised. They even told me that we (mrdangam makers) are not eligible for the membership card as it is meant only for artists. When my father turned sixty, we applied for pension through them. But they rejected the application saying makers are not eligible.'

Melgies moved into his own house decades after he moved to Chennai. There was no way he could have bought the land or built the house with his own earnings. Whatever he earned covered the household expenses and the education of his children. His son now works in Canon, one daughter studied pathology and the other works in an export company. He was able to invest in the house he now owns only because his mother-in-law and brothers-in-law helped. The independent house made things easier. But, unlike his cousins and competitors, Melgies does not have a shop of his own. He still moves between the houses of mrdangam artists such as I. Sivakumar, Neyveli Venkatesh and J. Vaidyanathan. And this means that the majority of the skin work is done at home and on his terrace. 'Only after we got our own house could we let it dry up on the terrace and not worry too much,' said Arogyamary.

Not that those with shops have it easy. The Mylapore makers all nail the varu on the pavement outside Vivekananda College, because there is absolutely no other place in that congested area. They have to constantly keep the cops happy and stay out of their way. And then there is the swamiji from

Ramakrishna Mission who does not want to see skin drying outside the college, of which too he is a part. When they know he is coming to this side of the compound, the makers quickly clear things away. All they need is a place to work with skin where they will not be harassed, but there is no such location in the city. The makers hope that the government will take note of their plight and do something, but no help seems to be forthcoming. To be able to address this issue, several makers spoke of the need to organise themselves into a union, but admitted that unity seems a very distant dream.

Preparing the varu from the buffalo skin is also a step-by-step process. After the central part of the buffalo skin is dried under the fan in the maker's house or shop, it is again soaked in a bucket of water overnight. The next day, the maker wakes up early and begins cutting the skin into one long continuous

Arogyam taking out a roll of varu from a bucket of water

varu the width of a thumb. This is a tedious process that takes three to four hours. Out of this varu, the maker already knows that the skin that is further away from the vertebrae will be mottha–melisu and hence can only be used as pinnal varu. The rest will be used as the final varu that binds the two sides of the mrdangam together.

According to makers, on an average, they get about ten to eleven bagams of varu from one buffalo skin. Once the long thong is carved out, it is dipped in water again. The next day, the varu is rolled out, stretched to its maximum, nailed to the floor on both ends and left to dry in the sun for a day. By the following day, the varu actually gains a little more length. It is only after this that the maker cleans the varu of all remaining javvu and unevenness. It is then bundled and kept ready for use. The old timers did not stop here, though. They would then dump the varu in a tin of creamy curd, or apply the curd on the varu, and keep it aside for a day. Once that was done, a thick layer of castor oil was applied. Much like how we varnish our wooden furniture to protect it from termites and deterioration, this extra seasoning was protection for the varu, they said, and would keep it strong and damage-free. But all this is in the past. With urgency and immediacy being the keywords of today, these practices have been discarded and are only spoken of nostalgically. 'In order to make the varu soft, they used to soak the varu in curd and hang it from the ceiling,' Murthy recalled.

SO FAR, THE TWO SIDES of the mrdangam, the two muttus, have remained largely independent of each other. It is time to bring them together. Once the valandalai muttu dries, the maker removes the malkuvaru, poivaru and both the muttus from the wooden shell.

This section of the making was demonstrated by Surendar, one of Antony's many grandsons working out of Mylapore. A quick recap: on the valandalai, there are forty-eight kannus and thirty-two on the toppi. We need to do some simple math now. The final varu that holds the muttus together will be strung through sixteen kannus on each side, so what will be the gap between each strap on the two sides?

Valandalai: The pinnal sattai goes through forty-eight kannus. So, the varu will go through every third kannu.

Toppi: The pinnal sattai goes through thirty-two kannus. So, the varu will go through every second kannu.

Surendar had the valandalai in his hand. He first cut out any extra leather that might be hanging off the sides of the muttu beyond the pinnal. Then, very carefully, he inverted the muttu and made sure that the okkarara and kottu thattus were not stuck together. Surendar slid a small piece of leather in the gap between the two to protect the kottu thattu, and then cut out the okkarara into a narrow strip—its diameter just as wide as the rim of the wooden shell. If this layer had extended under the playing surface, it would muffle the sound of the valandalai. Castor oil, the only lubricant they use, came into play again. Surendar applied the oil on the wooden edge of the toppi side to prevent the skin from sticking to the wood. If it sticks, the toppi sound, which needs to be an elongated resonance, is stifled. Sometimes, especially during the monsoons, the skin sticks to the wood in spite of the castor oil. This is solved by dripping castor oil through the cranny between the wood and the muttu, and by positioning a piece of wood below the pinnal and hitting at it hard to loosen the muttu.

The thanguvaru routine began again, for the final time. Surendar looped the thanguvaru at four equidistant kannus in the toppi and valandalai pinnals, and made sure that the tension on each was equal. Then he put in place the real varu that would hold the two membranes together permanently. With the mrdangam between his two feet, he began stringing the varu and removing the thanguvaru as he went around, and thus finally linked the two playing surfaces of the mrdangam.

As he worked, Surendar told me that there are three kinds of difficult clients: those who are old school and want their mrdangams only a certain way, others who torture the makers and make them work double time because that's just how they are (but pay very well and are, therefore, tolerated), and a few who refuse to listen to anything the makers say and want everything done their way.

All this while, Surendar was also tightening the varu, making sure that the muttus were seated well and balanced on the two sides. Finally, the varu was tethered on the toppi muttu side by tucking it in and around the varu loops.

Surendar now needed to make sure that the valandalai was well placed on the wooden frame. For this, he tightened the varu with that now-familiar hook; tight-hand grip and steady-feet hold, he knocked on the edge of the muttu with a smooth stone. He went around a few times until he was satisfied that it was tight enough and the muttu was perfectly and evenly settled on the wood. What he was actually looking for was the sound of wood. And if that was missing at any location on

Krishnamurthy and Sowriar working in tandem

the circular muttu, he would know that the varu needed to be pulled a bit more in that direction and that the muttu needed a few more knocks. This process also ensures that the muttu itself is not uneven.

The toppi muttu has the benefit of being pushed down by the weight of the shell when the valandalai is being worked on. This helps it truly fit like a toppi, a cap, on the frame. In any case, Surendar upturned the mrdangam and confirmed that everything was okay. The process of placing the two muttus in their final position and fortifying them is called padiparkardu— making sure it is settled.

As you might remember, the buffalo skins on the toppi side and the cow vettu thattu on the valandalai side already have a small hole in the centre, giving the layer below some exposure. This has to be increased. As the last act involving the skins, Surendar used a compass, and marked a circle that covered more than half the circumference of the toppi. He then cut out the two buffalo skins at that marking. Now, the goat allu thol on the toppi side was a very large central section of the toppi, while the two buffalo skin layers were a ring around it. On the valandalai side, the kottu thattu was made larger and the vettu thattu narrower and annular. It was only at this stage that he removed any remaining buffalo skin hair on the sides of the toppi muttu.

Courtesy: A. Sowriar

Arulraj pulling at the kayaru

In the past decade, another modification has been incorporated. Instead of harnessing the two muttus together with a varu or kayaru, makers screw each muttu on to the kattai separately using an improvised nut-and-bolt system. This makes the muttus easily replaceable, which means an artist can use one kattai for a wider range of pitches just by changing the muttu. This system was adapted from the dholak or dholki. Opinions on whether it affects the sound is divided. One side vehemently claims that there is a difference, while the other contests that it is all in the mind.

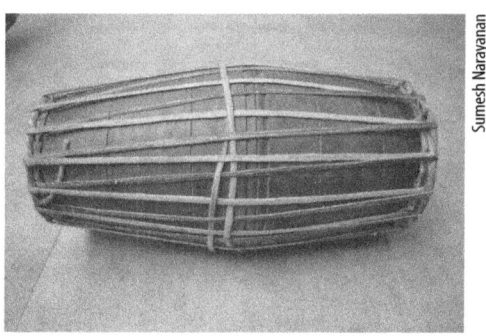
Valandalai, toppi muttu bound together with varu

As he was about to finish, I asked Surendar whether his work was art or just labour.

'When we enter the field, it is labour for money, but then, as we grow and people appreciate our work, it becomes art.'

There is one question that I asked every maker: how long will a valandalai muttu last? There was no unanimous answer. Some said a couple of years and others said four years. One maker claimed that he knew an individual whose muttu had lasted thirty years or more. In an extension of his thoughts on the life of the skin, Ravikumar proposed a theory: 'The life and longevity of the cow is there in the muttu. Imagine that a cow lived for thirty years, and you killed it to make a muttu;

that muttu will last for as long as the cow would have lived if it had been alive.'

Over the years, there has been another minor change. At one time, the makers did everything, from procuring the skin to the padiparkardu. But now, to some extent, a part of the skin work has been outsourced. Many makers buy readymade skin, prepared by others, from skin dealers. So, the raw-skin work has moved to another set of people. Sometimes, the apprentices and trainees have to do it when they start out. This has resulted in some social mobility for the makers. Even among the skin suppliers, there are some shifts. Kumar of Ambur is getting more and more involved with the making of instruments. This is stage one of moving vertically in one's social strata. He now hopes that, with his son entering the mrdangam-making field, he can move further upward. The mrdangam, after all, is the instrument of the classical, the brahmin. A day may not be far when his son completely gives up skin dealership and becomes a mrdangam maker. Someone else will then take Kumar's present position on the socio-cultural ladder.

'After all, this is a godly profession. The mrdangam itself commands respect. It is divine and that is why they respect us,' said Sundar (name changed). So are you saying that it is not because you work for brahmins, I asked. 'But brahmins are also god and the mrdangam is also god. Both are pure.'

We both laughed.

7

OF LABS AND LAVA

A typical meal at a brahmin wedding—indeed, any traditional social event involving a meal—in Tamil Nadu is incomplete without the mandatory vetthalaipakku (betel leaf and areca nut, a digestive) on a messy tray close to the exit door of the dining hall. It is considered very auspicious. I have very many memories of uncles and aunties loudly discussing politics, cricket and gossip with their mouths full, and a peculiar manner of speech born out of trying not to spray their audience with red vetthalaipakku juice. The combination is also supposed to possess aphrodisiacal qualities, perhaps because it lends the lips a dark red tinge that is considered arousing. Old Tamil films had cringeworthy 'first night' scenes where the bride and groom would share a vetthalaipakku.

Its north Indian counterpart, the paan, is usually filled with a complex assortment of condiments and spices; even the sada (simple) paan has a few fillings. The betel leaf of every region has a distinctive taste and aftertaste. The Varanasi leaf is tender and melts in the mouth, while the Kolkata variant has more body. The southern Kumbakonam leaf is known for its large size, dark-green colour and sting.

While the betel leaf–areca nut amalgam was being readied, many older relatives in my family would ask for 'the third' and point to a small round plastic box on the vetthalaipakku tray. This was box of sunnambu, slaked lime, which no one asked for by name. The sunnambu, always moist, was applied on the inner side of the betel leaf.

Slaked lime is a very interesting material. In its natural form, it is calcium carbonate ($CaCO_3$, limestone), which is found in limestone or in shells. When limestone is heated, it loses carbon dioxide (CO_2) and changes form to calcium oxide (CaO, quicklime)—hard and dry, and not of much use. But once water is added to it, CaO transforms into calcium hydroxide ($Ca[OH]_2$, slaked lime). This is what we call sunnambu.

Why am I going on about slaked lime? Because, incredibly, this edible sunnambu plays an important role in the leather industry and is used in a process called liming. This technique is also used by mrdangam makers to make what they call sunnambu thattu.

When I first heard about this technique, I presumed that it was some way of thinning the skin in order to increase its sonority. But when I asked the makers, they said, 'No, it reduces the skin's weight or strength.' I asked several makers, and never understood the difference. My own educational arrogance kicked in too. I assumed that, while experientially the makers knew what they were doing, they did not possess the knowledge to understand chemical changes. I needed a

Harvard scientist to validate what they were talking about. It was necessary evidence of my inability to understand knowledge that has a different operating system from the one I grew up with.

But let me tell you about sunnambu thol first. After removing the flesh and fat from freshly peeled goat skin, the maker applies a generous amount of sunnambu to the inner side. He then folds the skin into a bundle and soaks it in water for a couple of days. 'On the third day, when it's taken out, no human can bear that stench. We wash the skin with our hands like we would a shirt and let it dry. The sunnambu takes all the power out of it. Once the skin has dried in the sun, it becomes easy to roll. We store it and use as required,' Johnson said. The liming process also makes hair removal easy. It is the valandalai side—the kottu thattu—that the sunnambu treatment is generally reserved for. The cow skin on the same side and the buffalo and goat skins on the toppi side are untreated. Untreated skin is known as paccha thol (raw skin).

What exactly does sunnambu do to the skin? Hide is 64 per cent water, about 33 per cent proteins, and the rest is mineral salts, fats, pigments and so on. The protein component is made up of structural proteins[4] (29 per cent is collagen, 2 per cent is keratin and 0.3 per cent elastin) and non-structural proteins[5] (albumins or globulins 1 per cent and mucins 0.7 per cent). The liming process dissolves and aids

---

4. Proteins that give structure, i.e. shape and strength, to an organ; like keratin gives shape to hair.

5. Non-structural proteins function in ways other than giving structure. For example, enzymes: if you drink milk, the enzyme lactase helps digest it. Or take the protein haemoglobin, which helps absorb oxygen.

the removal of some structural proteins such as keratin, and all non-structural proteins such as albumins, globulins, mucins and mucoids. These non-structural proteins convert into a glue-like material, which hardens the skin when it dries. Liming helps remove these proteins, making the skin supple and soft. Collagen is a structural protein that is organised into soluble fibres of great tensile strength. Liming weakens intermolecular collagen interactions, and the influx of water loosens the fibre network of collagen and makes it swell, rendering the skin easy to work with. In the leather industry, this also allows colour pigments to be absorbed into the skin.

Johnson made a rather curious observation when I asked him whether the skin thins as a result of the treatment. He said, 'Sometimes the skin becomes thick after the sunnambu process; it depends on the nature of the skin.'

In the mrdangam-making arena, sunnambu thol is looked down upon, especially among the old-timers, and even more so among members of the Thanjavur clan. When I strolled down the by-lanes of Appar Swamy Koil Street, having conversations with makers from Thanjavur, each time I asked if they used sunnambu thol, they would retort sharply, 'No. Only paccha thol.' It was as if I had said something demeaning. In their view, a maker who works mainly with sunnambu thol is lesser, not hardcore enough, and the mrdangam artist who plays on such an instrument does not want to put in the required effort; he just wants more sound. The fact is, sunnambu thol helps increase the decibel of the valandalai and makes the mrdangam's tone sharper. But these are not universally seen as enhancements.

Upon reflection, I realise that the bias against sunnambu thol is in line with a deep-seated attitude in the inner quarters of Karnatik music. A vocalist who is only told she has a great voice, or a violinist who is applauded as a dexterous instrumentalist, knows that these are backhanded compliments. They are meant to point to a lack of toughness, or of depth in their musicality. Similarly, mrdangam artists are unhappy if they are told that their instrument had great tonality. In order to prove deeper understanding of music and insightful artistry, musicians prefer to underplay, reduce or even, in some extreme cases, nearly eliminate the effervescence of the instrument's harmonics. A case in point was Palghat Raghu, an outstanding mrdangam artist who conceptualised a radically independent way of approaching Karnatik music from the rhythmic front. But in the last few decades of his career, he adjusted his instrument's timbre in such a manner that the harmonics had very little strength; he nearly removed resonance from his valandalai. Raghu was trying to prove that it was his own hard work and intellectual brilliance that mattered; not the brighter tone, greater resonance or the harmonics of his mrdangam.

This is a very Karnatik trait, where anything connected with energising the presentation is viewed as fluff and superficial. Sunnambu thol is seen as the easier way out—a cover that hides a lack of musical understanding and mathematical complexity. Built into this hand-wringing about processed and unprocessed skin is that old preoccupation with 'purity'. Paccha thol is recognised as purer, more original compared to sunnambu thol. Mrdangam artists who never discuss the details of skin procurement will be the first to proclaim the superiority of paccha thol. Purity has indeed come a full circle!

Sunnambu thol is widely used today, both among concert-playing mrdangam artists and those who play for

Bharatanatyam performances. When we speak to makers about this trend, they point fingers at the artists. They are critical of a trend that, in their opinion, reduces the intensity of their work and consequently their own artistic satisfaction. In fact, Navaneetham even said, 'The sound (with raw skin) is good enough for us. But it is not enough for the players.' However, everyone agrees that muttus that use sunnambu thol do not last long. Britto called them 'use and throw'.

There is one more facet to this debate: gender. Some artists argue that sunnambu thol works better for higher tonics, that is, female vocalists, while the original raw hide is ideal for male tonics. This creates a categorisation among mrdangam artists—those who predominantly accompany men versus those who often share the stage with women. Needless to say, the latter are seen as being of a lower grade. A male singer is understood to be bestowed with higher knowledge merely by virtue of his gender. He is the base, the standard by which music is judged. The female singer is expected to strive hard to match this ideal. This discrimination trickles all the way up to the kind of hide used for the mrdangam. It is true that the paccha thol chosen for higher tonics is relatively thinner than those used for lower tonics. This thickness too is interpreted as indicative of arduousness and commitment. Sunnambu thol only makes the discrimination worse—the weightless feminine (sunnambu thol) versus the tough male (paccha thol).

A common argument, one to which I too subscribed for a long time, is that the sunnambu thol creates a shrill sound that is not true to the mrdangam. Players point to a distortion in sound, and say that it affects pitch correctness. But this so-called mrdangam sound is only a construct to which we are habituated, and which itself has been influenced especially by Palghat Mani Iyer and his descendants. Therefore, I am no longer certain about my own original sensory objections. I have heard distortions of so many kinds in non-sunnambu thol mrdangams, and people do not oppose those quite as vociferously. Does this dislike have roots in an ingrained sense of masculinity that calls for a certain kind of rugged endeavour as proof of higher calibre, I wonder.

Umayalpuram Sivaraman, though a student of Palghat Mani Iyer, has made it a point to counter this anti-sunnambu thol discourse. Johnson, who has been making Sivaraman's mrdangams for about twenty-two years, described how the artist moved to using sunnambu thol. 'He kept asking for more sound; he wanted to hear that rinkaram (clearly audible harmonics that stay on as reverberations). He even told me, "You can make the muttu with paper if you want, I don't care." So I decided to make one muttu with sunnambu thol. His father was also alive then. In his old house, he had a well, and since it was breezy, I worked out of there. When he checked the sound, he seemed to like it. And from then on, it has been sunnambu thol. But he still keeps asking for more and more sound!'

Sivaraman was also very clear: 'I want resonance. This is an instrument of nada. It is not a time marker.' He discovered another advantage. Remember the story about my colleague who struggled to get past customs at Sydney airport? Well, Sivaraman said that the sunnambu makes it easier. 'When the nadam is good and when there are travel-related conveniences, why not do it?'

While some simply say it is easy to work with sunnambu thol, Johnson is far more nuanced in his description. 'It is a knack; you cannot tighten the varu too much because it will stretch to become like the hanging earlobes of old women in the villages.' Johnson is still trying to satisfy Sivaraman. 'Even though it has been found through tests that he has the maximum harmonic resonance, he still wants more!' said Johnson. Sivaraman has now gone a step further. He has eliminated cow skin entirely from the equation. His kottu thattu and vettu thattu are made of goat skin and both are sunnambu thols. This is why the colour of his kottu thattu is a sparkling white. How much this removal of cow skin from the instrument is connected to the brahmin cow obsession is anybody's guess.

It is quite possible that this entire sunnambu thol business came from observing the leather industry. Since the community that worked in both industries overlapped, knowledge was shared. But when did this experiment begin? There's no clear answer. From the mrdangam makers we hear that sunnambu thol found its way into the Karnatik circuit via Tamil cinema, where it was already in use. 'Krishnamurthy did it for Cheenakutty and it was used for film recordings,' said Muruganandam. Navaneetham had much the same to say: 'It was used only in recordings, not at concerts. Then others began using it.' Ravikumar had another interesting observation: 'Krishnamurthy's clients were those in the light music field (cinema). He also did a lot of tabla work.' The skin used for the tabla is sunnambu thol. Ravikumar was suggesting that Krishnamurthy replicated the same technique in the mrdangam. Britto thought along the same lines, but he believed that Antony, who was a tabla and mrdangam maker for the film industry, was the first. 'He used the tabla techniques in the making of mrdangams.' But Melgies countered all this by saying that sunnambu thol has always been synonymous with the Madras muttu.

However, we do not know if the older generation of mrdangam artists who resided in Madras, such as Venu Nayakar and Madras Kannan, used sunnambu thol. Though Kannan himself said nothing about it to me, some mrdangam artists think that they played on sunnambu thol. The thing about the Madras makers is this: they catered to multiple industries, cinema, Karnatik and other music genres. Which means that, right from Munusami onwards, they were working on dholaks, dholkis, tablas, base tabla or Karnatik tabla, and probably other instruments like the parai and pambai. Their exposure was wider than those who came from Keethukara Street in Thanjavur.

Arulraj said something about Palani Subramania Pillai's mrdangam that is sure to raise the hackles of the artist's followers. 'Palani used sunnambu thol, but there is a difference between sunnambu thol then and now. In those days, just before we began the muttu work, we would apply the sunnambu and soak it in water for just an hour.' In other words, the effect on the goat skin was limited, which meant the calcium hydroxide would not have removed all the proteins and the skin would still be less supple. But the fact that Palani might have used any variant of sunnambu thol is going to be contested as it signifies a drop in his stature, thanks to the prejudice about the process. With the threat of Mani Iyer's image always looming large, the Palani camp will not take this lying down.

Palani himself had a very unconventional perspective on the mrdangam. His focus was far more on the toppi than the valandalai. 'For him, the toppi must be perfect. The valandalai could be average, but toppi had to be just right,' said Sankaran. To reiterate, this was—and still is—very atypical. Most mrdangam artists do not pay much attention to the toppi but would want a perfect valandalai. Arulraj remembered, 'It was all in his gumki. He would play softly on the valandalai.' This shift had a strong impact in Palani's playing style and people's perception of it. Unfortunately, it has also led to a reductionist view of Palani's art. Most people, including his most ardent admirers, can only speak about the speciality of his toppi, which was unparalleled. The splendour of his mind and valandalai prowess have been forgotten.

'I observed minutely how my teacher worked on the toppi. That's how I learnt the secret. Like in the valandalai, there is a balance for the toppi,' Guruvayur Dorai recollected. Arulraj remembered an incident in Thiruvaiyaru. 'Palani had a concert with Semmangudi Srinivasier that evening. Around 4 p.m., my father, Shetty, opened the cover and showed him the mrdangam. The valandalai was already tuned to Semmangudi's tonic. Then Palani began checking the toppi.' I am going pause the story here to explain something.

Mrdangam players apply semolina paste on the central area of the toppi's goat skin after wetting it. This gives the toppi a deep tone. The amount of water and paste applied varies with the depth of sound that the artist is looking for. As a concert progresses, the artist needs to keep the skin wet and add more paste because it dries and falls off. This maintains the toppi's sonic contrast with the valandalai. The balance between the valandalai and toppi gives the mrdangam multiple aural complexions. Karaikudi Mani called this coming together of the two sides of the mrdangam the 'distribution of the left', which is the mingling of the sound of the toppi on the left with the valandalai on the right.

Before semolina, artists used ash mixed with boiled rice, and at times even whole wheat flour. 'The ash mixture was amazing. That sound cannot be replicated. But, because of the wetness, the ash would spread all over the place, making it messy,' V. Kamalakar Rao recalled. Mrdangam artists have moved away from semolina too, and tried many kinds of sealants. The favourite high-end version in use today is Plastic Fermit. How deliciously ironic that an art form and a set of artists who pride themselves on ritual purity use a glue commonly used in toilets!

Muttus drying on the road next to a sign that reads 'Krishna Plumbing Sanitary Works'

On that day in Thiruvaiyaru, Palani applied the semolina paste on the toppi, checked it, and then did the unthinkable. He made Antony pull the varu for the toppi side. To do that, the mrdangam would have to be kept upside down, with the valandalai on the floor. This is never done, because any change in toppi-side tension will disturb the tuning on the harmonic valandalai side. Even during the initial stages of making the two muttus, makers do not worry about the varu pidi for the toppi. But Palani tuned the toppi to a notional pitch. I call it 'notional', but Arulraj and many others swear that he tuned it to an actual pitch, specifically half the frequency of the tonic. I find that hard to believe, because the toppi is non-harmonic and it is impossible to identify any actual pitch on it. All the same, Palani would have tuned it to an intense, low, expanding, sustained tone that provided the needed acoustic counterpoint to the tonality of the valandalai. This was Palani's inner sensibility. If a very particular booming, pliable, elongating sound emanated from his toppi stroke, he achieved the perfection that was in his mind and imagination. Guruvayur Dorai and his student Babu called it the 'dhommmmmmmmm' sound—nothing at all like the abrupt 'dhom' of the mrdangam. Adjusting the varu on the toppi side would have affected the pitch of the valandalai, but Antony rectified it by tightening the varu on that side to compensate. The sound of the toppi also depends on the way the goat skin is tied to the back of the muttu. As Sankaran pointed out, 'There should be no wrinkles when you tie the goat skin.'

WE NOW COME TO A critical inorganic element that provides the mrdangam its oomph factor. And if we go by Thanjavur family legends, then the best of this element is to be found in Rattipalayam, Thanjavur. With Karnatik music, it appears all roads do lead to Thanjavur.

This magic particle is a stone—kittankallu, also known as chittankallu. It is no ordinary stone either; Selvaraj claimed that it also has medicinal values. 'They use it in traditional medicine. Even in West Mambalam, there is a shop that sells traditional medicines where you can ask for chittankallu. They know all about it. When we had a sty in the eye, we would slice lime, put the powder of the kittankallu in it and use it as a compress on the eye. The sty would disappear. We also brushed our teeth with a mixture of kittankallu and salt.'

Before I explain the use of kittankallu in the mrdangam, let us travel to the place where it is found: Rattipalayam.

When Selvaraj described Rattipalayam, I had imagined it as a remote, unreachable location somewhere in the bush forests around Thanjavur. Even the much younger Soosainathan had given me the impression that it was a far-off, unsafe and difficult-to-access place. 'In Rattipalayam, there is a small hill with an Amman koil. You will find kittankallu there. It is also found near Gandharva Kottai and Manganur … in fact, all the way up to Pudukottai. You will find this stone where there are a lot of cashew nut orchards,' Selvaraj said. The old man from Thanjavur, T.K. Murthy, had this to say, 'You can find it on riverbanks. There is an insect found on those banks. Wherever the insect lives, the stone can be found.' Others added more stories to this narrative. Karaikudi Mani said, 'This is their secret, only they can identify the stone.' The Thanjavur makers, he meant.

Sowriar said that there was a banyan tree near the Amman temple, and you could find the stone around it. Another maker told me that they used to need police permission to go there. There were many snakes in and around the place too, he said.

The more I heard these semi-mystic narrations, reminiscent of Tamil supernatural films from the 1980s, the more inquisitive I got. I had to check it out for myself.

As we approached Rattipalayam, Soosainathan began describing the area. 'We were scared to come this side. Some people have committed suicide here. You see this road, right? In the late evenings, it gets very dark. But we come all the way here for stones. This pond is called singaperumal kulam.' He seemed as thrown by the development all around as I was. 'When I used to come as a kid, there were only mounds and mounds here. This place was wild back then. I am surprised by all the houses that have come up; it has developed so much now.' It was obvious that very few makers personally travel to Rattipalayam in search of the kittankallu. But Soosainathan's father Gabriel and mother Jesinthamary regularly come here and supply their son and some others with the stone. And Johnson sends some younger makers to collect stones.

We parked our car at the head of a mud road that had a few buildings on the side. It had taken us about fifteen minutes from Keethukara Street, I think. Gabriel, Soosainathan, my student Vikram and I walked towards a temple. Gabriel confirmed that it was an Ayyanar temple. Ayyanar is one of the village guardian deities that has been subsumed into the Hindu matrix over the centuries, which is why Sowriar referred to it as an Amman temple. Yet, many of these temples retain very distinctive rituals and customs. Here, there were three or four minor shrines around the main one.

There was a twig fence on the right and Thanjavur's trademark paddy fields at a distance. No hills or mounds, which I had been led to believe was the distinctive feature of this area. The temple itself was not very large, but had been recently renovated and painted a sky blue. A grove of ancient trees served as a beautiful canopy, but no banyan tree was in sight. When we saw an old lady watching over a grazing calf, Soosainathan whispered in my ear, 'Women would not come here in the past. People brewed illicit liquor here.' Oh, wait, there was a banyan tree, a small one, right in front of the temple. Everywhere I looked, there were fields. Perhaps the hillocks here were very small, and they were flattened for cultivation.

'From those days to now, we have picked stones from here. When we dug for the stone in those days, scorpions would come out,' Soosainathan said. Past a paddy field, we followed a pathway towards a stream. The land was flat, dry shrubs all over, and palm trees—once Tamil Nadu's pride—lined the stream. There was not much water there, though, and bushy bamboo plants had grown close by. Before I knew it, Soosainathan and Gabriel were picking stones from all around. 'Here it is,' they said. After all the build-up, I almost felt like they were archaeologists who had excavated ruins.

The stone was blackish-grey with mud in its crevices and holes. To the naked eye, it looked like solidified magma, and in that, I was not wrong. My geography teacher would have been proud. When we tested the rock at the Indian Institute of Technology, Madras, and checked later with a scientist, he confirmed that it was of mafic parentage, meaning it was formed by the cooling of magma that rose from the earth's interiors. This was obvious from the high olivine content, which meant that the stone was some sort of basalt or gabbro. It had also undergone a lot of weathering and oxidation, indicated by the presence of ferrous oxide. Kittankallu is made up of fayalite (94 per cent) and hercynite (6 per cent), I learnt. The makers and many mrdangam artists were right when they said that the stone was high in iron content. Wüstite and fayalite have iron in the form of ferrous, while hercynite has iron in the form of ferrous and a bit of ferric (both being iron of different oxidation states).

By the time Soosainathan found a few small bits of stone, his father had gathered large ones. The rocks were heavy for sure. 'When it rains, it is easier for us to collect more stones. We used to get this stone from there also (pointing to another location), but now we don't.' Pointing to some small mounds, he said, 'See. All these mounds have been broken and there are snakes and scorpions around here. We need to be careful.'

Collecting these rocks and bringing them all the way back to Keethukara Street is no easy task. Gabriel, a tall, lanky man, is in his seventies, and Jesinthamary is not young either. Both of them told me that there used to be a large hill in the vicinity and flowing water, which made it much easier to collect and clean the stones. Now, bringing the rocks and stones back home is a long, slow ordeal.

The two of them leave home at around 4.30–5 in the morning, reach the spot at 6–6.30 and gather stones for two hours. 'We collect them and put them in one pile near the temple. Once we have made a few trips, I will have enough stones for one basket. Then I take a tea break, load the cycle with them and push the cycle home. We need to rest en route,' Gabriel explained. The stones are heavy, and by the time the couple reach home at 1 p.m., they are exhausted.

But there is more work to be done. Jesinthamary takes over. 'At home, I soak the stones in water for a couple of days to clear off the mud. Once that is done, I keep them aside for a day and start powdering the stones the next day. There is a steel pestle and mortar with which I powder it.' She showed me a plastic bottle full of the powder and said it was five and a half kilos. 'The powder is very fine. When we crush it, we sieve out the fine powder. Then the bigger pieces are crushed again into smaller pieces. If I sit for four hours (6 a.m. to 10 a.m.), I will be able to make two handfuls of the powder. That is all I can do. There is no machine to do this. Even today, the crushing is done only by hand,' she said. It is very hard to crush kittankallu; I know, I tried my hand at it. 'When a machine was used, the teeth of the gear broke. This stone is like steel. We can buy the skin and other things, but making this powder is very difficult. You have to see it to believe it. When you work, your chest and back will hurt and even urination becomes hard,' Soosainathan added. It is a curious fact then that the crushing is done by the women of the house, very likely because it is non-skin work and thus not an exclusive male domain. I found this to be the case in the homes of several mrdangam makers, irrespective of their geographical location. Wives, mothers and sisters crushed this nearly unbreakable rock with a pestle and have done it for years. Soosainathan had said, 'It is so easy for mrdangam artists to complain about the instrument; only we know how difficult it is to do this work.' Ideally, the 'we' here should be replaced by 'they'—the women!

Once again, there was an older process that has now died out, and I am recording it here because Selvaraj shared it with me. 'We used to add water to the powder, boil it and then sieve it again. Only after that was it ready for use.'

So what is this kittankallu used for?

There is a fairly prominent, black, round area on the mrdangam's playing surface, which faces the audience. This black patch is on the kottu thattu, the goat-skin second layer, and is made of a paste that contains finely powdered kittankallu and cooked rice. After the valandalai and toppi muttus are ready and harnessed together, the work of applying this paste begins. There is no exact measure for preparing it; the makers just know the ideal consistency from the feel of the paste. The mrdangam maker takes a few spoons of dark grey kittankallu powder and a small quantity of cooked rice, and adds some water so he can mix them into a semi-dry paste. When done, he rolls it into a tight ball and keeps it aside. The sight of it reminded me of my days as a fussy child, when my mother used to make balls of rice, dal and ghee, hoping that I would consume at least some of them. The stone-and-rice ball looked like a darker version of those, just not edible.

With the mrdangam standing erect, the valandalai facing up, Surendran cleaned the exposed kottu thattu area with a blade. Some people use a rough piece of leather instead. Then he dropped a few grains of cooked rice on the membrane and pressed it with his thumb, mashing and spreading it evenly around the kottu thattu. A few drops of water were sprinkled to moisten it.

Soosainathan had a more sophisticated system. He bundled cooked rice in a small piece of cloth, and used the bundle like a dispenser. As he pressed it down on the membrane, the rice squeezed its way out through the cloth's weave. He then let the rice-laden kottu thattu dry for a short while.

The kittankallu–boiled rice paste is called sadam. Sadam has only meant cooked rice to me, but to mrdangam artists and makers, it is this weird paste. The application of sadam on the kottu thattu is an art and one that is tough to execute, though the makers make it look deceptively easy. 'You should apply the sadam using only the thumb with a lot of pressure. Nowadays, they do it very lightly. If you do it well, you will be tired for a week,' Selvaraj said. Murthy too criticised the tendency of the current generation of makers to take this part lightly, and use other fingers to apply the sadam. 'It will not stay,' he said.

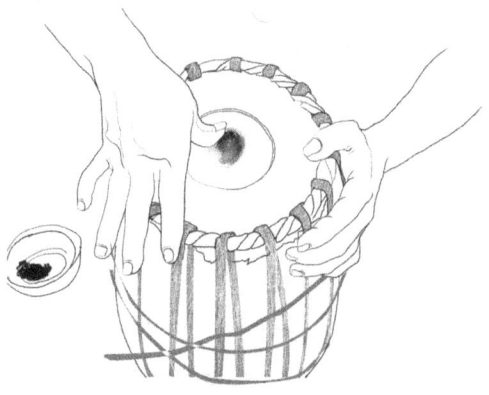

Taking a tiny ball of the sadam in one hand, Soosainathan started applying it in a circular motion in and around the central portion of the kottu thattu. His thumb kept moving, but the area covered was closer to the centre. He continued until all the sadam on his thumb was over. The continuous motion was carefully executed, the sadam evenly spread. Soosainathan then began rubbing the sadam with a large round smooth pebble so that the paste got compressed and affixed to the surface. It was now time for another small ball of sadam. This time, the spread was wider, covering almost the entire kottu thattu. The pressure that he exerted downwards glued the paste to the rice gum at the base. Soosainathan took a blunt knife and removed the loose particles on top with a few elegant movements. Again, he used the pebble to rub with force and speed until he was convinced that the sadam was tightly compacted and a mild sheen had appeared on its surface. He continued to switch between applying the sadam in a close circle near the centre and then a wider circle, all within the kottu thattu. He also made sure that there was a tiny gap between the circular edge of the kottu thattu and the annular vettu thattu—at the edge of the kottu thattu, some skin would remain exposed.

THIS PASTE OF COOKED RICE and kittankallu is crucial to the sound of the mrdangam. The sadam acts as a load (an added weight) on the membrane. It is this load that provides the valandalai its harmonics. Without it, the mrdangam cannot be tuned to the desired tonics. The harmonics of every single stroke on the mrdangam is the result of this load on the kottu thattu. And without a doubt, the way it is applied is cardinal to the musical effect of the valandalai.

The sadam adds a new timbral quality to the sound because the tones that emanate from the sadam at the centre and at the edge of the kottu thattu, at the juncture of the two thattus and on the annular are different, each one adding to the instrument's character. The mrdangam artist can then combine them in innumerable ways. As more and more sadam is added to the kottu thattu, the increased load brings down the pitch of the valandalai. Since the varu pidi tightens the membrane tremendously, the valandalai sound is at a very high pitch before the sadam is applied. This has to be brought down to the levels that match the tonic at which women or men sing.

It is true, of course, that the diameter of the apertures at the two ends of the mrdangam shell also determine the pitch range at which each instrument can operate. But, irrespective of whether it is a mrdangam shell meant for women's voices (typically between G and A), men's voices (usually between C and D) or instrumentalists (who tune their instrument sometimes at intermediary tonics around E or F), for turning the valandalai and synchronising it with any of these pitches, adding the load is absolutely necessary. The quantity of load will also vary depending on the artist's preference.

The second variable is the diameter of the opening on the annular thattu that exposes the kottu thattu. This too influences the amount of sadam that needs to be applied and the nature of the instrument's sound. Karaikudi Mani told me that when the muttu becomes old, he asks the makers to expose more of the kottu thattu, and also increase the width of that little gap between where the sadam ends and the vettu thattu begins. Varadan told me that, if the artist wanted more sound, he would just increase the exposure of the kottu thattu. All of these are important adjustments that makers and artists have discovered over the decades by observing how these materials respond.

As the maker adds layers of sadam to the kottu thattu, he constantly verifies the pitch of the mrdangam. 'As we add sadam, the pitch will keep dropping. So we need to adjust our work accordingly,' Selvaraj told me, adding, 'For every ball of sadam added, the sound will change.' This means the maker has to be deeply sensitive and attentive to any shifts in the pitch and tone of the instrument. He is watching for any discrepancy in the pitch across the entire surface, and responds as needed by tightening or loosening the varu at specific kannus. This requires multitasking, checking three kinds of tuning. One, bringing down the pitch of the valandalai with every layer of sadam, and two, ensuring that the pitch at all the kannus are aligned so that there is no ecchu–taggu. At the same time, the sound emanating from the vettu thattu and that which comes from the kottu thattu must also be in tune.

Constantly checking, the maker alters the way he applies the sadam depending on all these factors: closer circles, wider circles, maybe even closer to a specific kannu, hitting on the pinnal from below or above and fiddling with the varu tightness. This is a complex tuning methodology. I am not even going to try to explain the innumerable problems they

S. Anand

Jesudass checking and tuning the valandalai

encounter and the inventive solutions that have evolved. Soosainathan explained at least five different scenarios where he alters or modifies what he does, and I cannot explain what he said in words alone. But this much is clear: it is the goat skin, the kottu thattu, that is the most unpredictable and moody element, and needs a watchful eye. Soosainathan said, 'All this learning comes only from experience.' Another maker will, therefore, have his own set of tricks to deal with the vagaries of the mrdangam.

There are two mrdangam strokes that the maker plays to confirm that the outer tone coming from the vettu thattu and the inner tone from the kottu thattu are in sync. One is an open tap on the vettu thattu with his forefinger. As a musical playing area, the vettu thattu is referred to as the mittu. So, it is appropriate to say 'open tap on the mittu with the forefinger'. The other stroke is known as the chappu, where the player's hand is parallel to the valandalai and he strikes his little finger along the kottu thattu–vettu thattu juncture. In order to maintain the same pitch on both surfaces, the maker alternates between striking the mittu and playing the chappu all around the valandalai.

'As they keep adding layers of sadam, the mittu and chappu will keep differing. So they have to keep adjusting it. If the mittu is higher than the chappu, they will add sadam towards the centre of the kottu thattu, but if the mittu is lower than the chappu, they will add sadam to its edges,' Rajamani observed. There are specific terminologies to describe all of these applications. Sadam towards the centre is known as nadu-sadam (kittankallu–boiled rice paste at the centre) and sadam added towards the edges of the kottu thattu is known as ora-sadam (kittankallu–boiled rice paste at the corner).

The science of it is peculiar. If the pitch of the mittu is higher than that of the chappu, increasing the load at the centre pushes the kottu thattu downward. This automatically increases the internal gap between the kottu thattu and vettu thattu, decreasing the frequency of internal vibrations, bringing down the pitch of the sound that comes from the mittu. But why does the pitch of the mittu increase when sadam is added to the edges of the kottu thattu? This remains unclear to me. Perhaps when more sadam is added at the edges, it changes the weight balance on the kottu thattu, and that increases the pitch of the mittu?

Another way of increasing the pitch of the mittu is by scraping the sadam at the centre. Murthy did not like this practice. 'If you keep taking out the sadam from the centre, it will loosen up the particles, and in the long run, it will fall off.' The other problem is that it will cause a depression, which makes it quite uncomfortable to play on. But sometimes artists have to do this, especially when such a situation occurs just before a concert or on the performing stage itself. I have seen mrdangam artists use a knife to remove the sadam in the green room or on stage.

In order to explain the problem of the central depression, Sankaran narrated this anecdote. 'Kuppusami Pillai used to accompany T. Balasaraswati (the iconic Bharatanatyam dancer) and was in Madras for a performance. Muthaiah Pillai (father of Palani Subramania Pillai) told Kuppusami Pillai that he will prepare the latter's mrdangam for the evening's performance. Feeling that the mittu was lower than the chappu, he went on removing sadam and finally caused a big dent right at the centre. An exasperated and upset Kuppusami Pillai said, "What is this, sir? Look at what you have done."'

I forgot to mention that the final shape of the sadam is idli-like, concave and thinning towards the edges of the kottu thattu. That is, there is more sadam at the centre when compared to the edge. The concavity varies from maker to maker, and depends on the tonic to which the mrdangam is being tuned. Besides, the mrdangam artist does not just need the tone to be perfect, it has to feel right on his hand as well. Some players prefer less of a hump, while others want a thick idli-like sadam. 'When Shetty put sadam, it used to be rough and uneven, but my father's sadam was like a tortoise's back,' Selvaraj remarked. As a result, in Antony's sadam, the probability of mittu and chappu not coinciding was higher; it was just hit or miss. Sankaran described Rajamanickam's sadam thus, 'His sadam would look like a chain that had been beautifully strung. The edges were beautiful and that was his stamp.'

At times, the sadam looks fine on the surface, but its inner layers, closer to the skin, would have detached, creating a shaking sound. Artists and makers use an unusual term for this kind of shaky sound: velitthi. This is the sound one hears when multiple frequencies are heard prominently even when the player is holding one note. A good analogy would be the voice of a singer much past his or her prime who is trying to hold a note. The uncontrollable shake in such a voice is velitthi. There are many reasons why this would happen in a mrdangam, of which badly applied sadam or the detaching of sadam are a couple. The older the muttu gets, the tonic to which it can be tuned will also keep coming down. When there is too much wear and tear in the muttu, velitthi may make an appearance. This means it is time to change the muttu. Velitthi is also used as a derogatory term to describe a person who does not know the niceties of life, say someone given to making inappropriate statements. The word comes from the root 'vellai', meaning white, referring to a lack of shades. Songs that lacked depth were even referred to as vellaipatu. So it is possible that this musical colloquialism indicates a lack of depth in the sound, an unnecessary oscillation that is frivolous and superficial.

There are other expressions that describe specific variations of bad sound arising from the mrdangam. 'Kalasal' refers to non-uniform, disturbed sound that is off-pitch. The other derogatory word is 'tambalam'. As such, tambalam is a large copper plate. When it falls to the floor, there is a sharp, ear-shattering sound that continues unabated until the plate becomes stationary. This ugly sound is called tambalam sound.

It usually takes between twenty-five and forty small balls of sadam to complete the layering. 'Makers usually stop after about fifteen balls of sadam to let the wetness dry a little bit and then continue,' Rajamani stated. When done well, the sadam looks beautiful and sparkles. The maker would have cleaned up the edges so that there is also a visual contrast between the black sadam, the whitish border from the exposed goat skin and the cream or light brown colour of the vettu thattu's cow skin. The inner ring of the valandalai will then look like a complete solar eclipse.

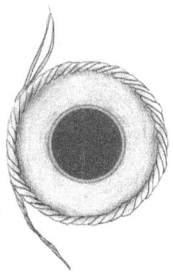

The sadam lasts anywhere between one and five concerts, the longevity depending on how well it has been applied, the style of playing and the artist's hands. If the artist plays with great force, chances are the sadam will loosen soon. Similarly, if the player has sweaty hands, he or she will need to change the sadam often. The sweat percolates into the sadam and loosens it, affecting the sound of the mrdangam. I have seen the sadam break away into small pieces and fall off the mrdangam face on stage.

Palghat Mani Iyer was extremely finicky about this. He removed a part of the sadam at the edges after every single concert, because he wanted a fresh coat. The reason he removed it at the edges, and not near the centre, was because he was afraid the maker would just fill the hole in the middle with a small bit of sadam. He needed it completely replaced; patchwork was unacceptable.

Britto gave me this beautiful explanation about how sound reverberates through the sadam. 'There are a lot of pores and hairs on the skin. If you remove the hairs, you are left with the pores. The pit from where the hair is removed is the place where the sadam sticks to the leather and that is what makes the cracks in the sadam. Basically, the sadam sticks to the pore holes, which causes cracks to appear. The nadam comes from the vibrations coming through the cracks.' The cracks he spoke of can be seen on the surface of the sadam, which looks like a dark glossy version of cracked arid land. Britto suggests that the sound emerges through these fissures in the sadam. C.V. Raman, in his paper 'Musical drums with harmonic overtones', published in *Nature* in 1920, concludes with this observation on the sadam: 'The central load also improves the musical effect by increasing the energy of vibration, and thus prolonging the duration of the tones.' Britto, from his experience, informs us that these tones come from the crevices in the sadam.

Over the years, because musicians have to travel all over the world for concerts with just one mrdangam, makers have had to find a way for the sadam to last for many more concerts. They have changed the base gum that glues the sadam to the kottu thattu. Nowadays, they use Fevicol or Vajram, an adhesive made out of cow fat and some chemicals. This keeps the sadam tightly fixed to the membrane and lasts the entire duration of a concert tour, which can sometimes be over a month of more than fifteen concerts. The only downside is that these powerful adhesives dull, or stifle, the sound in the beginning. After a few concerts, the base gum begins to loosen its hold on the sadam, and the sound then has greater tonality and decibel.

ACCORDING TO THE THANJAVUR MAKERS, the kittankallu is irreplaceable in the preparation of sadam. But makers in Madras, Peruvemba and Andhra use stones found in their own localities. Madras makers get their stones from Red Hills, Manimangalam or Maraimalai Nagar. Some claim that Rajagopal from Red Hills—known in classic south-Indian style as Red Hills Rajagopal—was the first to source this stone. However, Munusami and other makers who lived and worked in the city from before his time must have known about this source.

Muruganandam was the first to go to Padappai for stones, Navaneetham said proudly: 'They (his father and other family members) used to go to the temple there. They saw the stones and bought back a few to try and found that they were good. These stones were of the same colour as kittankallu.' But Padappai is inaccessible now because the Central government has taken over the piece of land where the stone could be found.

Maraimalai Nagar and Manimangalam are Balaguru's sources. Those from Peruvemba, Vijayawada, Vizianagaram, or the Tada region have always used stones found in their locality. Somehow, just by looking at the stones, and trial and error, they have all stumbled upon rocks that give them the desired sound.

Along with the kittankallu (Thanjavur), I also got samples of stones from Peruvemba, Maraimalai Nagar, Red Hills and Tada analysed to determine their chemical composition at the Indian Institute of Technology, Madras. Every one of these stones was high in iron content, but it was the sample from Tada that had the highest percentage of iron (ferrous), 73.2 per cent—much more than the much-touted kittankallu, which contained 53.4 per cent iron (ferrous and some ferric). Other than the Tada stone, all the other samples also revealed the presence of quartz. This is unusual and, according to Juergen Schieber, professor of Earth and Atmospheric Sciences at Indiana University, 'Under normal circumstances, olivine and quartz cannot coexist in magma. Thus, the presence of quartz indicates a later overprint, probably tectonic fractures that were filled with quartz as hydrothermal fluids percolated through the rock. The variability we see here could easily be found in a single outcrop of mafic rocks that were affected by later hydrothermal overprint and then weathered to variable depth.' There was also the presence of aluminium in the samples from

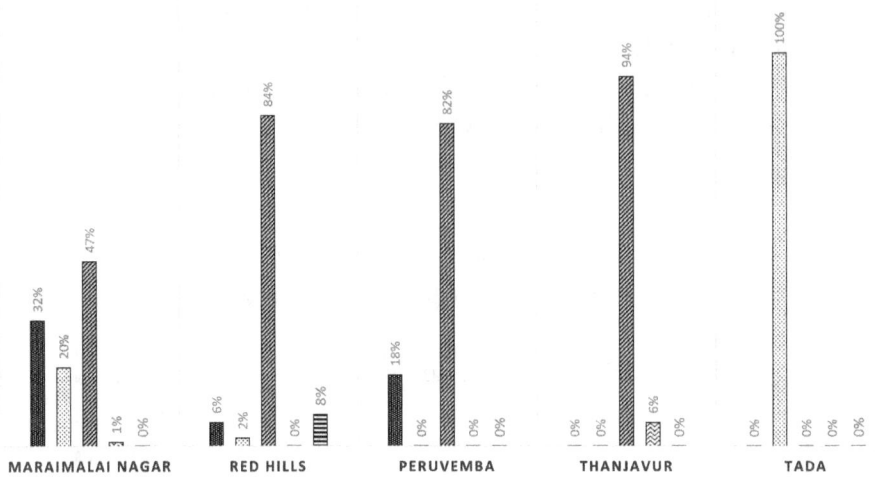

Stones were analysed for their chemical composition by X-Ray diffraction (XRD) using the Rietveld method. The relative composition of the various minerals from stones used by mrdangam makers sourced from five different regions are shown.

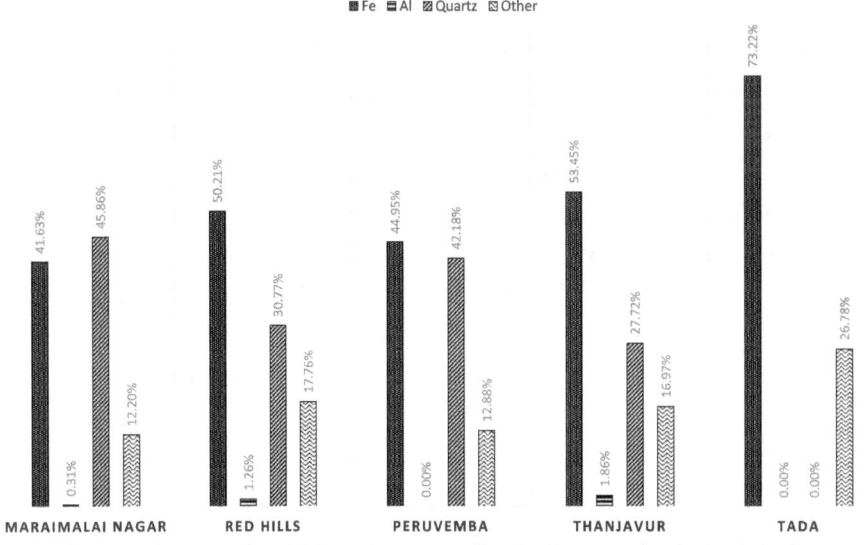

The percentage composition of the individual metals (Fe, Al) and quartz (SiO2) was calculated from the XRD data.

Maraimalai Nagar (0.3 per cent), Red Hills (1.3 per cent) and Thanjavur (1.9 per cent). The stones from Peruvemba and Tada have absolutely no aluminium.

The question is: how much does all this impact the tonal texture of the mrdangam? We really do not know. It is even harder to argue that any one sonic palette is the most ideal. Each stone, and the sadam derived from it, gives the mrdangam a distinct aesthetic presence. There cannot be 'only one'. Needless to say, the Thanjavur makers will swear that theirs is the best.

Selvaraj claimed, 'In the sadam made with other stones, ten balls are equivalent to one ball of kittankallu sadam.' Sankaran believes that the application of two small balls of kittankallu sadam causes the pitch to drop by one semi-tone because of its weight.

Navaneetham uses Red Hills stone, but also buys kittankallu from the Thanjavur family. He has a lot to crib about. 'They (Thanjavur makers) have relatives who gather the stones, grind them and sell the powder to their shops. We used to have a couple of workers just to powder the stones. There were always three or four paint buckets full of powder in the house. Once a bucket was used up, my father would go and gather more stones and powder them. Today, I am buying the powder from the Thanjavur people. We pay Rs 700–900 per kilo, but the quality is not always good. They cheat us. Sometimes the powder is coarse and, when we sieve it, we lose half a kilo of the powder. *(Laughs)* The increase in the price of the instrument is also because of this. The cost was less when we did everything. Now that so many people are involved, and each one is marking up their part, the cost has become very high.'

Balaguru used the special quality of the kittankallu to claim that there is nothing unique about the Thanjavur making style. 'I think that it is the speciality of the soil. Whoever uses that (kittankallu) will get extra-good sound. The maavu (paste) from there is special. I get different types of stones, but the stones from Thanjavur are a class apart.'

There have been experiments with replacements for this kind of stone: sand, crushed bricks, talcum powder, turmeric powder, but nothing worked. T.V. Gopalakrishnan attempted the most outrageous thing, causing makers to literally shed blood. Arulraj remembered, 'He gave me a powder and went away. When I mixed it with rice, it felt just like our paste but was white in colour. When I applied one or two small balls, my hand became rough and then my skin tore. I asked Soosainathan to try and, within two rounds, his skin also tore. When TVG came back at night, I told him what happened and he responded by saying, "It's okay, throw it and the muttu."' Little did Arulraj and Soosainathan know that they had been handed diamond dust for sadam. The realisation came only when TVG actually informed them why they were bleeding.

Mrdangam makers charge anywhere between Rs 600 and Rs 1,000 to apply sadam to a mrdangam. Some seniors recall the days when it used to cost much less. Sivaraman recalled, 'Azhaganambi Pillai paid only 6 annas (about 37 paisa). Later, he gave them 12 annas. My father gave them something similar, but also used to provide consultation for free.' Sivaraman's father was a doctor. Melgies remembers that, in the 1970s, he received just Rs 5. Slowly, over the decades, it has crawled to Rs 800 on an average.

C.V. Raman conducted important experiments on the harmonic properties of the mrdangam in 1919. When looking at different ways of striking the mrdangam on the valandalai side, Raman's first method is 'bringing down the flat of the palm of the hand on the centre of the drum head and then quickly removing it'. He states that this results in a deep hum without overtones. Mrdangam artists play one hard, tight stroke right at the centre of the sadam with their forefinger. This produces an abrupt and harsh 'TA' sound. To my unscientific mind and musical ears, it lacks overtones. It is important to note that the tuning of the mrdangam only means matching the mittu and chappu. It excludes any stroke played at the very centre of the valandalai head. Even in mrdangam-playing techniques, only on rare occasions is the very centre of the sadam sounded independently. This inharmonic stroke is, in fact, used as a contrast to the multi-tonal harmonic sounds that other mrdangam strokes generate.

8

THE GREAT DEBATE

C.V. Raman does not mention the name of the maker who prepared the mrdangam for his experiments in 1919. It is someone from a generation before Parlandu's. At that time, Raman was in Calcutta, so we do not know if the mrdangam he used came from his hometown of Madras, or someplace else. Was it young Munusami, an elder from Munusami's family, or Sevittian's father Arogyam perhaps? Unfortunately, we will never know. Raman's findings will remain etched in the history of science. But the person who created the instrument that gave him those beautiful sand formations known as Chladni figures (it is a way to visualise the resonance patterns of a membrane, and is used to determine its harmonic properties), and helped him prove his hypothesis that the mrdangam is a harmonic instrument, that uninteresting nobody has been buried.

There is another aspect to Raman's mrdangam which requires some investigation—the fact that the instrument itself would have been a slightly different beast in those days. And depending on whether it was a Madras- or Thanjavur-based maker, the nature of the instrument might have been different. In the early part of the twentieth century, once the sadam had been applied and all pitch-related anomalies settled, the mrdangam would have been ready for concert use. Thanjavur Vaidyanatha Iyer would have most definitely used such a mrdangam. 'Sound came from the sadam resonance,' Selvaraj explained. The vibrating membranes and the sadam-load on the valandalai gave the instrument its harmonic tones, and artists and audiences got the aesthetic dimensions they wanted.

While this seems to have been the practice in Thanjavur, makers and players in Madras were not satisfied with the resonance and came up with an ingenious idea. The grass broom, omnipresent in Indian homes, is made of tiger grass, *Thysanolaena latifolia*, also known as broom grass. The Madras makers slid thin strips of the grass stick between the vettu and kottu thattus. The annular vettu thattu and the kottu thattu below it are braided together along with the okkarara thattu at the base. By placing sticks between the two layers (kottu thattu and vettu thattu), the makers got a sharp, metallic string-like tone, because the sticks vibrated every time the mrdangam was stroked. Even more spectacular was the fact that, depending on where the stroke was played, the tone emanating from this innovation had a spectrum. Everything from a soft buzz to a pointed clean twang was now possible. It also meant that the aural reach of the mrdangam increased. Remember, this was the pre-microphone era. Even when microphones came into use, there was only one multidirectional mike in front of the stage, at some distance from the mrdangam. The addition of these tiny sticks—known as kucchi—to the structure dramatically changed how the mrdangam was perceived. With a larger aural presence, the mrdangam became that much more significant in a concert.

Kamalakar Rao, then a young man and a resident of Rajahmundry, who listened to artists like Madras Kannan and S.V.S. Narayanan via the All India Radio, said, 'Madras Kannan also played with kucchis. His mittu had that "choin-choin-choin" sound. That was one style of playing. It used to attract people. He had some special technique of striking the mrdangam. When he played, the kucchi would shake. We heard S.V.S. Narayanan play for the Vadyavrunda (All India Radio's orchestra). It used to be so beautiful.'

An instrument in which these grass sticks are inserted has come to be known as kucchi mrdangam, though Trichy Sankaran felt strongly that expressions such as kucchi mrdangam or kucchi muttu are erroneous. These are just mrdangams in which kucchis have been placed, he insisted. Usually, one thin stick is placed at every kannu; that is, sixteen in one valandalai. But makers and artists may reduce the number if there is already enough resonance from the skins and sadam. The sticks are slid in towards the kannu. Varadan explained this process, 'You have to split the grass into four equal strips and place it inside. We collect this grass from the villages. We use the entire grass, except for the bit at the very end that is thin.' According to Kamalakar Rao, makers in Andhra would at times place thirty-two kucchis instead of sixteen, which would mean two kucchis per kannu!

Another artist credited with being an early explorer of the kucchi mrdangam on the concert stage is

C.S. Murugabhoopathy. Kalidas narrates an incident that Palani had shared with him. 'I have heard my teacher say that kucchi was introduced by Murugabhoopathy. The two once travelled together and, on the way, he asked Murugabhoopathy about the sound of his mrdangams. Murugabhoopathy responded that he hadn't done anything different. "What have I done which you have not?" he asked. Murugabhoopathy was five or six years younger than my teacher and two years younger than Mani Iyer. So his response was meant to show humility. But my teacher noticed the kucchis. Madurai Ratnam was the one who had done that.' So are we to infer that kucchi was in use in Madurai? Once again, the credit for this innovation goes to the artist, while the actual thinker and doer is mentioned only in passing.

Several other musicians too say that Murugabhoopathy was the one who brought the kucchi mrdangam into play. I am not convinced. From all that we hear about the mrdangams used in Madras, it must have been in use from an earlier time.

Selvaraj believed that, while he still lived in Palakkad, Mani Iyer would have used a non-kucchi instrument. However, in those years, there was a parallel kucchi tradition in Palakkad. We know from Guruvayur Dorai that, even in the early 1940s, kucchi was in use there. T.V. Gopalakrishnan gave me more details. 'In Kerala, the kucchi used to be from palm leaves. There are three types of kucchi. The first is from the coconut tree, thennam kucchi. It is hard and the sound is harsh. The second is from the palm leaf. Here (in Tamil Nadu), they use thodappapullu (broom grass). Those days, the Kerala makers used to make fun of us, saying you are using what you use as brooms in the mrdangam.' In fact, Dakshinamurthy Pillai is said to have commented, 'O Lord, the thodappam (broom) must not be kept inside a mrdangam.'

As far as I have been able to ascertain, the practice of inserting kucchi between the membranes was in vogue in Madras and Palakkad. It also seems certain that kucchi mrdangams were in use in the Vizianagaram belt in the 1940s. Thanjavur seems to have remained largely unaffected by this trend. Selvaraj suggested that Shengol, the oldest but weakest among the three brothers, may have done kucchi work, but I do not know for whom. Thanjavur was considered the capital of Karnatik music, and its refusal to accept the use of kucchi was doubtless the result of a stuck-up attitude—the 'Karnatik attitude' I described earlier, where such enhancements are seen as fripperies. The mrdangam artists in Thanjavur played only on the sadam-loaded surface, with no other material to enhance resonance. However, as the sadam was changed many times over, some of the dried sadam might have crept into the lower edges of the vettu thattu. This would have added some extra resonance to the mrdangam.

In the world of Tamil cinema, kucchi mrdangams have long ruled. Guruvayur Dorai recalled, 'I took a kappi mrdangam (another method, similar to kucchi) once for a recording. Vazhuvoor Ramaiah Pillai (the renowned dance guru who choreographed dance sequences in Tamil cinema) was present. It was a recording in Revathi Studios on Mount Road, Madras. Rangaswamy was the sound engineer. I tapped on the mrdangam, and he said, "What is this? It doesn't sound like a mrdangam at all", and told me to get another one. I went home and brought another one, and that was also kappi. Whatever I played, they were not willing to accept. Then I took a kucchi mrdangam and played on it, and that chaan-chaan sound was heard. They immediately said, "Aah, that's the sound of the mrdangam.'"

Until the early 1950s, mrdangam artists were either using kucchi mrdangams or ones without such enhancements. Then came a major breakthrough—an inspired idea from Parlandu, the creative genius. Why not use the uncrushed, slightly larger granules of the kittankallu instead of the kucchi? When makers processed kittankallu for the sadam, the pieces that remained unpowdered were thrown away. Parlandu decided that these could be placed in between the vettu thattu and kottu thattu. At that point, he was working closely with Mani Iyer and made a mock-up version for him to try. Iyer fell in love with what he heard. The sound was unusual, bold, tight, had gravitas and presence, did not rattle like the kucchi and, above all, gave him an edge over his contemporaries, another differentiating factor.

Makers place granules of different sizes in the gap between the two thattus—an operation that requires a great deal of attentiveness and dexterity. The really small ones are pushed deep inside, closer to the wooden frame, so that they do not fall out. The medium-sized ones are the next to go in, and then bigger pieces close to the exposed kottu thattu. There is no hard-and-fast rule, of course, and the maker constantly tinkers with it, keeping the artist's desire in mind. These granules are called kappi, hence the term 'kappi mrdangam'.

The process of inserting these stone granules is a beauty to watch. The maker picks up a few kappis and smartly drops them on the sadam. Due to the sadam's curvature, they roll towards the inner edge of the vettu thattu. A little shake of the mrdangam and the granules are spread evenly around the inner perimeter. Then, by slanting the mrdangam just a wee bit, and using a screwdriver to open up the gap between the membranes, he lets the kappi roll into the gap. He keeps turning the mrdangam, making sure that the granules are evenly distributed, checking the tone at every kannu, and adjusting the kappi placements to be certain that not one is loose or out of position. In the maker's language, he 'settles' the kappi and the mrdangam.

Parlandu's innovation required a rethink of the entire mrdangam structure. The nature of the skin chosen and the extent of poivaru pidi had to be reassessed. Placing stone granules between two membranes meant that, over time, the kappi would scratch the skin and might even tear it. In order to avoid this, the makers decided to use thicker skin (both goat and cow) for the kappi mrdangam. But the skin selection process is not just about finding ideal individual skins, Rajamani pointed out; they have to work in combination. 'I do not know how he (the maker) knows, but only he knows. He checks by flapping the skins together.' A younger mrdangam artist added that either the two skins need to be of more or less equal thickness, or the kottu thattu (goat skin) needs to be thicker than the vettu thattu (cow skin). The other way around will not work. Soosainathan had a pragmatic explanation: 'That is because every time we remove the sadam, we also scrape off the skin, and so it thins over time.'

It also became imperative that the poivaru pidi be super tight, because the two thattus had to hold the kappis firmly between them. If the stone granules moved and got repositioned, the mrdangam would go out of pitch or a velitthi sound could emerge. Artists often speak of how Mani Iyer always brought along a minimum of two mrdangams to a concert. No doubt, as an early adapter of the kappi, he needed to be careful. There was always a chance that the kappi would move or fall off, and Mani Iyer could not take a chance with just one mrdangam. Umayalpuram K. Sivaraman was candid, 'You can trust the kucchi mrdangam; you can't trust that.'

A tighter poivaru pidi also changed the maker's focus. Mrdangam-making now involved brute physical strength, a certain toughness. While the kucchi mrdangam called for three or four rounds of poivaru pidi, the kappi mrdangam needed six or even seven rounds. By the end of the session, the maker would be bone-tired. The kappi mrdangam needed makers who were strong enough to keep going.

But tightening the poivaru to this extent causes two things to happen. Firstly, the pitch of the valandalai increases exponentially—even higher than that of a kucchi mrdangam. Tauter skin means higher frequency. Secondly, the skins are less flexible and the sound tight; much like a human voice is when the area around the throat is inflamed and thickens and the voice lacks its lingering quality. When kucchi is used, after the first or second sadam-loading, the pitch of the mrdangam will come down enough to be tuned to either male or female tonic, depending on the size of the kattai. But in a kappi muttu, this does not happen. Therefore, the makers devised a method called thattu murukardu, or breaking in the valandalai.

'To make the skins flexible, the stiffness must go, so they (artists) give the new mrdangam to their students to practice on,' Rajamani said. These Young Turks, full of energy, are free to hit it as hard as they want, attempt all that they know, and in the process, make the skin more pliable. 'They have to play a lot, for hours, either lessons or even to accompany a singer,' Rajamani explained. This suited everyone well—the students worked on their art, while the master got his instrument ready. As students practice on these mrdangams, the sadam is replaced at least three or four times. Each time it is changed, the pitch drops. Only after at least three or four such sadam replacements is the mrdangam ready for the stage. It used to take at least three or four months before a kappi mrdangam was considered concert-worthy. Even today, a few mrdangam artists follow this arduous procedure. And if I think about it, the process is rather similar to breaking in new cricket bats. After the application of linseed oil on a new bat, a wooden mallet on which a cricket ball is fixed is used to knock on it. The bat is also used to knock a suspended cricket ball. This helps tighten the wood, increasing the longevity of the bat.

In Thanjavur, Mani Iyer had a person whose task it was to break in the mrdangam. Rajaram said, 'For thattu murukardu, there was one Gurappa. He was always practising! *(Laughs loudly.)* My father would sometimes say, "Don't practise like Gurappa." He would say that practising in a smart manner is much more effective than just sitting and blindly practising for seven–eight hours. "Look at him, practises eleven hours a day! What is the use?" But if the thattu had to be broken in, it was Gurappa who had to play.' They even gave it a name: Gurappa practice. T.K. Murthy remembers seeing Gurappa's grandfather Anganna Nayakar's curious practice methodology. At the end of every lesson, he would pick up one grain of unhusked rice and keep it aside. At the end of the day, he calculated that he had practised for 'n' number of grains.

Once kucchi and kappi came into play, the final checking of the valandalai pitch was done only after the stones or sticks were put in place. This part of the making is known as suddham panradu—to clean up the mrdangam, the final check. The sadam is wiped at the edges, the varu is checked, tightened or loosened to make sure that the pitch is identical at all the kannus, and if there is any difference between the mittu and chappu, sadam is added or removed.

Palghat Raghu checking the mrdangam as a young Soosainathan watches

This is the actual final step. It is only during this stage that most mrdangam artists actually sit with the maker, personalise and finalise the instrument. In fact, makers insist that the artists need to be present at this stage. They say that the strength and feel of everyone's hand is different. Though the mrdangam may seem fine when the maker strikes it, it can be totally off when the artist plays on it. Therefore, the makers need the artists to play, test and express satisfaction.

Kucchi and kappi were not the only things placed between the membranes. Mrdangam artists did not think it peculiar to ask makers to insert the poonal/janeu and stick it with glue on the inside of the cow skin. Tambura strings too were tried, as were cut-up credit cards!

'My uncle's (Antony) working style was strenuous and hard. His body was also like that. He could do the work of four people. I am also like that,' Selvaraj said proudly. Although he did not think much of Antony's sadam, calling it 'rough', there was respect for his physical abilities. Arulraj too cheered his father's varu abilities: 'I remember my father braiding the varu. There is a knot where the braiding ends. Sometimes we had to apply sadam and pull the varu again, but the knot will just not move. The varu was so tightly pulled that loosening it was impossible. Even an elephant cannot loosen the varu that has been tightened by Shetty.'

It was clear from the accounts of several makers and artists that the physicality involved in the process of mrdangam-making is much lauded. Somehow, the respect associated with being able to match the artist's varu demands was (and is) seen as a sign of the maker's prowess and seriousness. This bodily power thus translates to respect, and hence, social standing. A combination of physical masculine power (something the brahmin player is seen as lacking) and the ability to prove one's own worth. At the same time, every extra round of poivaru pidi satisfies the artist's delusion that he is somehow more specific and knowledgeable about the instrument.

I am not in the least denying that there is a great need for perfection in tuning the instrument, or that the poivaru pidi plays an important role in achieving it. But after watching many interactions between makers and players, my sense is that, for the artist, there is vicarious male chauvinistic bravado also at work. They are not the ones pulling the varu with their entire body. Yet, many mrdangam artists speak with arrogance about how they need very strong poivaru pidi. To demand that, and get strong men to listen and do as they say, is a show of machismo.

Rajamanickam may have faced a bit of criticism even within the family about the lack of physical force in his methods. 'His work was very clean, and he was a smart worker who had a knack for doing things. He would not strain himself too much physically. His strength was in the skin that he chose and materials that he used. His was not hardcore physicality. It was about getting things done with minimal effort,' Melgies had said. Though it appeared to be a compliment, the repeated mention of the lack of hard body effort suggested to me a different register.

At the root of it all, of course, is the institution of caste. It is an intellectual, emotional, psychological and physical assertion of power. In this case, a community that considers its own abilities as being beyond the physical, derives power from instructing another to do the corporeal work. Bundled in this is an underlying feeling among the artist community that their work is above all these temporal activities. However, they are able to control and push people who are physically better endowed. That their elevated virtuosity depends on material effort is explained away as a willing contribution by the makers—imagine, these people (makers) are able to associate with the likes of Mani Iyer or Palani. Perhaps many players have not consciously thought in this manner, but it would still be a pretence not to acknowledge the inner workings of the player–maker equation.

Michael (name changed) had a humorous quip about mrdangam artists who gave them hell with poivaru pidi. 'All those artists who would break our hips and knees by asking us to go on and on are thankfully dead. (*Folding his hands and looking up.*) They would kill us with the varu pidi. If there was even the tiniest difference, they would not let go. They would call their wife and say, "Give him some tea." Or "Give him some water." Only to get more work done. Once we drank the tea or water, we would get some immediate energy, feel satisfied and forget the hardship and the fact that they were the ones causing it. We would tell ourselves that it's okay do the varu pidi to equalise that minute discrepancy.' Though Michael does not articulate it, I wondered how much of the temporary relief also came from the emotional satisfaction derived from that 'act of kindness'. That such a great artist was pausing, recognising his fatigue and trying to provide relief.

Almost the entire Thanjavur clan prides itself on the poivaru pidi, which is their speciality. T.V. Gopalakrishnan had said as much in our conversation. It is good to remember here that this demanding poivaru pidi was necessitated only by Parlandu's kappi muttu. The poivaru that Soosainathan had tightened, when showing me how it was done, was also for a kappi muttu, which is why he went on and on. And he wanted to do that extra round to prove a point to me.

THE VALORISATION OF THE POIVARU pidi has in turn led to a hierarchy among the kucchi and the kappi—the stick and the stone. We will be revisiting some of the subliminally discriminative and gender-associated aesthetic judgements that appeared in the case of the sunnambu thattu. Every kucchi mrdangam maker will tell you that their mrdangams do not require that much muscle work. Not that it is not present; just that, in comparison to its stony cousin, the labour is less intensive. All his life, Varadan has specialised in kucchi mrdangams. 'A person who works on a kappi mrdangam has to work hard (physically), use skins that are thicker, pull the vettu thattu a lot when he first places it, tighten poivaru, make forty-eight kannus and, while braiding, make sure that it is tight enough so that the kappi stays inside. For kucchi, we need not do all this; we leave it a little loose. Only then will you get the choin-choin-choin sound. Kappi muttu sound is gonagonagona. If you over-pull the kucchi muttu too much, the sound gets stifled. When it is loose, there is that jilujiluppu!' At another point in the interview, Varadan called the kappi sound 'dhimma'. It is obvious that the difference in the making has more to do with the sound that the artist desires than anything else. But if we place the sound emanating from the kappi mrdangam at a higher pedestal, the language changes. And this higher stature of the kappi is also connected to the fact that mrdangam artists usually use kucchi mrdangams for women vocalists and kappi mrdangams for male vocalists.

'The quality you get in a kappi, you will never get in a kucchi,' said Rajamani. In the core Karnatik circles, 'choin-choin-choin' is not a compliment. It indicates lightness, easiness, casualness—a lack of effort. Somewhere, there is also an implication that anyone can get good sound out of a kucchi mrdangam, but only a real player can make a kappi mrdangam sing. Great mrdangam artists speak with pride about how they moved from kucchi to kappi. Karaikudi Mani said, 'Between 1965 and 1976, Rajamanickam used to work for Mani Iyer. He came to me of his own accord and said he will work on one kattai for me. He used to live near Ice House. I handed over a mrdangam, but he insisted that I should only play on kappi. Those days, I did not know much about kappi or kucchi, but of course, I knew of Mani Iyer's mrdangam sound. I felt the difference when I played on a kappi mrdangam. The clarity was much more. In a kappi mrdangam, an echo comes from inside the instrument; once we experience that, we get new openings in artistry.'

Those who have moved the other way, from kappi to kucchi, struggled to explain why. Some just blame it on the demands of the profession; more concerts and not enough intervals between them means no time to work on and maintain the tougher kappi mrdangam.

Rajaram too spoke of a time when Mani Iyer found out that his prime disciple, Palghat Raghu, was using a kucchi mrdangam. 'During the Palakkad Festival, Raghu mama brought a kucchi mrdangam. My father called him and asked what mrdangam he was using. He knew by then that Raghu had started using kucchi mrdangams. Raghu said he had brought his own mrdangam. My father asked to see it. When he saw that it was kucchi, he told Raghu, "You do not need this." Raghu mama had changed to kucchi mrdangam because it was expensive to maintain a Thanjavur mrdangam.'

This is the other thing that is often spoken of. 'To maintain a kappi mrdangam using Thanjavur workmanship is very expensive. One needs to be very patient, like with a naughty child,' Karaikudi Mani said. There is no doubt that, because of the variables they bring into the picture, kappi mrdangams need to be constantly watched and monitored. But does that make them better, of higher quality? The inference is that those who play kucchi mrdangams need not worry so much; in other words, they need to expend less effort.

This is a notion that Sivaraman vociferously disagrees with. 'Not at all! Everything is the same. People say this on purpose (in order to bring down the image of the kucchi mrdangam),' he said.

Let us examine now how this discrimination is connected with gender-prejudiced notions of the masculine and feminine. Both the processes that give the kappi its sound are laden with masculinity. Whenever the sound of the kappi mrdangam is discussed, it is about the heaviness, roundedness, a bell-like ring with a lingering resonance. Some use the word 'gambhiram', or majesty. In these discussions, kappi is respectful and traditional, while the kucchi is titillating. Karaikudi Mani even said, 'Kappi is like a woman wearing a saree, while kucchi is like one wearing jeans, nothing wrong, but there is a difference.' Even those who play kucchi mrdangams agree, and blame singers and audiences for the fact that they are not using kappi. The tabla-like reverberating, chiming tonality of the kucchi is visualised as superficial beauty, whereas the more weighty, sustained knell of the kappi is inner strength. Needless to say, the former is associated with female imagery and the latter with male. Consequently, many artists and makers argue that it is okay to use kucchi for women vocalists, but for men it must be kappi.

T.K. Murthy was proud he did not fall into that trap. A regular mrdangam artist for M.S. Subbulakshmi, he stressed that, even at her higher tonic, he used a kappi mrdangam. This is highly interesting, because here is a person who never shied away from sharing the stage with women (as many of his contemporaries did), but still takes pride in the fact that he did not give up his kappi—a stamp of masculinity and sturdiness.

Falling under the kucchi's spell is equated with giving up integrity, becoming commercial. And if we correlate this with gender, everything suddenly makes sense. Mrdangam artists often speak in private about not needing to put in too much effort when accompanying women; that they can get away with just playing one stroke or providing light, feather-like touches. Among themselves, they speak of such concerts as ones in which a kurta retains its iron-creases. The sound of the kucchi is in some manner associated with this sort of experience.

The consequence of all this is that, even if the mrdangam artist demonstrates great effort in a concert, the kucchi sound can blind the listener from recognising that effort. At one point, Vellore Ramabhadran was possibly the busiest mrdangam artist in the field. He belonged to the old chauvinist school and did not accompany women. He finally agreed to do so only after receiving the 'Sangita Kalanidhi', the highest honour a Karnatik musician can receive. Interestingly, having received the award, he felt secure enough to share the stage with women. Until then, he was probably afraid that he would be belittled by his contemporaries and considered less worthy. But his style of playing itself was soft, uncomplicated, unextravagant—and he played on the kucchi mrdangam. Clearly, this was an intellectual disaster. His playing did not conform to the male-constructed idea of gravity, and his mrdangam's tone displayed playfulness.

He was not truly respected by his colleagues. Sangita Kalanidhi notwithstanding, Ramabhadran died an unheralded hero.

We also find that many mrdangam artists who use kucchi mrdangams convey their masculine musicality by playing in an aggressive and mathematical style. Softness and retreating to the background are nearly non-existent. Are they unconsciously also compensating for the unspoken accepted norm that kucchi mrdangam is feminine?

These days, there are more women singers than men in Karnatik music. This also means that most mrdangam artists who are active today play on kucchi mrdangams rather than kappi, yet this hierarchy remains. Proponents of the kappi argue that there is greater clarity in what they play, more perfection, less chance of hiding behind the veil of attractive sound. The counter argument is that kucchi provides scope to play strokes with greater nuance, softness and delicacy, and provides uniformity in resonance.

Even as I lay out the qualities that celebrate each format, you can see the sexist connotations that creep in. One mrdangam artist who plays on kappi mrdangams said with egotistic resignation, 'Playing with kappi mrdangams is very hard, but if some people say they like only kucchi, how can we argue?'

In this testosterone-filled game, makers of the kappi mrdangam preen. This machismo cuts across caste and class. Many say pointedly that kappi is the real deal, and that mastering it is the high point in the evolution of a maker. Anyone can make a kucchi mrdangam, but only 'we' can do this. The kappi mrdangam originated with Parlandu, so this tradition belongs to the Thanjavur school of makers. Peter (name changed) said, 'Thanjavur work means kappi muttu. We work for hours on the sadam, they do not.' The Thanjavur makers often snidely remark that the Madras makers only use kucchi muttu. The family believes that, while they can make any kind of mrdangam, the Madras makers are only good at kucchi stuff. Oddly enough, all makers, including the Thanjavur lot, make more kucchi than kappi mrdangams today.

The prejudice gets worse if a maker works with kucchi and sunnambu thol—useful skills, no doubt, but he is not someone who is looked up to. And, by and large, it is the Madras muttu that is associated with this kind of work. In truth, though, there is little to demarcate the Thanjavur and Madras muttus these days. All of them work with sunnambu thol and kucchi, even if they *also* make kappi mrdangams and use paccha thol. I have to wonder if there is much left of the acclaimed Thanjavur work. There are very few who do it now, and even fewer artists who make use of such mrdangams. Of course, this has only made it the more elite option. Which means, very rarely will anyone question the presumed superiority of kappi mrdangams, even if they themselves use kucchi. Madras muttu dominates the market, but Thanjavur muttu is the aspirational perfection.

Balaguru spoke of the predominance of sunnambu thol now. 'Ninety per cent use this today. The reason is, you don't have to take the javvu (the layer of flesh just below the skin) off physically. It is easy.' And then he said something particularly interesting. 'For those using kappi muttu, there is no connection between the skin and the sound. This is my argument. It only depends on the sadam, the muttu, the width of the mouth.' Many makers from other communities sniggered at the Thanjavur mrdangams, truth be told. They would say that, in spite of cutting the vettu thattu quite wide to expose so much of the kottu thattu, and applying a truckload of sadam, the Thanjavur mrdangams still do not have sufficient sound. When Murugabhoopathy played with Karaikudi Mani's mrdangam, which was made by the Thanjavur makers, he apparently said, 'I asked for a mrdangam; you gave me a stone.' Karaikudi Mani understood this as being an acknowledgement of the enormous physical effort involved in generating resonance with his mrdangam. But was Murugabhoopathy's comment tongue-in-cheek, I wonder.

People like Mani Iyer, though, would never use a mrdangam made by the Madras makers. Everything had to be from Thanjavur: skin, stone and maker. On the other side of the spectrum was Madras Kannan who played on kucchi muttu, which might also have occasionally been sunnambu thol, made by the Madras makers. He thought the kappi hype was unnecessary. 'You can make a mrdangam with kappi or kucchi, there is no difference. Looks like Palghat Mani Iyer did not understand this,' he said bitingly.

Even within the Thanjavur family, at least until a generation ago, there was a hierarchy based on whether the family member made more kucchi or kappi mrdangams. People like Parlandu and Selvaraj pass the test as kings of kappi, and have the validation of the Mani Iyer clan. Rajamanickam is somewhere in between, while Antony and his family, the present rulers of the industry, are seen as kucchi people.

Now comes the twist in the tale. Antony did a lot of Palani Subramania Pillai's mrdangams. When I spoke to Antony's son, Arulraj, he said that Palani played on a kucchi mrdangam. He even specified that, instead of using the usual poonthodappa (broom grass) kucchi, Palani used toothpicks. Sankaran countered this: 'Palani sir used to carry a container full of toothpicks. But I don't think he ever used it, except maybe as a temporary solution during an emergency.'

Selvaraj clearly did not agree, because he casually criticised Palani by saying, 'Only if we kept kucchi would Palani's mrdangam have sound.' He believes that Palani did use a kucchi mrdangam. Arulraj too compared Mani Iyer's and Palani's mrdangams: 'Palani wanted a lot of sound but Mani Iyer did not; so that (Iyer's mrdangam) was a challenge.' He also attributed this beautiful thought to Palani: 'Palani would say that, if a fly sat on the sadam and flew off, sound should emanate from it.'

But here is the problem. Palani's students categorically say that he never used a kucchi mrdangam. Kalidas said, 'Palani only played with kappi, never kucchi.' Sankaran and Dorai too confirmed this.

I was confused; the makers and the artists were saying two diametrically opposite things. Whom was I to trust? However, Kamalakar Rao also remembered seeing Palani Subramania Pillai play on a kucchi mrdangam.

Later, Sankaran conceded that there was a short period when Palani played on the kucchi mrdangam. Dorai had also heard about Palani's experiment with toothpicks but was sceptical that he actually used kucchi mrdangams. He only remembered one occasion on which he had lent his own kucchi mrdangam to his teacher. Umayalpuram Sivaraman was sure that Palani played on both kucchi and kappi. It is quite possible that Palani's students have erased from their memory their guru's use (even if limited) of the kucchi mrdangam.

BUT THE BIGGEST SHIFT THAT has taken place since the arrival of the kappi mrdangam is in the playing methodology and aesthetic imagination. Oral history and anecdotes about the mrdangam artists of the early twentieth century always hovered around two strokes: the chappu and arachappu (a variation of the chappu). Artists such as Azhaganambi Pillai, Dakshinamurthy Pillai, Ramdas Rao and Alapadi Natesa Ayyar were well known for these strokes. I have heard many seniors speak of this. Both strokes involve at least a part of the sadam area. This meant that sound from the mittu on the vettu thattu was not in focus. It was the sadam and the juncture of the two thattus that were the important playing areas. In a kucchi mrdangam, playing on this juncture vibrated the sticks and created a ringing sound. This changed with the kappi, which added heaviness to the mittu.

With use of the kappi below it, the mittu developed a stronger body and tighter tone. This shifted the acoustic intent of the instrument, and the player's focus too shifted from a chappu-based style to a mittu-dominant one. This is evident in Mani Iyer's playing. With the arrival of the kappi, the thought process of mrdangam artists changed forever. Many seniors belonging to the Palghat Mani Iyer school used kappi mrdangams and were active even until the early 2000s. Therefore this intellectual shift has come to stay, even though many artists today use kucchi mrdangams.

When Selvaraj speaks of the kind of work his father or even Rajamanickam did, he mentions this. 'In the old days, when my grandfather and my father had begun work, there was hardly any sound on the mittu,' he said. Another time, he said that Rajamanickam and Antony's mittu had no weight.

This 'weight' he speaks of comes from the tighter varu pidi and the kappi.

The tone of the mrdangam most definitely affects the nature of its art. Sankaran described it crisply when he said, 'If the chappu works well (meaning that its tone is attractive) in a concert, my artistry orients itself towards that stroke and my mind begins exploring all its possibilities.' This fact is necessary to understand the impact of the mrdangam's metamorphosis when the kappi was introduced. This means that Parlandu single-handedly changed the nature of mrdangam-playing. But a large section of the Karnatik community would reject such a statement. That honour, first and foremost, would be bestowed upon Palghat Mani Iyer.

The advent of the microphone may also have had a role to play in the changed artistry of the player. In the time before there was any amplification, the chappu had to be loud to draw people to the instrument, and the kucchi helped enormously. The downside was that the mittu sound would not have been strong enough to reach the audience. But with the advent of technology, every tap became audible. Which also meant that the mittu was heard and, combined with the kappi, the mrdangam's musicality changed.

While we were discussing the negative opinions about the kucchi mrdangam, Sivaraman suddenly blurted out the words 'male chauvinism'. It was odd to hear this from a man who has never accompanied women singers on the professional stage. It felt as if Sivaraman was experiencing chauvinism towards his own choice of kucchi, and that, unexpectedly, this led him to empathise with how a woman feels when she is valued unfairly. Unlike Ramabhadran, Sivaraman is widely respected for his felicity and astonishing skill, yet even he appears to be facing the prejudice against kucchi. There have been whispers in the corridors of the artists' parliament that Sivaraman uses only sunnambu thol these days, and that he has done away with cow skin entirely. This means his vettu thattu and kottu thattu are both made of sunnambu goat skin. On top of all this, apparently he uses Chinese bamboo—an increasingly common replacement for broom grass—as kucchi. All this makes the sound he produces on the mrdangam distinctive, explosive with heightened resonance. He loves it. In fact, he calls the kappi 'thool', which means leftover particles. Sivaraman clarified that this was an old usage, but his pointed use of it held meaning all the same. He said this categorically about the kappi mrdangam: 'Chappu does not have nadam. When you play an arachappu, the sound is dull. When I cannot hear it on the kappi, what should I play on?' he asked rhetorically. He went on to say that those who claim to hear nadam on a kappi mrdangam are hallucinating. It is not an accident that Sivaraman's playing is also known for the chappu and the arachappu. Sankaran too said, 'I preferred kucchi for reasons of continuity in resonance and tonal quality, especially in the arachappu and muzhu (complete) chappu.'

Sivaraman narrated a very interesting incident concerning the sound of Mani Iyer's mrdangam. In exchange for a mrdangam made from wood used for idols, Iyer offered one of his own mrdangams to a gentleman named Thanjavur Rajendran. 'He told Rajendran, "You can take any mrdangam you want from the collection I have." He had a big collection of mrdangams. Rajendran went up and came back down very soon. Mani Iyer asked him, "Did you take one? Are you satisfied?" He said, "No,

I didn't like any." My teacher asked why. He said, "There is no nadam. I want a mrdangam like Madras Kannan's.""

During our conversation, Sivaraman made a stunning observation countering the criticism that the kucchi mrdangam had too much sound. 'When there is a lot of nadam, controlling and playing it is difficult. If there is less nadam, playing it is easier.' In this one line, Sivaraman summed up his entire argument: it is up to the artist to control the sound of the instrument. Your inability to master something cannot be a reason to devalue it.

The one point on which makers and artists agree is that the present state of affairs is dismal. They all bemoan the hurried nature of the music scene today, and complain about the disastrous dip in standards, both in making and playing. 'If there is a concert at 6 p.m., they will come to my shop at 5.30 p.m., because they know I can get it done. There are many artists who have changed their clothes here and gone directly to the concert hall. I will not blame them; they just do not have the time,' said Peter (name changed). 'Now there is no time for thattu murukardu and all that. People do not even know what that is. They want the mrdangam "live", which means it will not last long. But they do not care and are willing to just replace the muttu. We have all changed.' Senior mrdangam artists convey their displeasure at the very soft manner expected of accompaniment today. 'There is less intensity and even less involvement in playing,' a veteran complained. This, they say, means that the makers too need not care about how they make their instruments; everything is slipshod.

Karaikudi Mani was thankful that makers work with him even in these hurried times. 'These people come to work for me because of affection. Instead of spending one-and-a-half hours with me, they can easily make five hundred rupees.'

In order to cater to this new professional space, the makers too have made changes. They need to ready the instrument at lightning speed. Ravikumar spoke to me in detail about the minute revisions they have made to satisfy their customers. It is not the best thing to do, but they have no choice.

Ravikumar was also critical of how quickly trainee makers open up their own shops. 'To learn this art of making, one needs nine to ten years. But people learn for just four or five years and start up on their own.' When I pushed him further to concede that this leads to a loss in quality, he responded, 'Customers want it. Quality will surely reduce. See, when the customers themselves like what they are getting, we can't do anything.' The makers have always made the point that it is up to the artists to ask for things, give them new challenges, up the ante. They feel that the artists of today don't care very much about their instruments. When I asked Jesudass how much artists know about his work, he replied, 'We should start from the makers. Today, many makers don't know how to check the mittu and chappu.' Among artists, he said, 'There are very few today like Karaikudi Mani, T.K. Murthy, Sivaraman, TVG, etc. who know. It is very rare for someone in this generation to know. We can count them on our fingers.' But Sowriar and Navaneetham were not happy with such a sweeping generalisation. They were quick to name artists among the younger lot who are attentive and knowledgeable.

Navaneetham said, 'One guy will join as a worker, and

within a year will open his own shop. There is no apprenticeship or training. He will just accept the money given.' This also causes prices to drop, affecting everyone. Johnson explains the costs involved: 'I have a shop, a rented house and one person working for me; my overheads have increased, which means I have to increase the price to cover my expenses.' But the younger trainees at these shops are itching to stand on their own two feet. Therefore, even if Johnson is unhappy about it, these youngsters will still attempt to make a living in an already minuscule market.

There is a lot of anger directed at the Thanjavur family who the rest feel indulge in poaching and cheating. Only the new generation of makers, though; everyone exempts the older Thanjavur generation of any wrongdoing. Makers also cited instances of mrdangam artists pitting one Thanjavur maker against another. Instead of giving two mrdangams to the same member of the family, they split the work between two cousins or brothers. Or when one is away, they shift loyalties without informing their usual maker. This keeps the makers on tenterhooks, and also means that they are, at times, willing to undercut each other. Ultimately, the entire business environment becomes tense.

IN THIS COMPLICATED SOCIAL AND aesthetic scene, the answer to the question of where the sound stems from remains elusive. Britto had an explanation: 'There are three parts to good sound from a mrdangam; that which is due to the player, kai nadham (the sound in his hands), thol nadam (the sound in the leather) and mara nadam (that which is due to the wood). All three have to come together for good music.' Like everyone else, Britto too forgot the maker.

Who is the source of the sound? How did the dead and the alive come together in this composition? When the cow, goat and buffalo skins listen to each other, respond to one another's movements, collide and partner, music happens. Who created the sound? I do not know. Perhaps Ravikumar was right when he said that the animal comes alive through the sound of the skin; perhaps sound itself is a living being.

What about the mrdangam artist? Is it his sound? How can he take sole ownership of something that comes from so many elements? One element in this chain moves away from its designated place and the music stops.

The mrdangam artist receives the rhythm not just through the ears but through every part of the body. And it is not just the sound; it is a relationship between the artist's fingers and the animal skins. In that touch, a sensory relationship is formed every time an artist plays a new instrument. Like any relationship, it grows with time, and soon the player and the mrdangam are inseparable. His skin and the skins of the cow, goat and buffalo form part of one musical body. The wooden frame placed on the artist's legs anchors everything. But, before the artist enters the picture, it is the maker who brings various textures, colours, sounds and shapes together by twisting, turning, stretching, breaking, crushing, washing, coating, cutting and binding it all together with his body. The maker is the Cupid. He understands the dead, the alive, the lifeless and the artificial, and finds a way to marry them. He looks and he knows, and feels in his fingers the beat of the mrdangam. And, when he strikes it for the first time, the mrdangam is born.

But no one cares. 'After the mrdangam gets on stage and merges with the song, it takes us somewhere else. (*Smiles and gestures with his hands*). It is like heaven,' Ravikumar said joyfully.

9

THE ANDHRA STORY

While the Madras and Thanjavur muttus dominate conversations around mrdangam-making, there have been parallel traditions in other places across south India. Kingdoms across the Indian subcontinent have been patrons of the 'high arts'. To the south of the Vindhyas—from the big centres, like Thanjavur, Mysore or Thiruvananthapuram, to other smaller dominions, like Vizianagaram and Bobbili—Karnatik music was central to high art, even if northern winds occasionally destabilised its grip over the southern royalty. It is then but natural that instrument-makers have lived in these regions, and evolved their own different ways of doing things.

In what is today Andhra Pradesh, the mrdangam-making tradition is found in two main regions: Vizianagaram and Vijayawada. But many other towns, such as Rajahmundry, had makers who constructed mrdangams for the local musicians. As with Thanjavur, Peruvemba and Chennai, I have been able to trace names of makers back to about eighty years, not more—although this is by no means a comprehensive exercise. Unlike folk from the Tamil Nadu border regions who migrated to Madras and became synonymous with the Madras muttu, these makers lived and worked in Andhra Pradesh, only rarely encountering mrdangam artists from the Mecca of Karnatik music—Madras, which later became Chennai.

Mrdangam artist Kamalakar Rao is the son of G. Varada Rao, a Tulu-speaking brahmin who migrated from southern Kerala to Rajahmundry and set up a thriving hotel business. When he was about five years old, his father saw him tapping on a mrdangam that a local artist, Raju, had left behind. 'He used to come to the hotel for firewood at 6.30 in the morning. He would leave his mrdangam at our home and go to the hotel to pick up wood to burn sambarani (incense). I used to wake up, go and tap on the mrdangam. My father thought I had some talent, and I began learning from Raju garu himself. Then he put me under the tutelage of another local artist, Varanasi Yagnanarayana Sastry,' Kamalakar said.

This was the early 1940s, and Kamalakar remembers an elderly person, Chittappa, who used to make mrdangams. A young lad then, Kamalakar's understanding of the instrument was negligible. It was enough that the muttu looked beautiful; no one bothered too much about the sound, and he himself had no clue about the technicalities involved in the making. The stone for the sadam was procured from a local hill, and Chittappa would somehow get the mrdangam ready. 'He was from a community of dancers. He used to play at dance programmes and at weddings where women danced.'

His brother, Ramchandran Venkatratnam, used to play the mrdangam too. 'He played really well,' Kamalakar told me.

Chittappa belonged to the danseuse (devadasi) community, he said. In Andhra, young girls from the bogam and the sani castes were also dedicated to the temple. According to the *Castes and Tribes of South India* (1909), 'In Telugu-speaking districts, dancing girls are called bogams and sanis, just as the dasis are, but there is only one temple in the northern part of the presidency that maintains a corps of these women in the manner in vogue further south.'

It appears likely that they belonged to the bogam community since, further south in Vijayawada, the makers are from this caste. However, we do not know if Chittappa's father too was a maker.

Kamalakar Rao sought advanced training in Vijayawada, another musical hub. The Vijayawada region was, and continues to be, well known for its traditional music, dance and storytelling, which use the mrdangam for percussion. This means there must have been at least a few families that catered to these artists. However, it was only in the twentieth century, after an All India Radio station was established there in 1948, that this riverside town became musically relevant. AIR employed Karnatik musicians as 'staff artists'. They accompanied musicians who came from outside and were members of AIR's own orchestral outfit, the Vadyavrunda. This meant the need for mrdangam makers too increased.

Poombula Bhashyagarulu from Gudiwada lived in Vijayawada, and Kamalakar remembers working with him. 'He used to do better work than what I got done in Rajahmundry. The sound used to be good.' His use of skin was like Madras and Thanjavur, and Bhashyagarulu paid more attention to tuning. 'But, compared to the Thanjavur makers, the varu pidi was less.' Poombula Bhashyagarulu worked at AIR as a mrdangam repairer, and had a near-monopoly over the Vijayawada market. Dandamudi Rammohan Rao, a student of Palani Subramania Pillai, trained one of his own students who belonged to the goldsmith community from Nasarannapeta, in mrdangam-making in order to challenge Bhashyagarulu's stranglehold. Kamalakar Rao did not think much of this new man's workmanship, though.

Bhashyagarulu's father, Keshavayya, both made and played mrdangams. Having learnt the craft from his father, Bhashyagarulu passed it down to his son B. Loyaraju, who, along with his nephew Nageshwar Rao, continued to make mrdangams. The baton has now been handed over to the next generation. L. Bhaskar, Loyaraju's son, having sharpened his skills under his father and cousin, joined the business. The Keshavayya family belong to the bogam caste.

Vijayawada is about 450 kilometres from Chennai, an overnight journey by train. Perhaps this is why the making here is influenced by the traditions in Tamil Nadu, mrdangam artist Vankayala Ramanamurthy theorises. To his mind, the real Andhra mrdangam-making tradition comes from north coastal Andhra Pradesh: from Vizianagaram. 'My great-grandfather Shri Vankayala Balarama Gupta is the author of the Turpu Bhagavatam, which the kings of Vizianagaram asked him to write as a parallel to the Kuchipudi Bhagavatam. Turpu means the east, and Vizianagaram is northern Andhra Pradesh. Shri Balarama Gupta was a vocalist, and his brother Shri Narasimha Gupta, a mrdangam artist. My father, Shri Vankayala

Narasimhamgaru, told me that Shri Balarama Gupta was the person who initiated the small-scale industry of mrdangam-repairing and making in Vizianagaram. So, under his guidance, the Bhagavata mrdangam was first made here,' Ramanamurthy explained.

This kind of mrdangam was initially made as accompaniment for the Bhagavata (musical storytelling tradition). The vettu thattu in the Bhagavata mrdangam is much narrower, exposing a larger portion of the kottu thattu. Naturally, the sadam covers a much larger surface area. On the toppi side, they use another paste instead of semolina. Ramanamurthy said it was surprising that, despite being brahmins, Balarama and Narasimha Gupta used to supervise mrdangam-making and hold a big pooja and ceremony around it. 'They treated the mrdangam as an avatara of Nandishwara.'

All the stories we hear are descriptions of how mrdangam artists organised a supply chain in order to satisfy their requirement for the mrdangam. Which part of the making was supervised? What was left to the makers alone? These are questions I have examined over and over in these pages, but they keep coming back. And the question of who owns the knowledge just does not go away.

At any rate, Ramanamurthy does insist that his great grandfather Balarama Gupta made mrdangams himself. According to Ramanamurthy, Kottiyada Sathyam was the first maker of the Bhagavata mrdangam. I must add the caveat that he is merely the first name that I have been able to trace. 'He belonged to a backward community and was living in a village called Korukonda. Bobbili and Korukonda were under the rule of the Vizianagaram Samasthanam. His son Sanjeevi also made Bhagavata mrdangams,' said Ramanamurthy.

As far as making mrdangams for Karnatik music concerts go, it is the descendants of Nimmala Somalingam who dominate. Somalingam belonged to the jangalu caste, also known as jangam. The jangalus appear to be lingayats who lived in these Telugu-speaking regions. Many of them were priests (to castes lower in the hierarchy), religious vagabonds and fortune tellers. Though Somalingam was the initiator, it is his son Nimmala Trinatha Rao whose impeccable work brought fame to the Vizianagaram mrdangam. According to Ramanamurthy, 'He took the quality of mrdangams in north coastal Andhra Pradesh to an unparalleled level.' He unfortunately passed on a few years ago, and his son Nimmala Srinivas now continues in the same line of work. According to Somalingam's nephew, Vurivi Sivalingam, it was Kolanka Venkata Raju—a professor of mrdangam at the Vizianagaram Music College, and a regular accompanist with Dwaram Venkataswamy Naidu (the man who gave the violin the 'solo' status in Karnatik music)—who taught his maternal uncle Somalingam the ways of making a mrdangam. 'Regarding measurement and selection of the skin, he guided and gave all instructions to the first maker of the concert mrdangam,' Ramanamurthy said.

Sivalingam began training under his maavyya (maternal uncle) Somalingam when he was twelve years old. 'I learnt how to repair the Karnataka mrdangam and the Bhagavata mrdangam from him.' After training under him, Sivalingam went to Korukonda to learn the art of making Bhagavata mrdangams from Kottiyada Sathyam. But since Sathyam was busy with Bhagavata performances, his son Kottiyada Sanjeevi taught Sivalingam. Now, Shekar, Sivalingam's son, too is a maker. 'This is how we have been supporting our families,' said

Sivalingam. Somalingam also taught his brother's son, Nimmala Rajyalingam, who is still making mrdangams.

For all their humility, these makers are very proud of their work. Sivalingam declared, 'Overall, in Andhra, in the making of the Karnatik mrdangam, Vizianagaram is very famous. There are others who make mrdangams, and I should not be saying this, but as they say, "Man is man's own enemy". However, people who know and the people who play the instruments vouch for the greatness of the quality of work here in Vizianagaram.' He was suggesting that, because makers in other places, like Vijayawada, are not good enough, they tend to underplay the superiority of the Vizianagaram mrdangam makers.

'In Andhra Desam, it is first my uncle Nimmala Somalingam and then myself—we have earned a good name for ourselves in this art,' he concluded.

10

A DIFFERENT REGISTER

I began my research with the citadel of Karnatik music: Chennai. I was not then consciously looking for mrdangam makers in other states. It took me a while to realise that there was much to explore beyond the confines of Tamil Nadu. I read and re-read transcripts of my conversations with makers and artists. Every reading gave me new insights and threw up passages that I had overlooked thus far.

When I spoke to T.V. Gopalakrishnan, he briefly mentioned a maker's enclave in the suburb of Palarivattom in Ernakulam. Like the Thanjavur makers, they were also from the paraiyar community and had converted to Christianity, he had said. Gopalakrishnan recalled that, when he was around six years old, Thomman, who was then in his thirties, used to come to his house to work on mrdangams. The maker's son, Sowri, had even come to Chennai and worked with Gopalakrishnan. 'They were three or four brothers. Their names were John,

Jacob or something. And then there was also Chandy from the same family. They must have learnt it the traditional way, maybe from Thiruvananthapuram, which has an older tradition.'

Speaking of people who worked in Thiruvananthapuram, Gopalakrishnan mentioned others like Parameshwaran, and said, 'But they are not paraiyans. They worked at the palace, right? So it is not possible (that they were paraiyans),' he said. He remembered that Parameshwaran had moved to Bangalore and worked there for a very long time. A few months later, I met P.V. Parameshwaran's son Krishnakumar at his Bangalore home. They were the family who took care of all suddha maddalam and mrdangam needs at the Thiruvananthapuram palace. Krishnakumar retold a story about his grandfather P.K. Vellai and great-grandfather Karuppusami.

'The king was very interested in my grandfather, but his bodyguard was jealous of the recognition my grandfather received from the king. So my great-grandfather (Karuppusami) plotted to give the bodyguard some mrdangam work. One day, he told my grandfather (Vellai) to stay at home and said he would go to the palace alone. On that day, on the king's insistence, he had to go to pull varu for the suddha maddalam because there was a concert to be held on that very day. My great-grandfather informed the king that there was no one to help him. The king said, "My bodyguard is strong; he can help." After that day, the bodyguard was absent for a week. My grandfather demonstrated that it was not just about strength, it was in the technique. You need to know how much to pull. They used to say that, if my grandfather pulled varu for the suddha maddalam, a vibrating sound would emanate from it even if a fly hovered over it.'

Just as the Thanjavur makers initially only made tavils, Karuppusami's ancestors were suddha maddalam makers for three or four generations. It is from Vellai's time that mrdangam-making became their livelihood. This makes sense historically, because it is only over the past 120 years that Karnatik concerts have proliferated in public spaces—exponentially increasing the number of participating musicians, and thus the demand for mrdangams. As Bharatanatyam too became the face of Indian 'classical' dance, the demand for mrdangams even quadrupled. From all that I have heard, it appears that the suddha maddalam and mrdangam makers who were engaged at the Thiruvananthapuram court, and later on in music colleges and by professionals in the city, came from a little village called Peruvemba, about 20 kilometres from Palakkad. Locals might have also been employed, but it was makers from Peruvemba who dominated the show.

I drove in and around Palakkad, and was strongly reminded of the Thanjavur belt, except for the low-lying hills in the background. We (my student Vignesh and I) had an appointment with P.R. Kasumani. His son K. Rajesh coordinated the interview, but warned us many times over that his father does not really speak much, that he would say very little. We persisted, and since P. Krishnakumar from Bangalore had also recommended our case to his cousin Kasumani, he reluctantly agreed to meet us along with his paternal uncle P.V. Ramakrishnan.

Though the family had settled in and worked out of Peruvemba, they actually belonged to Pallavur, which is about 13 kilometres away. Pallavur was their taravad, the ancestral home. We were extra vigilant so as to not miss the village, and were in touch with Rajesh on the mobile phone too. This was all unnecessary. As we meandered through the narrow two-lane roads of Kerala, we were suddenly greeted by the sight of fresh bull skin stretched and nailed to the ground on one side. I had never seen anything like this. So far, I had only seen such skin work done in closed compounds or on backstreets. Evidently, we had arrived at Peruvemba, the hub of mrdangam and chenda makers.

Everything about this place was different from Keethukara Street in Thanjavur. The homes here were more accessible, larger and well kept—a clear sign of economic well-being. It looked like any middle-class colony, and it would be hard to place the caste of its inhabitants. Rajesh waved from deep inside the street. We turned in, parked, and made our way into Kasumani's home and workplace. It was a typical village home: an L-shaped structure with a courtyard that had been roofed with asbestos sheets for shade. Red-oxide flooring, typical of the region, caught my eye, and a brown band of paint on the outer walls that went up to about two and half feet from the floor. Within the compound, mrdangam work was ongoing. Kasumani, his wife, mother and Ramakrishnan were all there. Kasumani now works with about five assistants. On that day, his assistant Achyutan was witness to our conversation, on occasion providing us some factual clarity.

As Rajesh had warned us, initially, Kasumani only gave us monosyllabic answers and gestures, and threw in a few technical words here and there. For some time, he was guarded and seemed disinterested in sharing knowledge or time with us. His uncle Ramakrishnan, on the other hand, was full of beans, generously sharing details of their family history.

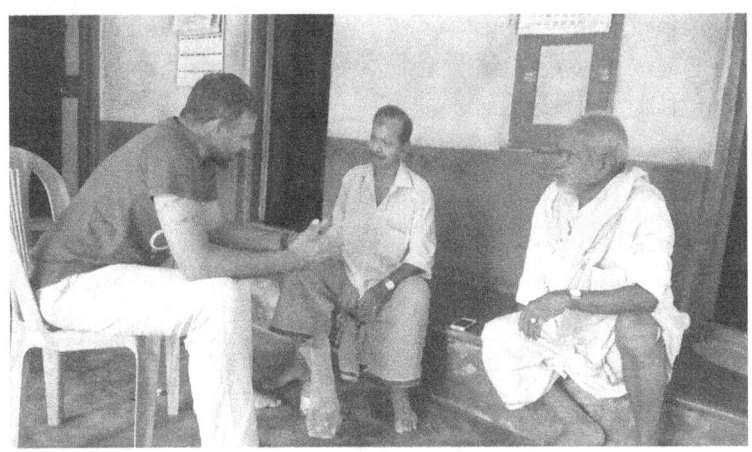

The author in conversation with P.R. Kasumani and his uncle P.V. Ramakrishnan

Karuppusami's son, P.K. Vellai, had three children: P.V. Rajan, P.V. Parameshwaran and P.V. Ramakrishnan—all of whom were involved in the industry. Rajan's son, P.R. Kasumani, studied in Coimbatore, across the state border, until class eight, and was inducted into mrdangam-making by his father. Once his father moved back to Peruvemba, their practice stabilised, and Kasumani took the family profession forward. His brother P.R. Nathan still operates out of Thripunithura. Kasumani's and Nathan's mother, Manikyam, actively participated in the work as well. Having lived with her husband for ten years in Coimbatore and another ten in Bangalore before returning to Peruvemba, she was in the thick of things. Now, at eighty-six, she watches over all the activities, and keenly observed my discussions with her son, grandson and brother-in-law.

Parameshwaran left Kerala and moved to an entirely new market in Bangalore. There, he became the specialist for professionals, maintaining very high standards, something his son Krishnakumar—who is today Bangalore's leading mrdangam maker—still talks about. The third son, P.V. Ramakrishnan, now seventy-five, lived for over four decades in Tiruppur, a place known for its cottonwear export industry, and in Coimbatore. He made mrdangams and harmoniums there. 'In those days, there were a lot of bhajan performances in Tiruppur, and there used to be a demand for the petti (harmonium),' he said. He is now an old man who makes harmoniums when orders come his way. The demand for harmoniums has dwindled, he said.

The late P.V. Rajan

Manikyam

There is more to the Karuppusami lineage. Vellai not only taught his own sons, but also trained three brothers, Krishnan, Narayanan and Velayudhan, who were not of his family. Guruvayur Dorai remembers Narayanan. Dorai was a very young boy living in Guruvayur, and had only one mrdangam tuned to one tonic. 'We needed one more mrdangam, for a different tonic. So when we asked people where we could buy one, we heard that there was a maker in Peruvemba village near Palakkad. It was Narayanan. He made many mrdangams for me. Before him, his father and his cousin Peruvemba Krishnan also made mrdangams, but I only know Narayanan well.' Narayanan's two sons are also makers: one lives in Koyilandy and another in Kozhikode. Vellai married his son Rajan to his student Krishnan's daughter Manikyam, and hence they are all now related.

Selvaraj and Melgies recalled Velayudhan of Peruvemba. Palghat Mani Iyer may have had scant respect for these makers, but Selvaraj remembers visiting Velayudhan with him. 'Mani Iyer took me in a horse cart from Kalpathy. Velayudhan was so happy and honoured to receive him. Mani Iyer introduced me as the person from Thanjavur who does mrdangam work. We went there to get something we needed, and Velayudhan said that he would have been happy to come and give it personally. He also asked about my work, and Mani Iyer replied by saying that I was good and did whatever he needed. Velayudhan had worked for Mani Iyer and Sathapuram Subbiar (Mani Iyer's guru).' Velayudhan had two sons, Vasu and Sathu. Vasu did both mrdangam and tabla work. Sathu's sons, Vishwanathan and Unnikrishnan, live and work in Kozhikode. Vellai also had a daughter, Ponni, whose son Appu became the main maker in Coimbatore. Today, his son Manikandan runs the show.

From Thripunithura in the south to Koyilandi and Kozhikode in the north, Coimbatore in the east extending up to Bangalore, the Vellai clan have a large tract of land covered.

BUT WHAT MAKES THEM SPECIAL? Some makers in Chennai had told me that the Kerala makers are able to generate a lot of sound from the valandalai in spite of cutting very little skin out of the vettu thattu. The annular thattu is broader than what is seen in the Thanjavur or Madras styles. Kasumani credited this to the quality and selection of skin. He claimed that the skin in Kerala is free and without 'temper'. I struggled to make sense of the word and finally came to the conclusion that it meant that the skin is softer and generates greater resonance. Unlike people who work in Tamil Nadu or Karnataka, the makers of Kerala source all their skin from within the state. They do not seek the goats of Andhra. For the wooden frame, however, Panruti remains the single source. Once again, the expression 'temper' cropped up. 'The temper in the trees here is less. Because of lesser rains in Panruti, the tree colour is different and the wood has temper. Panruti trees are good,' Kasumani said.

Describing the mrdangams from his home town, Krishna Kumar had said, 'In the Palakkad style, the mittu will have little nadam but it is attractive. The "dheem" (open stroke played on the valandalai) sound will be very good.' When I interjected and said, 'People still talk about your chappu,' he added that that was the main difference between the Palakkad mrdangam and the rest. There are also some minute differences in the way, and how much, the vettu thattu and kottu thattu are stretched.

Their work is also gorgeous in presentation. 'When the Thanjavur makers clean up after applying the sadam, it will be a little messy. The remains of the sadam will be around. But when the Kerala maker gives you the mrdangam, you will think twice before using it! And if you play one chappu, it will give you a ringing sound: thaaam,' a nostalgic Guruvayur Dorai proclaimed.

Even the reticent Kasumani could not resist taking a swipe at the Thanjavur makers. When I told him about the results of the test on the various stones used in the sadam, and that the differences between the stone he uses and those that Thanjavur makers source from Rattipalayam were not so great, he chuckled and retorted, 'Then why do they not get any sound?' I was in the unexpected position of defending the people of my state! When I said, 'The reason could be varu pidi and kappi. Skin here is thinner; they use thick skin, which is necessary because they make kappi muttu.' Kasumani was not one bit impressed. 'Hmmm, continue ...' he said, brushing all my explanations aside. But when asked directly about the Thanjavur mrdangam, he refused to respond. He kept saying he could not comment about that, but reasserted, 'The one thing I can say is that the skin has to be good ... in ours, it is good.'

There are a few more interesting localised variations in the process. Boiled rice or Fevicol are the preferred adhesives as the base layer for the sadam in the Thanjavur and Madras styles. But here in Peruvemba, and indeed other parts of Kerala, makers previously used something else. Krishnakumar said, 'You will find this in the Guruvayur temple. If you rub it on the stone nicely, you will get gum from it. We use that gum as the foundation paste.' Krishnakumar was referring to a seed that they call kunnikuru, kunnumani or guruganji, or *Abrus precatorius*. At the Guruvayur temple, it is kept in a large brass tub and devotees are expected to put their hands in and rake it up. Though it is a poisonous seed, it is said kunnumani also has medicinal properties. And in the mrdangam-making process, it is a fixative. 'Kunnumani will adhere twice as strongly as rice. Fevicol has double the strength of kunnumani's adhesive quality, of course, but the sound is better with the kunnumani,' Ramakrishnan said. Krishnakumar offered detailed reasoning: 'The kunnumani gum smothers the sound when you first apply it, but it opens up as you play. This is because the gum synchronises with the texture of the skin. When you mix this gum with water and apply it, it becomes one with the skin. So there is no distortion in the vibrations. If you use Fevicol, it is like a plastic layer that can be peeled off when it dries.' The other adhesive, vajram, will just not hold in Kerala, the land of the south-west monsoons. This also means that drying skin is a daunting task here.

Even in a place like Peruvemba, where mrdangam- and maddalam-making is so common, makers have to handle objections from neighbours who find the stench of fresh skin too much to handle. This is accentuated during the rains; the odour of wet skin is much stronger. 'There are complaints, but we just adjust and go on,' Kasumani said casually. Among his extended family are three people who make maddalams. It was their raw material—bull skin—that I had seen spread and nailed on the roadside.

A Peruvemba-made mrdangam is easy to identify. The pinnal on the valandalai side is prominently raised, a thick piping around the circumference. They call it a netthi muttu. Over time, it will come down a little bit but still remain visible. 'Every time you change the sadam, it will come down a bit. It will fold over and the protrusion will reduce,' said Krishnakumar. But it will not fold over to such an extent that the muttu loses its strength. This is called vazhiyaradu, or overflowing. I am not sure about the benefits of this netthi pinnal, but it is certainly a distinguishing feature. As we have already discussed, the region's other speciality, the madakku pinnal technique, has been entirely dropped. It was too time-consuming and difficult to execute. Interestingly, they continue to use cow-skin thongs for the valandalai pinnal. I have to wonder whether the pairing of the valandalai's vettu thattu, which is made of cow skin, with the cow-skin pinnal and the toppi's two-layered buffalo skin with the buffalo-skin pinnal has a structural logic that impacts the strength and the sound of the muttus. While all other makers have completely shifted to buffalo skin for the pinnal, the Peruvemba makers steadfastly use this older method.

Ramakrishnan and Kasumani had no doubt that it was kucchi mrdangams that were being made in the old days. 'No one played kappi then,' Kasumani said with conviction. This convinces me even more that kucchi mrdangams were prevalent all over the Karnatik music world for a very long time. The Peruvemba folk have a strange story about the stone they use for mrdangam sadam. My student was told by Kasumani that they are fallen iron fragments from nearby iron factories that over time have transformed into some form of stone. They call it keedakallu. A close cousin of the kittankallu?

A few minor things about the toppi also distinguishes their work from the rest. When the toppi goat skin is tied from the inside to the muttu, the Peruvemba makers only tie it with eight knots and not twelve like the rest. They also paste strips of skin on the knots to minimise chances of tearing.

IN THE 1940S, P.K. VELLAI, along with his sons, Rajan (Kasumani's father) and Parameshwaran (Krishnakumar's father), moved to Bangalore. That city clearly had a shortage of mrdangam makers, and the artists there needed to do something about this. Krishnakumar mentioned an artist called Ponniah Pillai, a native of Pallavur but living in Bangalore, who might have been instrumental in getting Vellai and his sons to move there. Vellai had twelve children, three sons and nine daughters, and one assumes he was looking for greener pastures to make ends meet and to fulfil that need of every Indian parent of the time: getting his daughters married. But the move to Bangalore was not as beneficial as he had hoped. The city then was not bustling with art and culture. There were only a handful of artists and not too many concerts. It must have been a struggle, and soon enough, Vellai returned to Palakkad, leaving his two children behind. Parameshwaran was just twelve years old when he went to Bangalore with his father and brother, and just a few years older when his father moved back. A little later, Rajan too headed back home, leaving Parameshwaran to fend for himself in that sleepy town. And he nearly gave up.

Bangalore Venkatraman, a ghatam artist, had given him a cycle to get around on for his work. 'We used to stay in Malleshwaram 8th Cross. My father went to return the cycle and inform him (Venkatraman) that he was shifting back to Peruvemba. Venkatraman was very upset. He told my father to wait for two days and that he would do something about it. My father said, "No sir, I am struggling here. Let me go." We were struggling for even one meal,' Krishnakumar narrates.

Musicians in Bangalore were in desperate need of quality makers whom they could call on when needed. Until then, they were getting most of their work done in Madras. Some professional artists believed that Parameshwaran was, in fact, superior to the Madras makers, and wanted to retain him in their city. It is distinctly possible that I am hearing only one side of the story. There certainly were other makers in Bangalore at that time. What was their work like? At any rate, it is true that artists like M.L. Veerabhadrayya, Bangalore Venkatraman and vina artist Mysore Doraiswamy Iyengar came together to convince Parameshwaran to stay back. Venkatraman used to work at ITI, and they pulled some strings to get Parameshwaran a job in the relay adjustments division. 'But he was given the work on one condition. He will only work the first shift and then dedicate his afternoons to mrdangams.' Somehow, they managed to broker this deal with the bosses on the shop floor. And, as they say, the rest is history.

Parameshwaran's move to Bangalore not only distanced him from his home town physically, it also moved him away from the Peruvemba gharana of mrdangam-making. Back then, Veerabhadrayya, a senior disciple of Palghat Mani Iyer, was a force to reckon with in Bangalore circles. He had also brought makers from Thanjavur to Bangalore for brief periods. A little later, in the 1960s and 1970s, Mani Iyer sent Selvaraj to Bangalore to work on Veerabhadrayya's mrdangams. Inevitably, the artist's influence on Parameshwaran was profound. A curious man, willing to learn and adapt to the needs of his clients, Parameshwaran would go to concerts and observe the difficulties of the artists. He was guided by mrdangam artists who believed in the Thanjavur style of playing and, consequently, making. 'My father would even play the tambura (at concerts). The artists would have to keep tuning the mrdangam on stage and the vocalist would not be able to concentrate. He also noticed that those who came from Madras did not have this problem. My father started thinking about it. Was it a manufacturing defect, or did the problem lie with the artist? He used to think deeply about these issues, ponder and research.' In saying this, Krishnakumar is also passing judgement on the other makers who lived and worked in Bangalore. He is implying that their workmanship was mediocre and this affected the quality of concerts.

Slowly, Parameshwaran's making moved closer to the Thanjavur school, and Veerabhadrayya showed him the way. 'At that time, my father used to go to Veerabhadrayya sir's house to work. One day, he asked my father to make a muttu. Veerabhadrayya sir had seen Parlandu's work in Thanjavur and had worked with him. So he bought skin, selected it and kept it ready. My father was working in the Palakkad style then. When he started working on the skin, it tore. That caused him to wonder what kind of skin it was. Then, Veerabhadrayya sir told him to use the entire skin and make one muttu, and that it did not matter if one tore. This motivated my father and we changed to the Thanjavur style.' With a few modifications, Parameshwaran has now made it his own Bangalore style.

WEARING THE TYPICAL SAFFRON-COLOURED KERALA veshti, fifty-eight-year-old Kasumani sat with a stoic face, shaking his legs impatiently and speaking only because he was obliged to reply. I was fairly intimidated, and did not know how to break the ice. He was not rude or aggressive—quite the opposite, in fact. He was polite and kind, even smiling, but visibly disinterested. I would ask a question and Kasumani would make a short comment or utter a single word; sometimes barely audible. He would let his uncle Ramakrishnan take over. Rajesh was video-recording the entire conversation on his mobile phone. It was only after about half an hour that I felt Kasumani had begun trusting me; that he felt there was some sensitivity to my line of enquiry.

And then, in his own way, he opened up. There was resignation in his tone. He was clear about his relationship with the mrdangam artists, and did not expect anything more from them. His life and economic or social conditions had not changed in all these years. Rajesh explained, 'He (Kasumani) asked me why a vocalist was making a documentary about this. I am telling you openly. Many people come, take videos and photos of my father, but there is no recognition and respect for us, or any improvement in our lives.' The makers know only too well that they have to keep working and keep their customers happy. Ramakrishnan said, 'It is an ancestral business for us. You need a mrdangam, you come to us. We will do our job and get the money that's all … we don't think of anything else.' Kasumani added, 'If the mrdangam is good, then the artists will call us. If they are happy, I will get work.' When I persisted about their being on the margins of the world of music, he dismissed me, saying, 'What can we do by thinking about it?'

This was true of many areas of work, Rajesh felt. 'Now, take a teacher who has many students; some are lawyers, collectors, etc., but not everyone gives credit to their teacher.' I responded by saying that nobody denies having learnt from a teacher, but mrdangam artists speak about making the mrdangam when they have nothing to do with it.

Rajesh also spoke about how mrdangam makers are recruited at the government music colleges in Thiruvananthapuram, Thripunithura and Palakkad. Many who apply have no background in making. Since the examiners (typically, mrdangam artists) know very little about the making process, the selection is unfair and haphazard. While he was also making the point that preferential selections are made, Rajesh's statement revealed that no senior mrdangam maker is ever an examiner, only mrdangam players. An appalling and painful state of affairs.

But Kasumani does not want to complain about all this. He just wants to continue doing what he does. People in Chennai know his name and mrdangam artists come to him because they like his work. He is contented with this and shoves all disappointments aside. Holding on to anger and negativity will only affect his work and his relationship with the artists. Kasumani had sharp opinions, it was clear, but he was unwilling to express them because he did not trust the environment. Why would he when no one has taken the time to ask him about his problems?

Ramakrishnan was explaining the greatness of his father's work when I added that no one knows about him because he works with skin. Once again, the pooja room came back into the conversation, and Kasumani added, 'Yes it (mrdangam) goes into the pooja room. Will a slipper go into the same room? It won't, right? This is skin and so is that. Everyone should think about this. No one thinks.'

All said and done, Kasumani is also an optimist, and believes things will change in the future. Even as he expressed this opinion, his wife, who hails from a family of chenda makers, laughed, and Kasumani joined in. The family had worked with the great and popular artists of Kerala, like Kunneseri Mani Iyer, Krishnankutty Nair, Velukutti Nair, and now for artists from Palakkad, Coimbatore and Trichy. Some Chennai-based artists too send in bulk orders from time to time. Much like the musicians who live and perform in Kerala, these makers too care very little for certification from the Chennai Karnatik establishment. A refreshing attitude indeed!

Rajesh is not certain about his future plans. He has completed his MA in music from the well-respected Kerala

Kalamandalam, a deemed arts university, and learnt to play the mrdangam from Palakkad Mahesh Kumar. Now he is working in a microfinance company. I asked him why he does not consider becoming a serious mrdangam artist. After offering the often-quoted reason of the hands becoming rough, hard and stiff, he made an incisive point. 'A mrdangam vidvan's son has a better chance to be an artist and gets better opportunities because of his father. My father is in this business, so my chances of success here are better.' This is not just about concert opportunities or connections; it was a cultural observation. He made that clear when he said, 'If this were an agraharam, there would be concerts and it would be easier to observe and learn. It's not like that here.' It is near impossible for Rajesh to climb the performance ladder because of the invisible knowledge sluices that remain permanently shut.

I realised that we were discussing two tenuously connected worlds: the upper-caste performance and learning environment on the one end and the marginalised mrdangam maker on the other. They overlap only for convenience, and remain socially and aesthetically disengaged. This separation conveniently reinforces the brahminical lie that caste is varna (occupation- or ability-based social hierarchy) and not jati (birth-based social hierarchy). And this results in cultural 'othering'.

After spending nearly one-and-a-half hours with the family, and sharing some lighter moments over tea, I broached the sensitive question of caste. All but Kasumani were willing to speak on this subject. Krishnakumar had told me in Bangalore that they were tholkollans who came under the vishwakarma umbrella. I had read that kollans specialised as iron smiths. But they are also further subdivided into groups such as theekollan, kadachikollan, tholkollan, theeporikollan and perumkollan. Tholkollans would have traditionally worked with skin, so their entry into the mrdangam-making sector is not surprising. Today, the kollans are classified as Other Backward Castes. Interestingly, in both the state government's Backward Classes Development department and the Kerala Public Service Commission websites, tholkollans are not placed within the vishwakarma ambit; they are mentioned separately.

When this discussion emerged at Kasumani's residence, there was a lot of debate and confusion. Were they perumkollans, kadachikollans or perhaps kadayan (a Scheduled Caste)? Opinions were divided. Ramakrishnan was sure they were not kadayan, because kadayans were those who dived into the seas for pearls, and vishwakarmas did not do that. I was later told by a friend that all this confusion may be the result of a local issue. Apparently, at the school level, at times, children belonging to the kadachikollan community get categorised as kadayan. Later, using this, they obtain a kadayan certificate and benefit from the Scheduled Caste categorisation. Naturally, objections had come from the kadayan community. Whatever may be the case, the tholkollan community is placed in the lower rungs of Kerala's complex caste design, though definitely above the kadayan community.

After Karuppusami's family established themselves as the leaders in mrdangam-making in 'God's Own Country', others joined in. In Peruvemba itself, another family has been at it for three generations. Another Velayudhan and his children are on the job. They too have taken over other territories and established themselves in places such as Thiruvananthapuram.

THERE WERE MANY TIMES DURING my interviews that I wondered about where pursuing a quest becomes plain insensitivity. When do I stop a line of questioning? How much do I push? Is it even correct to ask delicate questions of people who were not born with my privileges? Is my caste privilege blinding me? How do I place myself within the discussion? I am still to resolve these quandaries.

Kasumani and family were the last mrdangam makers I interviewed in my three-and-a-half-year journey of trying to learn about makers and the making, and they were distinctly different from most others. I might have been a well-known Karnatik musician, but they knew only too well that this made no difference to their complicated life. Hence there was no hoo-hah about my arrival. And this meant that, perhaps for the first time in a very long time, I was part of a conversation where I found myself self-conscious, seeking recognition and legitimacy.

11

WOMEN IN CHARGE

I distinctly remember the first time I watched Dandamudi Sumathi Rama Mohan Rao play the mrdangam. In my teens then, I was absolutely stunned by her skill and acumen, yet entirely uncomfortable watching a woman seated in a 'manly' position, playing with gusto and a great deal of animation. She is so unladylike, I had thought. I came to know much later that, in the nineteenth and early twentieth century, there were many women from the devadasi community who played the mrdangam. Unfortunately, along with the twentieth-century brahminisation of the music came all the interdicts associated with brahmin norms. Even today, women fight to establish their rightful place as mrdangam artists in what is accepted as a man's world.

Mrdangam-making too has always been a male-controlled territory. Women have always provided assistance in this home-based industry, but they are rarely spoken of. They do the physically taxing 'crushing the stone' job and help with drying skin, but there is a generally accepted notion that mrdangam-making is too difficult for womankind, especially the skin-related stuff.

But amongst them there have been those few who have ignored the boundaries laid out by men to earn their living.

The Hide Queen

Madhammal had a disarming smile, a carefree demeanour, and she brimmed over with confidence and happiness when we met. And why not? This woman had dominated the skin supply market for decades. Her father and grandfather were in the same business, and she continued the family occupation, supplying skin to makers in Tamil Nadu and Kerala. Her father had moved to Ambur in search of a better life when she was just three years old and trained her to follow in his footsteps. She worked assiduously, established new business relationships and expanded the business to get where she is today. A woman with no regrets.

Madhammal

'I have gone to many places—Kozhikode, Trichy, Mannargudi—all alone to supply skin. I have had no issues. I would take the overnight bus. Get myself a ticket and another for the bundle (of skin). Reach the place early in the morning at five or six. I would finish my business and they would buy me a ticket to Vellore. And I would reach home by ten at night. When I went to Chennai, it was better, I could come straight back to Ambur. I bought this house with my earnings. This is a good business. Like Rajinikanth said (in a film), only if you put in effort and struggle, will you get results! But you should work with focus on one job, not do this and that. I have no complaints about the profession.'

The shift to Ambur worked very well for her. From only supplying skins for mrdangams and tablas, she began supplying skin for and making thappu, pambai, udukkai and other instruments. 'Work has definitely increased over the years, it is much more now,' she said.

If there is one thing she is not happy about, it is that people do not care about quality anymore. 'In those days, artists cared about the sound,' Madhammal said. 'Earlier, everything was made with skin. Now, more and more, it is made with plastic. But that sound is not good. It is all about money now. The sound of skin instruments cannot be matched.' She blamed Sivamani, the immensely popular Indian drummer, for this trend, and said she would not be surprised if the same happened with mrdangams. Her statement was prophetic. A prototype synthetic mrdangam has been manufactured—its attractiveness appears to lie in its 'purity' advantage rather than any sort of animal activism. If it works, artists can erase the dishonour of producing music from a dead animal's skin, especially the cow.

Age caught up with Madhammal around three years ago. She could not travel as she used to. Her son Kumar, who only manned the shop thus far, began doing the rounds too. But her customers still remember her and that pleases her. 'Even now, they call me once in a while to Chennai. People in Chennai took good care of me. There is a Dawood bhai in Triplicane. He has a big musical instruments shop and I used to supply instruments and skins to him. Even yesterday he asked me to come.' To her, respect, fame and honesty mattered far more than money.

Kumar was not impressed with this idealism. 'Once you have money, people will respect you,' he retorted. She was combative: 'If you bother only about making money, people will accuse you of being a cheat, a thief. Why did Dawood bhai call me? Not because I have money. The monetary situation can change but not the name you earn. Even Arogyam asked for me. People should remember your work, that is good for us. He does not understand this; he is just after money. Did Jayalalitha amma take all the crores she made with her?'

Kumar ended the argument with a curt rebuttal. 'The other day, when you were sick in hospital, did respect or reputation help? Why didn't you tell the doctor to save you because you have earned these things?'

A Rebel Maker

In the late 1950s, R.S. Ashwathamma married a twenty-year-old Anantharamaiah. They lived in the village of Rajaghatta, near Doddaballapura in Karnataka. She is around eighty now, and hence I deduce that she was probably nineteen when she got married.

When I first heard of this village from Srinivas, their son, I was piqued by its rather regal name. I did not know that this little village had, over the past decade or more, gained a great deal of archaeological significance. The remains of a thriving Buddhist monastery and settlement had been unearthed during excavations conducted by the Department of Ancient History and Archaeology, Mysore University, between 2002 and 2004. More work is currently in progress.

Anantharamaiah was one of four children born to a Telugu-speaking, poor, Vaishnavite brahmin priest. As a young man, he used to act in Bayalu Kathe, a form of Kannada musical theatre, playing characters such as Anjaneya. As he acted, he would listen intently to the tabla artist who accompanied the musical drama, captivated by its rhythmic patterns and tonal variations. He just had to learn to play! And he did, in just a few years. From being an actor with the troupe, Anantharamaiah became its percussion artist. He did not realise then that, with playing the tabla comes the responsibility of maintaining it and getting a new instrument prepared, if needed.

'At that time, he was in Rajaghatta. He used to play the tabla but had not yet learnt the art of making and repairing. During those times (early days of marriage), he used to visit Bangalore once a week on Sundays and return to Doddaballapura on Monday,' Ashwathamma remembered. The trip to Bangalore was unavoidable because all his tabla repair work was done there by Venkatappa in Cottonpet. In the city, he would attentively watch Venkatappa at work. That led to him wonder why he should not do this himself. At that time—and sadly even now—this would be considered a revolutionary thought coming from a brahmin. Playing a skin instrument was bad enough, now he wanted to learn to make it. But Anantharamaiah's financial needs were acute and choices limited, which loosened other social considerations for him. His father was also supportive. And so, Venkatappa trained Anantharamaiah, along with another student, Rangaswamy, who also went on to become an important maker in Bangalore. (Rangaswamy is now retired and does not keep well. All my efforts to interview him failed.)

Having learnt this new craft that would provide a living for his struggling family in the mid-1960s, Anantharamaiah opened a shop on D Cross, Doddaballapura. But, in these small towns and villages, demand must have been minuscule and intermittent. Having seen Venkatappa work in the big city, Anantharamaiah knew that he needed to move to Bangalore to grow. So he left his wife behind in Rajaghatta and moved. Ashwathamma had to continue taking care of the joint family in the village. 'There were around ten or twelve people in the house. My father-in-law had three sons and three daughters; one of the sons had moved out. I used to do various chores, like cooking, cleaning, chopping firewood. I used to take ragi balls for the family members who worked in the fields, and also do chores there, like taking care of the cattle, etc.'

After a while, Ashwathamma's father-in-law told her that she should join Anantharamaiah in Bangalore. 'When my father-in-law took me from Rajaghatta to Bangalore, he told me that I should visit our village only if he was present and not otherwise. He felt that my brothers-in-law would not treat me well because my husband had taken up tabla and mrdangam repair. My father-in-law encouraged my husband (and me) to pursue this profession even though the rest of the family didn't want us to. He used to visit us every Saturday as long as he lived.' This unquestioning affection from her father-in-law is a treasured memory. Anantharamaiah's father was a special man, a priest known to speak directly with Lord Anjaneya. But his mystical orthodoxy had not robbed him of practicality or the capacity for unfettered love.

When Ashwathamma joined her husband, all he had was one plate and one tumbler. Her mother-in-law gave her two earthen pots. 'In the early days, we used to struggle to even buy half a kilo of rice,' Ashwathamma said. With no family or friends to help, the only person who cared for them was the old lady from whom they had rented the house, which was called 'Ajji Maney', or grandmother's home, in Sowrashtrapet. No relative visited them, as they found the work repulsive. His older brother, Chennakeshavachar, never acknowledged Anantharamaiah as his brother. When there was absolutely no one around, the landlady's support must have been overwhelming, an immense source of strength. Ashwathamma tears up even now when she speaks of the old lady.

What began as tabla work soon moved into mrdangam territory. Before opening his own shop, Anantharamaiah used to go to the homes of artists like M.S. Ramaiah, H. Puttachar and M.L. Veerabhadrayya. 'He also used to visit shops such as Bharath Harmonium Works and Aruna Musicals from where he got the instruments (both tabla and mrdangams). He would then work on them at home and deliver them back to the shops,' added his son Srinivas. He added that, in the beginning, there was much more tabla work than mrdangam. Even in the Mysore palace, the use of the tabla was frequent. He named a musician, Mysore Sheshappa, who used to play the tabla in the palace. Srinivas said that the use of mrdangam grew in the Bangalore–Mysore belt only later.

It is no surprise then that, in 1969, when Anantharamaiah opened his shop, he called it Shantha Tabla Works. 'My father used to say that SPR Arts, a professional board-maker in Balepet in the 1960s, made the board. Father wanted to name the shop after his first daughter, Kantha. But by mistake SPR Arts wrote it as Shantha, and that came to stay. My father wasn't very fussy, perhaps he thought the name Shantha was good too, and importantly it got him business,' said Srinivas. 'When he took the shop on rent near Balepet Circle, it was small—measuring 6x17 feet—and was in fact one half of a room. The other half was a charcoal shop.' In 1979, Anantharamaiah bought the shop and that has been the family place of work ever since. His shift towards the mrdangam happened because of the support of mrdangam artists like M.S. Ramaiah, who were then 'big people' in Bangalore.

But, even for Anantharamaiah, who broke so many taboos, skin-related preparation work was religio-culturally out of bounds. Skin for the instruments was bought readymade, from either Thanjavur or Palakkad, and that work was carried out by communities whose caste allowed for such direct contact with raw skin.

'The area where we stayed had families making agarbattis. Since I was at home while my husband was away at work, my neighbours would ask me to join them,' Ashwathamma said. But she was not very interested in that work. Ashwathamma had begun to develop an interest in the making of mrdangams and tablas. She would bother her husband at night, wanting to know how to do this and that, and he shared his knowledge with her. 'I learnt how to make the individual parts of the instruments but found "joining" them very tough, so I would ask him to do it,' she recalled. Over time, she became more and more involved in the work. 'I never found it smelly or repulsive. We used to keep the skins at home. After all, it was thanks to the skins that we were able to have a livelihood; it fed us. I even had my children in this house!' It was in Bangalore that the couple had their four children: Ashwathanarayana, Kanthamma, Pushpalatha and Srinivas.

Ashwathamma at work

Business began to grow, which meant Anantharamaiah needed more hands to help. Bulk export orders of twenty-five or fifty muttus would come from Aruna Musicals, a store owned by Arunachalappa, a harmonium player, and later taken over by his son, the violinist A. Veerabhadrayya. In order to execute these demands on time, Anantharamaiah would call in makers and helpers from Kerala or Tamil Nadu. They would stay in the shop and the Anantharamaiahs, on the floor above. Ashwathamma would take care of all their requirements, cooking for them and keeping them well.

As the years went by, almost all the leading mrdangam artists of Bangalore, such as V.S. Rajagopal, A.V. Anand, T.A.S. Mani, H. Puttachar, M.L. Veerabhadrayya, M. Vasudeva Rao and K.N. Krishnamurthy found their way to Shantha Tabla Works. This led to economic stability for the family, and along with it came respectability. Anantharamaiah became known as 'Dagga Mama' and as 'Ananth Miyan', the south Indian equivalent of Akbar Miyan, a famous tabla maker in the north.

But it was not only Anantharamaiah's fame that grew; Ashwathamma too began to be taken seriously as a maker. Balaguru in Chennai told me that Ashwathamma continues her husband's work, and that they could get about fifteen tabla muttus ready in a day. 'Some foreigners had an instrument made out of some kind of cloth that needed repair and they had given it to Aruna Musicals,' Srinivas remembered. And naturally an SOS was sent to Shantha Tabla Works. 'My mother repaired it so well that they expressed surprise that there were such skilled craftsmen in Bangalore,' Srinivas said proudly.

Even today, Ashwathamma applies sadam for mrdangams and tablas. 'I start from the morning. For higher tonic mrdangams, it takes less time, but longer for those in the lower tonic,' she said. She is happy that her son Srinivas has taken over

Ashwathamma at her workplace, Shantha Tabla Works

the reins of Shantha Tabla Works after her husband passed away in 2009. Not only has Srinivas kept his father's work alive, he has also maintained the family's priestly practice. From the age of seven, he has performed poojas at the Anjaneya temple near Vijayalakshmi Theatre, helping his guru and relative Shridhara Bhattar. Even today he goes there to 'serve the Lord'. He also plays the mrdangam at small concerts and for bhajan singing.

But there was a time when Srinivas, who is a B.Com. graduate, had a job offer at the post office. The offered salary was Rs 3,000, but Anantharamaiah told him that he would pay Srinivas the same amount if he joined the mrdangam-making profession. Srinivas had no choice but to obey, and I detect some regret in his tone. But now Srinivas too is hoping that his younger son will enter the mrdangam-making fold. 'My elder son has finished his B.Com. and is now doing his M.Com.,

CA and articleship. He has clearly told me that he is not going to do this work. If he leaves home at 9 a.m., he comes back only at 9 p.m. He will not come here. This generation does not want to work hard, sir. They just want money to come,' he said unhappily. The other son is still doing his B.Com. and wants a regular job. He will do this 'on the side', and Srinivas hopes this will turn fulltime. But, for now, the future of Shantha Tabla Works is unclear.

The acceptability that Anantharamaiah and his family eventually received from their own clan and society needs to be placed within the larger conversation of caste. Their eventual acceptance is a function of caste privilege. None of the makers belonging to marginalised castes have been able to eliminate stigma, because their caste and work are conflated to mean the same: the 'impure'. Which is why a dalit who works in glass high-rises inside techno parks still faces discrimination, or is compelled to hide his cultural background. When a brahmin 'lowers' himself to work as a mrdangam maker, he faces immediate rejection because he is handling the untouchable. But when he rises financially, and his excellence is proclaimed by other 'upper' castes, the perception takes a turn for the positive. He becomes the person who sacrificed everything (meaning caste privilege) to follow his vocation, or he is credited with having raised the status of this low profession. This upliftment never happens for the people of marginalised castes who have toiled for generations as mrdangam makers.

Interestingly, a Google search threw up the names of many mrdangam makers, but the only website of a maker that popped up was that of Shantha Tabla Works.

The Skin Expert

Kasumani had informed me that it was his daughter-in-law who nails and dries the fresh cow and buffalo skin, but somehow it had not registered. At the end of our conversation, he took me to the adjacent house and then it hit me. In between the two homes was a small Bhagavati temple. The front yard of his daughter-in-law's house was covered with three large buffalo skins that had been spread out and nailed perfectly. Kasumani was explaining how many thattus they might be able to get from one skin when a young Palakkad-based mrdangam artist arrived. Instinctively, all conversation on skin and skin-work was terminated. There was no agreement, no word of caution; it just ended. The young artist was surprised to see me there and was inquisitive about my presence. I avoided giving out too many details. Group photographs followed, in which Kasumani's daughter-in-law stood a step behind all of us, dressed in a nightie, the modern small-town south Indian casual wear.

I left for Palakkad without even asking for her name. A short telephonic conversation with my wife about what had transpired, and her utter shock that I did not speak to the 'daughter-in-law', brought me right back to Peruvemba. Now dressed in a beautiful green saree, she welcomed me into her home.

Turns out, she is not exactly Kasumani's daughter-in-law. Her name is A. Geetha, and her brother Manikandan is married to Kasumani's daughter. But, as is common among insular Indian families, there is another connection. Geetha's paternal grandmother, Ponni, is Kasumani's paternal aunt.

A beaming Geetha

I had observed that the women in almost all mrdangam-making families contributed to the work, but this was usually limited to powdering the stone or applying the sadam. This was the first time I was meeting a woman in a maker's family who took care of the skin processing entirely on her own.

Geetha's father was a well-known Coimbatore-based mrdangam maker, and she grew up watching him work. 'My father, Appu, used to work out of our home. He could even play the mrdangam. When I was a child, I used to help him, and so, I never had any feeling of disgust looking at skin. One day, a person brought a skin, and there was nobody to nail it because my father was ill. Due to high blood pressure, he was half-paralysed. Skin cannot lie around for a long time; it has to be cleaned and nailed as soon as possible, otherwise it starts smelling. But my brother, who was in his teens then, was scheduled to return only at 3 p.m. So my father told me that he would give me instructions and I should just follow. I agreed, and learnt the job.'

Geetha moved to Peruvemba after her marriage, but life was not easy. They were struggling to make ends meet. She wanted to find a way to contribute to the family income. With two little children at home, going outside to work was out of the question. Her husband Shankaranarayanan was already working with skin processing. She began helping him out. Today, she has taken over completely, and it has become her profession. 'I may well be the one lady who is doing this skin-beating job,' she said with a beaming smile. Rather than being disapproving, her husband's family are proud of her.

The skins are chosen and supplied by Kaja Hussain from Pudunagaram, near Palakkad. But Geetha advises him on how to choose. 'I tell him: that is thick, this skin is thinner, this has got knife marks, that has a hole ...' She then went on to describe their process for preparing the skin. 'We nail it and remove the flesh and fat. If it is not removed, the varu will tear. We then leave it under the sun for two days and nights. Sometimes, if it is really hot, the skin might even dry by the end of the day. So we remove the whole skin and hang it on a bamboo pole. The next day, we dry the other side (the hairy side) for a couple of hours. If the skin does not dry properly, it may curl in different places, and then my customers will not be able to remove the hair. At times, I work from 9 a.m. to 1 p.m. without a break.' Geetha buys cow and buffalo skin from

Kaja Hussain for about Rs 1,500. The price varies, depending on the size. She adds to it her 'kooli' (wages), which works to about Rs 400, marks up the price accordingly and sells it. Her selling price is anywhere between Rs 2,000 and 2,500 (price varies depending on the size of the skin). Geetha's customers primarily make mrdangams and chenda, and they come from all over the region, including Thalasseri, Thrissur, Trivandrum, Ernakulam and Coimbatore.

'In a week, we may sell ten to fourteen skins. We have the facility to nail four skins in our home. So, we dry the skin and store it. Some people come and buy in bulk. We have to sell minimum two a day to meet our kooli. If we sell more, it is profit,' Kasumani's son Rajesh added.

Fresh buffalo skin drying in Geetha's yard

For the chenda, she prepares bull skin and says that, if it is thin enough, which is rare, it could work for the mrdangam too, replacing cow skin on the valandalai. 'You will get good nadam,' she claimed. She even sends bull skin for the Nashik dhol. According to Geetha, bull skin has veins but cow skin does not. This gives bull skin the tone needed for the chenda and the dhol. Geetha reserves goat-skin supply exclusively for her brother Manikandan, who runs Appu Mridangam Tabala Works in Coimbatore. The affection in her tone when she mentioned her brother spoke volumes.

When it rains—and it does pour down in this part of the country, especially in June and July—work becomes an ordeal. 'We use tarpaulin during the rainy season to keep the skin dry.' They cover the stretched and nailed skin with a tent-like structure, but if the rains are too heavy, even that does not hold. Work comes to a standstill. On normal days, they roll and store the dried skin for up to a month because customers buy only when there is a requirement. But during the rains, fungi could destroy it.

Geetha's seventeen-year-old son has watched his mother pull, nail, clean and dry these skins day in and day out for years. 'It is under the hot sun, very tedious and a hard job. But I am used to the smell now. When the skin is fresh, it does not smell, but after some time, around mid-day, it will start smelling. My mother continued working even when she was pregnant with me. If she asks me to do it, I will,' he said. Initially, when Geetha began working, she would do everything behind the house, so that people did not see her. Not anymore. In fact, her brother-in-law and his wife have followed in her footsteps, doing the skin-processing in their yard, just next door.

'My family is surviving because of what my father taught me. I am educating my children with the profits from this job. My father always told me that, "You are not a girl child, you are my older son,"' Geetha said, voice cracking. 'I feel so emotional whenever I speak about him. He is no more, but all the credit goes to him.'

12

THE MASTER MAKER

There are heroes and there are heroes. Only a few of the idols of any time truly endure, remaining relevant and influential long after they are gone. In Karnatik music, there are two unchallengeable personages: Ariyakudi Ramanuja Iyengar and Palghat Mani Iyer. One could argue endlessly about the rightness of placing them on that pedestal, or the wrongness of doing so at the expense of others. But no amount of feverish disagreement will displace either of them from the head of the table.

There is only one such phenomenon in the history of mrdangam-making: Parlandu. For the makers' community, he is that one universal reference. A person whom not just the makers but also the artists acknowledge as special, and the latter is significant. In truth, the exception that is Parlandu only highlights the overall apathy of the artists towards makers. The special status Parlandu occupies remains reserved for him alone.

In order for anyone to even come close, they have to be better than the best, so unique and unparalleled that their caste and social standing is at least momentarily forgotten. Sometimes I also wonder whether Parlandu was treated with such reverence when he was still alive.

Parlandu represents the quintessential excellence-seeker. A man with natural talent who pushed the envelope. Anything he touched turned to gold. It also struck me that almost my entire collection of stories about him came from mrdangam artists. Even the tales that the makers shared came from senior artists who had worked with Parlandu or seen him at work. At times, several people told the same story with minute alterations, adding colour and depth to it.

A complicated long-term relationship with a culturally distant and powerful community can be emotionally debilitating. But the legend of Parlandu gives the makers hope and confidence. Like Jesinthamary, his daughter, told me happily, 'Ayyars would not let him go. They were at peace when he did their work.' This professional power gave him and his colleagues strength. And without a doubt, subsequent generations have drawn from that strength too, deriving value, relevance and a sense of achievement from what they do.

The non-Thanjavur makers may not have a blood-bond sort of connection with him, but they too are fascinated by Parlandu. He is not just a person; he is an idea, the musician among makers. In fact, that is exactly what T.V. Gopalakrishnan called him. 'Parlandu was more musician than maker. He had a very discerning ear. Much like how we can make out whether a student will sing well or not, he would just take a piece of skin, tap it with his fingers and reject it, saying it is not good enough. He was so sensitive.'

Mani Iyer and Palani were born in 1912 and 1908 respectively. Parlandu was their contemporary, and I am going to guardedly postulate that he was born in 1910 or thereabouts. There is a wonderful photograph of Mani Iyer and Parlandu that gives you a sense of the man. To the right of the frame, seated on a small wooden plank is a thin, bare-chested Parlandu with a small brush-like moustache. He is holding the top of a large mrdangam with his left hand and rubbing the sadam with a pebble in his right. But it is Parlandu's eyes that draw our gaze. Deep-set, sharp and small, yet soft and arresting. On the other side of the frame is Mani Iyer. Two mrdangams—a really small one and another large one—block him, so we don't get a complete measure of his posture. There appears to be the mark of sandalwood on his right arm, so I am guessing that he had just finished his morning pooja and joined Parlandu at work. His hair is buzz cut as always, and Mani Iyer's face too is typical of how people describe him: expressionless. His body language, though, speaks. He has a mrdangam on his lap, causing him to sit at a slight angle, but he exudes confidence and command.

Melgies said, 'This was taken in Thanjavur. Mani Iyer had a room upstairs. If you go to Thanjavur even now, you will still find the house. One doctor amma lives in the house today. All the mrdangam work used to happen there.'

'Oh, so this is taken upstairs?' I asked.

'Yes. It was taken a long time ago. Mani Iyer's son Rajamani took this photograph, and it is published every year for the Mani Iyer Day celebrations.'

The iconic picture of Parlandu and Mani Iyer

There are umpteen stories about Parlandu's mastery over mrdangam-making, and I will narrate a few here. Let me begin with an insightful description from Selvaraj: 'He had a raga inside him for each of the singers.' It is as if Parlandu remembered a rendition that he associated with every musician. Through this melodic memory, he internalised their musical landscape, vocal range and tonic. 'If the tambura was strummed, the mrdangam would be in perfect tune with it,' Selvaraj said. That Parlandu was hard of hearing makes it all the more astounding. Much like Beethoven, who composed even when he could not hear, Parlandu readied the mrdangam by paying attention to the music that he had preserved in his mind. Did he have the rare ability of absolute pitch? That is, the ability to identify pitches by merely hearing the frequency. We will never know for sure, but I would not be surprised if he did. Because everything that older mrdangam artists, who were then up-and-coming juniors, say about him points to such a capability.

Rajaram said, 'During Rama Navami and Navaratri, he (Mani Iyer) would have played three or four concerts using the seven–eight mrdangams he took with him. Before leaving, he would have given instructions to Parlandu.' Iyer had a unique way of doing this. On a small piece of paper, he would write instructions like 'Muttu GNB' or 'Sadam Ariyakudi' or 'Alathur Brothers Sadam'. Parlandu knew the tonic to which he needed to tune each of these mrdangams, and the extent of variability to factor in if any of these singers increased or decreased their tonic a little. 'They (makers) had to cut up invitations that came into small pieces and store them. He (Mani Iyer) would write on them "Sadam Alathur Brothers" and insert them in the varu. At one point, my father hadn't played for Madurai Mani Iyer for about two or three years and didn't know his tonic. But he heard him on the radio and noted the tonic. He told Parlandu the tonic and asked him whether it was right. Parlandu said, "I will take care of it, Ayya." And he prepared the mrdangam perfectly. My father had doubts, but Parlandu was confident and told him, "If there are small adjustments to be made in the tuning, don't worry. I have provided for that." Such was his work. My father used to always say that he was very smart.' It is said of Parlandu that he knew the tonic by the names of the artists, not by the numerical or alphabetical measures that are usually used.

In the afternoons, apparently Mani Iyer took pleasure in listening to the work happening upstairs as he lay down for a siesta. He was so drawn by the changes in tone after every round of sadam that he would often rush back to the first floor where Parlandu was at work. 'He would be lying down at home at 1 p.m. When Parlandu pulled the varu and struck the mrdangam, the pitch would rise. My father would get excited. We would be pressing his legs, Lalitha (Mani Iyer's daughter) and I, and he would be enjoying it. Just when he was falling asleep, Parlandu would play a chappu. He would exclaim, "Oh, he is not letting me sleep … look how good his work is. I am going up … how can I sleep when such good work is going on? I am going up." And would go join Parlandu. He loved sitting there, watching when they put sadam,' recalled Rajaram.

It is not often discussed that the maker, even if he has not formally learnt to play the mrdangam, must know to play its strokes in order to make sure that the instrument is in ideal musical shape. Rajaram remembered Parlandu's exquisite arachappu. 'Parlandu used to play the arachappu really well; you could listen to it all day. After applying two rounds of sadam, he used to test the mittu and chappu for any incongruency and play the arachappu, and it used to resonate. There is no one to play arachappu like him.' If Mani Iyer was angry with Parlandu for anything, the sound of that arachappu on a well-made and tuned mrdangam would make him forget everything.

Parlandu was outstanding at every part of the making process, but his speciality was in the way he finally got the mrdangam perfectly tuned, absolutely no approximations. After everything else has been perfectly put together, it is in this final operation that the artist gets the mrdangam aligned to the nature of his or her hands, style, strengths and needs. So it is not just about a tunefully made instrument. Through the making process, the maker himself would have tested pitch accuracy over and over, but the moment the playing hand changes (from maker to artist), everything can go awry. Parlandu's brilliance lay in making an instrument belong to the artist who owned it. Mani Iyer apparently used to say, 'Rajamanickam must apply the sadam and Parlandu should do the final suddham.'

That was the one aspect where Rajamanickam had the better of Parlandu: the durability of his sadam. Selvaraj and Rajamani both spoke of how excellent Parlandu's sadam was but mentioned that it did not last long. Somehow, Rajamanickam was able to extend the life of the sadam. This helped Mani Iyer reduce the number of mrdangams he needed to carry to concerts. Of course, carrying so many mrdangams was a luxury that only Mani Iyer could afford; something even senior mrdangam artists today cannot.

Parlandu was largely the chief maker for Mani Iyer, though he did do some work for Palani and the others too. When he went to Trichy to work for Palani, Mani Iyer would get nervous. 'These guys (Parlandu and his brothers) would bunk and go there (to Palani's house), and Kitta Ayyar used to get yelled at,' said Rajaram. Kitta Ayyar was the person who liaised between Mani Iyer and Parlandu, which also meant that he played his own little games. He would needle Parlandu with barbed comments, and at times quietly reduce the amount paid to him. 'One time, Kitta Ayyar would have said something or the other to tick Parlandu off, or reduced his payment, or done something of that sort, and Parlandu was angry about it. So, when Kitta Ayyar went to see Parlandu, he said, "If you enter the slum, you brahmin, I will cut off your sacred thread and slap you." Kitta Ayyar ran back and complained to my father, "Sir, see what he is saying!"' Rajaram recalled, laughing as he told the tale. Kitta Ayyar addressed Parlandu as 'para payale', which translates to 'paraiyan fellow', a reference to his caste. There were many skirmishes between the two, and Parlandu rarely held back.

Maybe it was easier for him to lash back at the manager rather than the big man himself. Thiruvaiyaru Krishna Ayyar, a student of Thanjavur Vaidyanatha Ayyar, used to jokingly say that Sevittian had asked him to take care of all his children. Using this as a reason, Mani Iyer used to complain to Krishna Ayyar that Parlandu was not following his instructions.

But aesthetically and professionally, Mani Iyer and Parlandu were a perfect fit, making Iyer most possessive of his prized maker. Since he maintained an iron grip on Parlandu's movements, other artists were sometimes left in the lurch. 'Palani would have concerts with G.N. Balasubramaniam or Madurai Mani Iyer and would inform him (Parlandu) that he needs two or three mrdangams. But it would not be ready on time. So, he would get upset with Parlandu and Mani Iyer. That is when Shetty came into picture,' Kalidas explained.

Players vied for Parlandu's attention. Even the mighty Dakshinamurthy Pillai had to wait. 'He was dying to have Parlandu work for him, but my father was not interested,' Selvaraj said. 'Dakshinamurthy Pillai's student, Ranganayaki, I think her name was, came home and asked my father to come to Tirukokarnam and work for him. Even his son Swaminatha Pillai made a request. But my father was hesitant because he did not know the style of work Dakshinamurthy Pillai expected.'

Sankaran gave me a different story. 'When in Madurai for a concert, apparently Dakshinamurthy Pillai was struggling with his mrdangam. Shengol was supposed to come and sort things out but sent his brother instead. In the evening, there was a knock on the door. Parlandu had to explain to Pillai that he was from Thanjavur and had been sent by Shengol. He assured Pillai that he would get the mrdangam ready. Immediately, he corrected the ecchu–taggu, did some varu pidi and the final suddham. Dakshinamurthy Pillai was so impressed that he proclaimed loudly, "Wisdom lies here".'

Parlandu was Mani Iyer's man and Antony became Palani's. This division of the two biggest players between the Thanjavur brothers meant that the two makers' work was also compared and contrasted. Jesudass, Antony's son, describes it succinctly: 'Their work was the same. Some people liked Parlandu. It was in the nuances that they were different, and that is because of their relationship with the artists for whom they were working. The artists also had confidence in the makers of their choice ... Parlandu worked for Palghat Mani Iyer and that is why he is spoken about so much. My father, Shetty, was working for Palani. In those days, Palani and Mani Iyer were in competition. And much like that, my father and Parlandu were also similarly competitive.'

Palani's students feel the need to assert their teacher's might in the face of a near-constant Mani Iyer onslaught. Similarly, Antony's sons want to place their father's work on par with their illustrious uncle's. I have noted earlier in this book that Antony's work was not considered great, but perhaps my perception too was clouded by the 'Parlandu–Mani Iyer camp' within the Thanjavur family and in the world of Karnatik music.

At any rate, when it came to putting Parlandu or any other maker in his place, the two giants would come together. Rajamani had this incident to narrate, 'One of the times that

Parlandu was fighting with my father, he had gone to Palani's house to work. At that time, my father needed a mrdangam for a concert and borrowed one from Palani. After the concert, he returned the mrdangam through a student. In those days, they charged Rs 1 to apply a new sadam. But Parlandu told Palani that he needed Rs 3 for this mrdangam since Ayya had played on it. Without batting an eyelid, Palani sent him away, saying that he need not work for him.' Palani may have been deeply hurt by Mani Iyer bossing over the makers, but if any one of them, even the most revered, overstepped a line, indicating even an iota of assertiveness, he was put down.

ALL THE STORIES AROUND PARLANDU speak of the special treatment he received. Artists respected his mind and listened to him. Selvaraj said, 'Both of them (Mani and Parlandu) listened to each other.' Gopalakrishnan said, 'Even Mani Iyer would not say anything to Parlandu. He would say, "Ayya, this is how it is", and Mani Iyer would accept it.' His greatest contribution to the art of mrdangam-making is creating the kappi mrdangam. Most unusually, everyone unambiguously acknowledges that this was Parlandu's idea, his contribution. As far as I have been able to determine, Parlandu probably came up with the idea of the kappi mrdangam around 1953: an innovation that influenced the modern interpretation of the 'dignified mrdangam sound'. In all my fieldwork, this was the only occasion when mrdangam artists wholeheartedly gave credit to a maker for an idea. Parlandu was the exception, and his contribution—even if it is not publicly recognised—is accepted without hesitation in the inner circles of Karnatik music. To reiterate, no one else, absolutely no one, has been accorded this privilege.

Only one mrdangam artist refused to accept that Parlandu had the ability to come up with the kappi muttu. Umayalpuram Sivaraman said emphatically, 'I am not prepared to accept that Parlandu had that level of knowledge! He worked well. He had a natural talent.' According to him, the idea must have come from Vaidyanatha Iyer, who would have learnt it by watching someone from an earlier generation. 'I don't think it was his idea,' he said.

However, like everyone else in the family, Parlandu was not forthcoming about his methods, not even to his own son. Selvaraj would ask Mani Iyer to explain Parlandu's work, hoping that someday he could understand it. On one occasion, Parlandu entered the room when this conversation was going on, and Mani Iyer told Parlandu about the questions his son was asking. By the late 1950s, Parlandu could not work anymore because of diabetes, and Selvaraj had taken his place at the master's house. So, Parlandu would drop by at Iyer's house to give his son a few suggestions and then just leave. At one point, Selvaraj lost patience. He told his father to either teach him systematically every day or leave him alone. And Selvaraj was left to fend for himself. When I met Selvaraj, he was at the end of his life, still in awe of his father. 'When he applied sadam, irrespective of the pitch, it would look like the back of a tortoise. In my father's mrdangam, there would be absolutely no ecchu–taggu. He would make only one muttu a day. He wasn't concerned about money. What he wanted was for his work to be respected and appreciated,' Selvaraj said with pride.

What is difficult to comprehend is the exact nature of the relationship between Mani Iyer and Parlandu. There is no doubt that Iyer's respect for him was enormous. He would often hand over the gifts he received at concerts, like shawls or flasks, to Parlandu because he was thrilled with a mrdangam. Rajaram saw this differently. 'My father only spoilt him. If the muttu was good and the kutcheri went well, he would come back and give him 100 rupees. Or sometimes if he went for a concert in Delhi, he would get these Kashmiri shawls ... and give it to him.' So pleased was he once with a mrdangam that he gave Parlandu a gold coin. This was Mani Iyer's way of saying thank you. But he did not stop with material awards alone. When Parlandu fell sick, Iyer got the best doctor in Thanjavur to attend to him and sent money to the hospital regularly. 'Parlandu had diabetes and was in hospital towards the end of his life,' Rajamani said. 'The hospital was about a kilometre from our house. At that time, my father was not on talking terms with Parlandu but would send him 30–40 rupees every month through money order. My father was very concerned about him.' Not just that, when Parlandu was sick but not yet in hospital, Kitta Ayyar was designated with the task of collecting Parlandu's urine every morning for testing. Something Kitta Ayyar did with great reluctance. He would go to Mani Iyer's house to complain about it before he headed out to the hospital. 'Why is Parlandu's urine my headache?'

Was all this just respect for Parlandu as a master maker? Or was it an expression of personal affection? I am unable to put my finger on what this relationship meant to Iyer. I specifically asked, 'So there was a close bond between the two?' And Rajamani said yes emphatically. Mani Iyer was without doubt a person of his times, limited by the caste edifice that he grew up in. This was not something he addressed; in fact, the thought would never have arisen. Yet, at the very centre of his life was this man from the margins of society, a section that Mani Iyer probably never recognised as intelligent and creative and had no other association with. Even Iyer's wife would complain that Parlandu was more important to him than she was. A musical bond held Iyer and Parlandu together, and created a personal closeness. But Mani Iyer could not transform this relationship into an equal friendship. It was instead a hidden friendship. I believe it was not just a functional and opportunistic affiliation. Without confronting caste, though, Mani Iyer could not have made more of it. Iyer believed in the life he led as a brahmin, and that made him who he was. Yet, in this one case, he might have been touched by something bigger. He was just not ready to allow himself to recognise it.

Perhaps the most repeated story about Parlandu is that he told Iyer that the toppi sound he so desperately sought came from Palani's hand not Parlandu's muttu alone. He was insinuating that Mani Iyer could not achieve the same on a toppi just like Palani's.

Why was this so significant?

It was a rare occasion when Mani Iyer revealed his own insecurity, maybe even to the surprise of his own inner circle. And what brings everything together is the fact that it was revealed by the master maker, Parlandu. In speaking of his soft 'bringing down' by Parlandu, was Mani Iyer also displaying his immense respect for the man? Rajaram's version of this story ends with Mani Iyer asking: 'Then will my toppi never sound like that? I asked you to make a good muttu, but you have said that it is in the hands. Are you saying I will never achieve that kind of a toppi sound in my lifetime?'

There is something I want to reiterate here. I found it baffling that all the musicians, including Mani Iyer's children, who admired Parlandu for his workmanship, did not use the grammatical phrasing that implies respect. This separation between the professional and the individual is revealing.

When I asked Rajamani about Parlandu the person, he had nothing to say. He began with 'Parlandu was a nice person', and later said, 'I knew him very well'. But all that he shared was work- and skill-related. Parlandu did not exist outside his identity as a maker. I kept prodding Rajamani to explain why the Iyer–Parlandu connection was unusual. Rajamani acknowledged that it was, but added nothing more. In fact, his brother Rajaram spoke of how Parlandu would get angry and stop coming for a while. 'They would fight on and off. Parlandu would suddenly ask for 500 rupees and, if my father was in a good mood, he would give it. If not, he would refuse. Then, Parlandu would say that he won't come to work.' Rajamani had earlier made this general observation: 'Whatever you do for these people, they have no brains.'

There was just one personal thing that Rajaram remembered. 'Ayyo, his smile was sinister!' And he demonstrated how Parlandu would speak with his hand covering his mouth. He was very intelligent, Rajaram added.

It is nearly impossible to know what Parlandu felt about all this. Did he even have the luxury to explore his emotions? 'Parlandu hardly spoke,' said Selvaraj. 'Shetty was not like that; he spoke a lot. I do not speak much, only to some extent. Johnson and Arulraj are more talkative.' Selvaraj was using the metaphor of speech to mean obedience. He was implying that his cousins and uncle were more combative and, he thought, out of line. Their outspokenness was not to be emulated. To his mind, the job of the maker was to quietly obey, without asking questions. He should express an opinion if needed, but only when asked or if something really went wrong. In Selvaraj's estimate, Parlandu was non-combative, submissive and stayed within the lines. His occasional outbursts and walkouts were possibly the release of mounting emotional pressure. Living in a personal and social context where oppression was customary and rights non-existent, yet realising that he himself was special, and at the same time feeling honoured by his association with upper castes—all of these conflicting elements must have been emotionally draining and would have remained unresolved until the very end.

Consider also how brahmin mrdangam artists would have looked at any maker who was even marginally self-assured. It is, of course, why Rajamanickam was considered difficult. It was an accepted norm that when the dalit mrdangam maker speaks to an artist his hands cover his mouth and his upper garment is taken off his shoulder. For Rajamanickam to have put in place professional norms at that time is nothing short of revolutionary. These caste-inflected displays of servitude are still present, if in a less naked form. They can still be seen in the way respect is automatically accorded to the brahmin, the way makers stand up when speaking to mrdangam artists, how they play down their own achievements and contributions, and continue to consider this cross-caste association special. Irrespective of their seniority, every maker I spoke with addressed me with unquestioned deference. Above all, there is the pacifist approach towards all that happens around them.

These lines are constantly being redrawn by the powerful in an unrecognised casteist negotiation with the other side. Any perceived action that crosses the currently acceptable limits is put down to lack of respect and decorum.

To return to our enquiry: so, who was Parlandu? I spoke to his son Melgies and daughter Jesinthamary. They described him as a gentle person who rarely got angry. Both of them reiterated that he hardly spoke. He wanted the extended family to remain together and tried his best to keep the brothers united. They had their own homes but made it a point to come together for all family events. But he really did not like discussing work with his brothers. Mrdangam artists, on the other hand, told Melgies that Parlandu was very helpful, telling them to practice hard, teaching them how to maintain their instrument and tune it well. Work was everything to him. Towards the end of his life, Parlandu was a worried man. He owned some land in Nadukaveri (this might be the land that Mani Iyer is supposed to have bought him), which provided paddy, but ill health meant his monthly income was negligible. Over and above economic troubles, on the personal front there was hurt. After his marriage, Selvaraj moved into a separate home, even though Melgies and Jesinthamary were still young at the time.

There was one thing Jesinthamary said that was at odds with everything else I had heard. 'If the Ayyars listened to him and followed what he said, he would work. They must fall in line. But if they tried ordering him around, he would not work.' So Parlandu did have another side, where he displayed self-esteem, confidence, arrogance and self-assured delight in his own wizardry. Maybe the junior artists of his time encountered this side to Parlandu. Jesinthamary also believed that there was a time when Mani Iyer himself came and apologised to Parlandu, calling him back to work. Whether or not this happened, Parlandu was most certainly someone who would have commanded that apology, if not for his caste.

As we know, Mani Iyer moved to Madras in 1964, and members of the Thanjavur family also began shifting base to the state capital around that time. But a weak and unwell Parlandu stayed back in his home town, remaining there until the day he passed on. Chronic diabetes, perhaps exacerbated by alcoholism, took its toll. Parlandu died in 1970. And I doubt any mrdangam artist went to bid him adieu.

Mani Iyer had said, 'My heaven is a place where Somu Asari has worked on good sandalwood and made the kattai, Parlandu constructs the muttu and I get to use that mrdangam to play a concert for Ariyakudi Ramanuja Iyengar.' I hope this happened in a heaven where all of them had shed their respective castes and were basking in each other's magnificence.

THE MAKERS' FAMILY TREES

*The lineages in these family trees attempt to trace individuals
who are directly connected to the art of mrdangam-making.*

THANJAVUR FAMILY (1A)

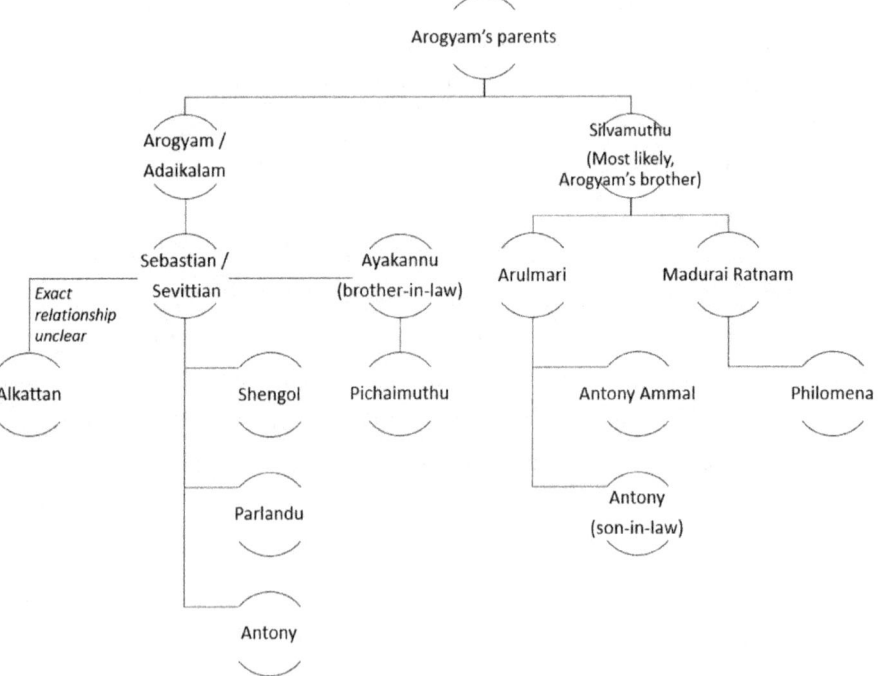

THANJAVUR FAMILY (1B)

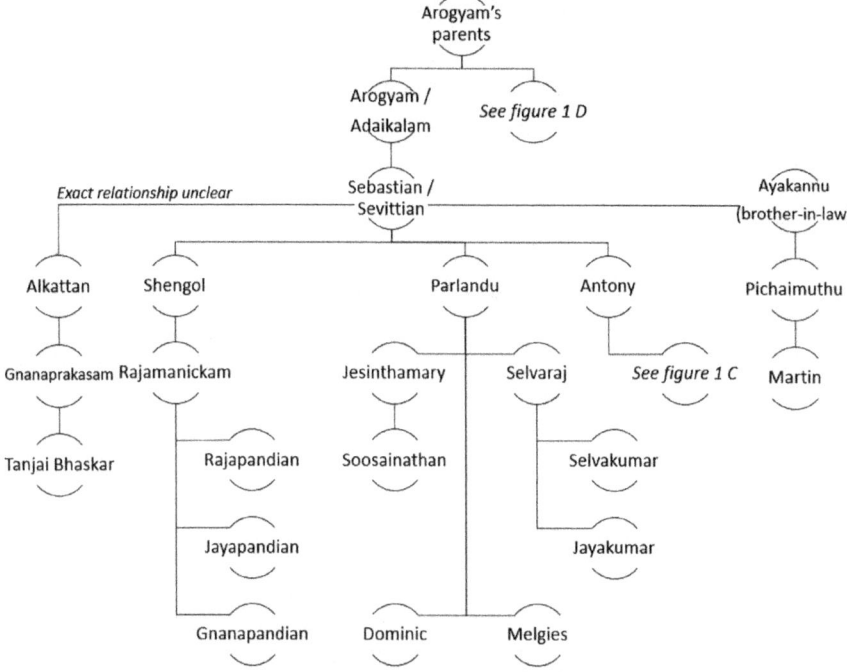

THANJAVUR FAMILY (1C)

THANJAVUR FAMILY (1D)

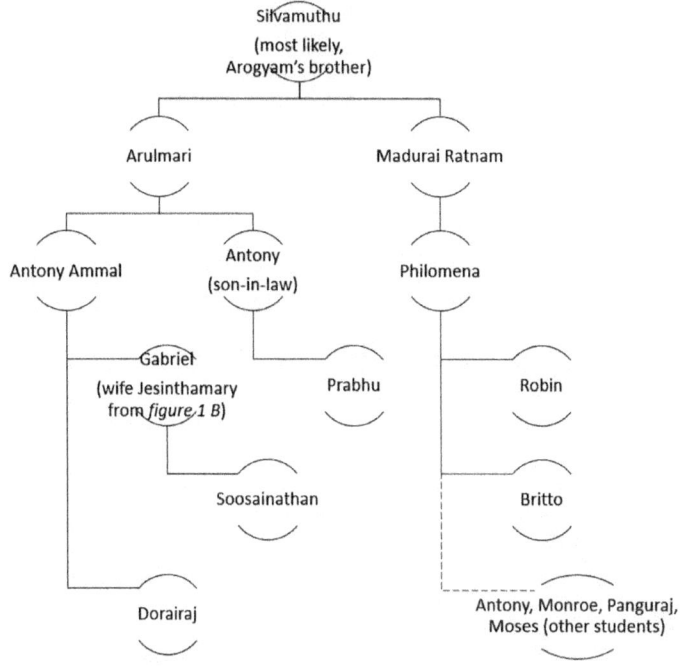

MADRAS MUTTU

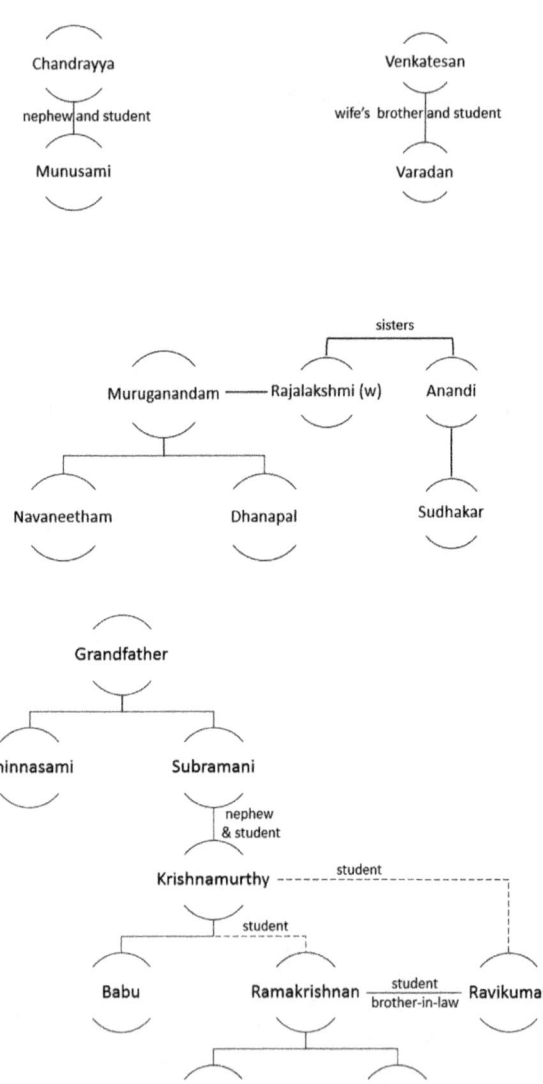

Chandrayya
nephew and student
Munusami

Venkatesan
wife's brother and student
Varadan

sisters

Muruganandam —— Rajalakshmi (w) Anandi

Navaneetham   Dhanapal   Sudhakar

Grandfather

Chinnasami   Subramani
nephew & student
Krishnamurthy - - - - student

student

Babu   Ramakrishnan — student / brother-in-law — Ravikumar

Jyotiprakash   Radhakrishnan
(sister-in-law's husband)

PERUVEMBA

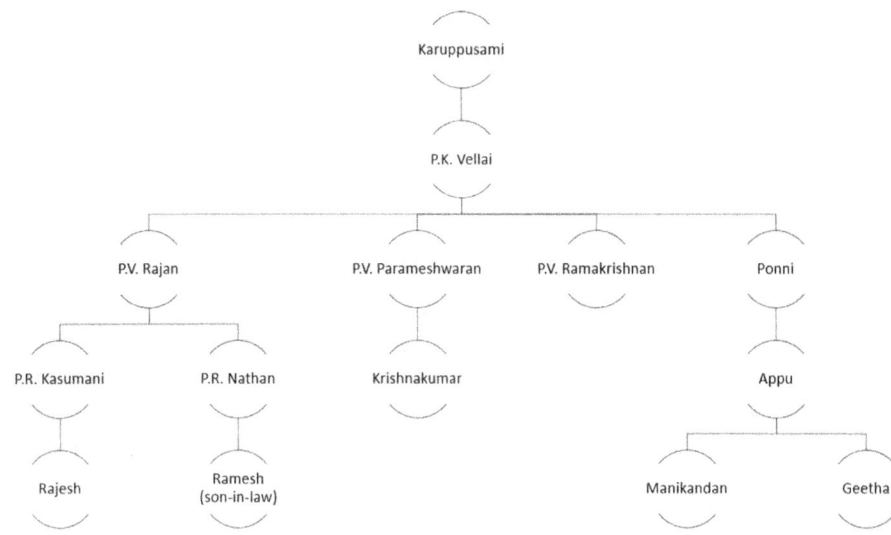

Karuppusami

P.K. Vellai

P.V. Rajan   P.V. Parameshwaran   P.V. Ramakrishnan   Ponni

P.R. Kasumani   P.R. Nathan   Krishnakumar   Appu

Rajesh   Ramesh (son-in-law)   Manikandan   Geetha

KARUPPUSAMI'S STUDENTS

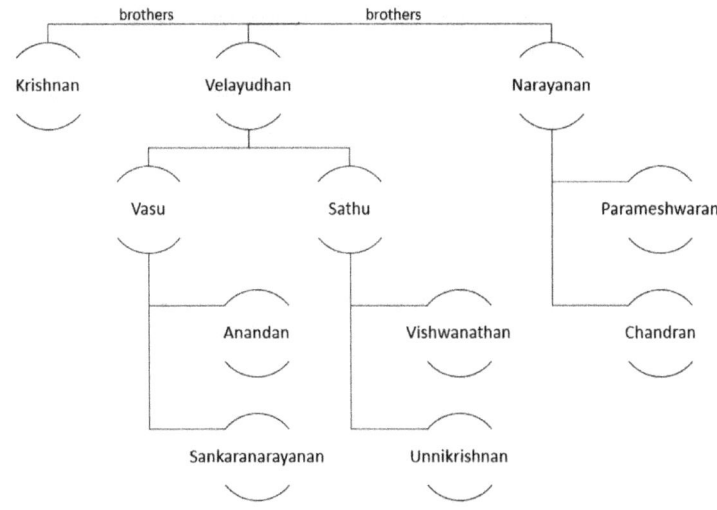

brothers   brothers

Krishnan   Velayudhan   Narayanan

Vasu   Sathu   Parameshwaran

Anandan   Vishwanathan   Chandran

Sankaranarayanan   Unnikrishnan

BANGALORE TRADITION

VIJAYAWADA TRADITION

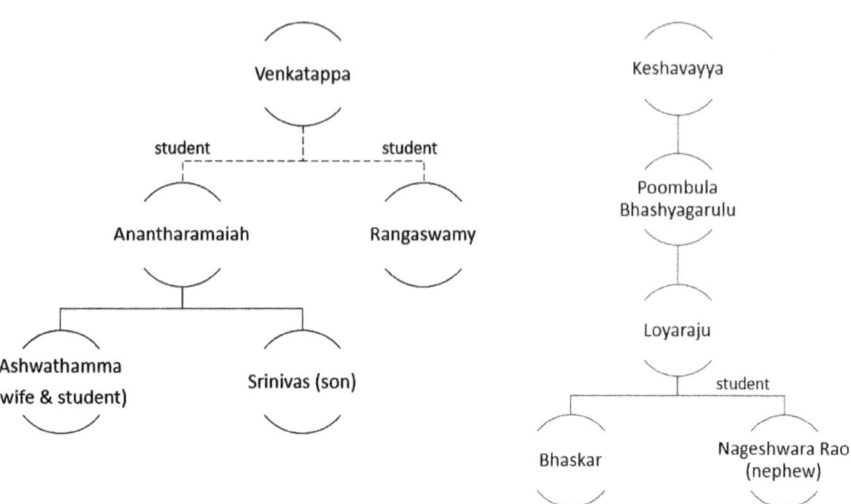

VIZIANAGARAM TRADITION

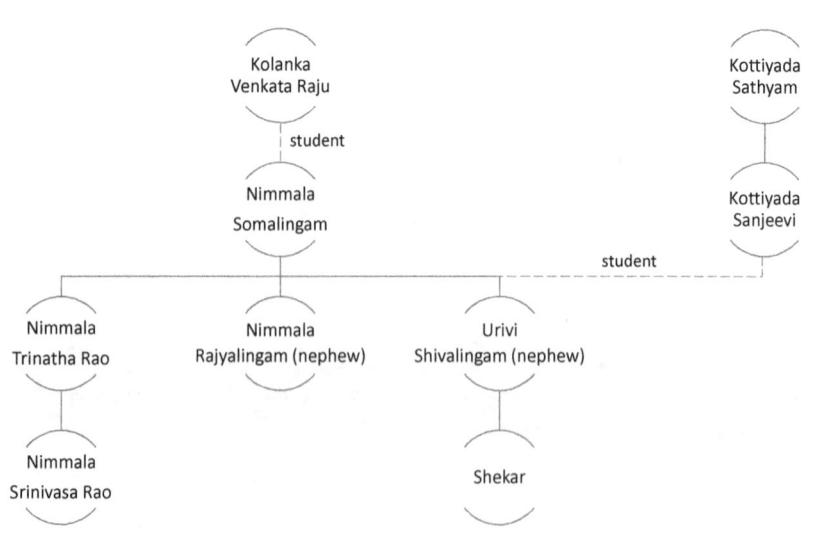

THE WOODCRAFTERS

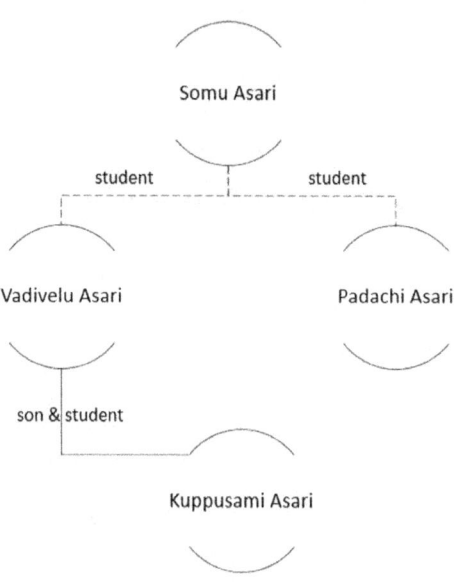

Somu Asari

student — student

Vadivelu Asari   Padachi Asari

son & student

Kuppusami Asari

AMBUR

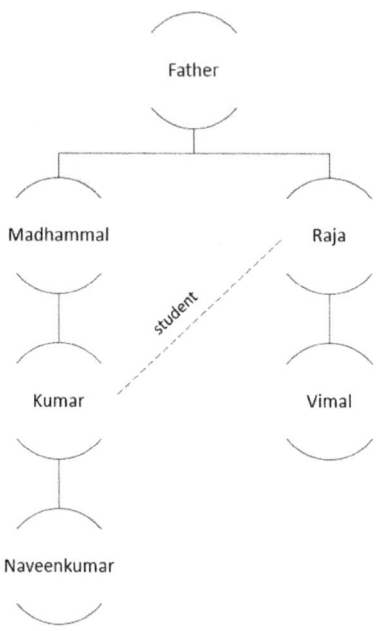

Father

Madhammal   Raja

student

Kumar   Vimal

Naveenkumar

A BRIEF PRONUNCIATION GUIDE

This is not a comprehensive list of 'making' words, but a selection that is not pronounced in the Tamil as the spelling in English indicates. Since many of these words are as unfamiliar to speakers of Tamil as anyone else, the guide seemed especially worthwhile. Tamil has a few hard consonants, such as D, L, N and T. You'd have to roll your tongue back to the top of your palate and slap it back down to pronounce these letters. They are often used as doubles, and that is indicated with a double capital: LL, NN and TT. Other capitals indicate sounds such as A as in a: (father) or U as in u: (too).

allu thol—aLLuthol   அள்ளுதோல்

asari—AsAri   ஆசாரி

bagam—bAgam   பாகம்

chappu—chAppu   சாப்பு

gambhiram—gambhIram   கம்பீரம்

jadi—jAdi   ஜாடி

kannu—kaNNu   கண்ணு

kattai—kaTTai	கட்டை
katti adi—katti aDi	கட்டி அடி
kittankallu—kiTTAnkallu	கிட்டாங்கல்
kodukapuli—koDukApuLI	கொடுக்காப்புளி
kolam—kOlam	கோலம்
kottu—koTTu	கொட்டு
kottuthattu—koTTuthaTTu	கொட்டுதட்டு
malku varu—malku vAru	மல்கு வாரு
	(மல்கு வார்)
mittu—mITTU	மீட்டு
muttu—mUTTu	மூட்டு
nadam—nAdam	நாதம்
nadasvaram—nAdasvaram	நாதசுரம்
nattu—nATTu	நாட்டு
netti muttu—netti mUTTu	நெத்தி மூட்டு
	[நெற்றி மூட்டு]
okkarara—okkArara	ஒக்காரர
	[உட்காருகிற]
padi parkardu—paDi pAkardu	படி பாக்கிறது
	[படி பார்க்கிறது]
pinnra sattai—pinnra sATTai	பின்ற சாட்டை
	[பின்னுகிற சாட்டை]
poivaru—poi vAru	பொய் வாரு
	[பொய் வார்]
poivaru pidi—poivAru piDi	பொய் வாரு பிடி
	[பொய் வார் பிடி]

ringaram—rIngAram	ரீங்காரம்
sadam—sAdam	சாதம்
sama thattu—sama thaTTu	சம தட்டு
sattai—sATTai	சாட்டை
soruguthattu—soruguthaTTu	சொருகுதட்டு [செருகுதட்டு]
suddham panradu—suddham panRadu	சுத்தம் பண்றது [சுத்தம் பண்ணுகிறது]
sunnambu—sunnAmbu	சுண்ணாம்பு
tambalam—tAmbAlam	தாம்பாளம்
tangu varu—tAngu vAru	தாங்கு வாரு [தாங்கு வார்]
tangukayaru—tAngukayaru	தாங்குகயிறு
thattu—taTTu	தட்டு
ulsattai—uLsATTai	உள்சாட்டை
vadyam—vAdyam	வாத்தியம்
valandalai—valandalai	வலந்தலை (வலந்தரை)
varu—vAru	வாரு [வார்]
velaipadu—vElaipADu	வேலைப்பாடு
velitthi—veLitthi	வெளித்தி
vetthalaipakku—vetthalaipAkku	வெத்தலைபாக்கு [வெற்றிலைபாக்கு]
vettuthattu—veTTuthaTTU	வெட்டுதட்டு

BIBLIOGRAPHY

BOOKS

Bhagavatar, Soolamangalam Vaidyanatha. *Cameos*. Chennai: Sunadham, 2005.

Bhagavatar, Soolamangalam Vaidyanatha. *Karnataka Sangita Vidvangal*. Kalakshetra, 1994.

Grafe, Hugald. *The History of Christianity in Tamilnadu from 1800 to 1975*. Bangalore: Church History Association of India, 1990.

Hemingway, F.R. *Madras District Gazetteers: Tanjore*. Madras: Superintendent, Government Press, 1906.

Krishna, T.M. *A Southern Music: The Karnatik Story*. Delhi: HarperCollins India, 2013.

Oddie, Geoffrey A. *Hindu and Christian in South-East India*. London: Curzon Press/The Riverdale Company, 1991.

Pearson, Hugh. *Memoirs of the Life and Correspondence of the Reverend Christian Fredrich Shwartz* (3rd edition, Vol. 1–2). London: J. Hatchard & Sons, 1939.

Seetha, S. *Thanjavur as a Seat of Music*. Madras: University of Madras, 2001.

Thurston, Edgar and Rangachari, K. *Castes and Tribes of Southern India* (Vol. 1–7). Madras: Government Press, 1909.

Webster, John C.B. *The Pastor to Dalits*. Delhi: Cambridge Press, 1995.

Webster, John C.B. *The Dalit Christians: A History* (Contextual Theological Education Series 4). Delhi: Indian Society for Promoting Christian Knowledge (ISPCK), 1994.

NEWSPAPERS, JOURNALS AND ARTICLES

Anand, S. 'Thyagaraja's Cow', *Outlook India*, 08 September 2003. Retrieved from https://www.outlookindia.com/magazine/story/thyagarajas-cow/221354.

Raman, C.V. 'The Indian Musical Drums'. *Proceedings of the Indian Academy of Sciences*, pp. 179–188, 1934.

Raman, C.V. 'Musical Drums with Harmonic Overtones'. *Nature*, pp. 104, 1920.

Sruti/Sruti Magazine for the Performing Arts: The Sruti Foundation.

ACKNOWLEDGEMENTS

Writing might happen in solitude, but without the generosity of so many who share their knowledge and experience, putting together a story of this complexity is next to impossible. In the past four years, there were many people who answered my questions and handheld me through the lives and histories of mrdangam makers. I want to make special mention of K. Soosainathan who not only showed me the nuances of the making but also guided me to the various places that mattered for this narrative. T.R. Rajamani, Prof. Trichy Sankaran, A.S. Johnson Kennedy, A. Sowriar, writer Perumal Murugan, Prof. A.R. Venkatachalapathy were there to clarify any doubts and/or send in detailed notes that added to the depth of my understanding. S. Anand generously granted me access to all the brilliant photographs he had taken in the year 2000 when he delved into the lives of the Thanjavur makers who lived in Mylapore, Chennai. My words first have to pass through rigorous editing by my in-house critics R. Krithika and Prema Rangachary, and it is very much the better for it.

Ajitha G.S. was the best editor I could have had. Having worked with her before, I knew that I would get feedback and suggestions that would make me think, redraft ideas and narratives with greater sensitivity and insight. The fifteen beautiful sketches included in the book are the work of the artist Rohini Mani, who not only went into every detail with me with utmost dedication, but also spent a day with Sowriar in order to really understand the mrdangam-making process.

I depended entirely on primary sources and below are all the individuals who took time out to be interviewed for this book. Some were detailed conversations, while others were short. Vignesh Ishwar was immensely helpful and followed up with many interviewees for clarifications and additional information. Unfortunately, from among the individuals below, F. Selvaraj and Madras A. Kannan have passed away.

A. Arogyam

A. Geetha

A. Jesudass, J. Edwin and S.P. Altrin

A. Sowriar and Sarada Sowriar

A.S. Johnson Kennedy

B. Loyaraju

C. Varadan

F. Melgies and Arogyamary

F. Selvaraj

G. Krishnamurthy and Rajam

G. Lawrence

Guruvayur Dorai

J. Ashok

J. Surendarpeliks

J. Vivek

K.S. Kalidas

K. Soosainathan

Karaikudi R. Mani

Kudanthai David

Kumar and Madhammal

Kuppusami Asari

M.R. Jyotiprakash

Madras A. Kannan

Madurai J.M.S. Britto

Nageshwar Rao

P. Krishnakumar

P. Ravikumar

P.R. Kasumani, P.V. Ramakrishnan and K. Rajesh

P.T. Martin

R. Arulraj

R.S. Ashwathamma

S. Arulraj

S. Balaguru

S. Gabriel and Jesinthamary

S. Muruganandam and M. Navaneethakrishnan

Srinivas Anantharamaiah

T.K. Murthy

T.R. Rajamani

T.R. Rajaram

T.V. Gopalakrishnan

Trichy Sankaran

Umayalpuram K. Sivaraman

Uzhavoor P.K. Babu

V. Kamalakar Rao

Vurivi Sivalingam

Some friends conducted a few interviews on my behalf and connected me with mrdangam makers. Ranjani Govind interviewed R.S. Ashwathamma and Srinivas Anantharamaiah, V.V. Ramanamurthy spoke to Vurivi Sivalingam and shared his own thoughts on the making tradition in Vizianagaram with me via a voice recording, Sai Giridhar provided me information regarding Vijayawada-based makers B. Loyaraju, Nageshwar Rao and L. Bhaskar, and B.S. Purushotham put me in touch with makers in Bangalore and accompanied me on my field trip to the city.

Archived material becomes that much more valuable when we are trying to understand people about whom very little is recorded by society. I am thankful that T.R. Rajamani shared with me his brother T.R. Rajaram's 1984 interview of Somu Asari. Similarly, Prof. Trichy Sankaran converted his 1991 camcorder recording of S. Rajamanickam's working methods into digital format and made it available for my use. G.M. Sumangala sent me the recording of a conversation that some of us from Chennai had with Koraga drummers in Maala, Karnataka in 2018. Praveen Sparsh sent me descriptions of precisely how certain mrdangam strokes are executed. I would also like to acknowledge Surendarpeliks, who demonstrated the final steps in the mrdangam-making process for me.

This book brings together socio-politics, aesthetics, chemistry, biology, acoustics, engineering and physics. There were many who helped me understand these nuances. My sincere thanks to Prof. P. Chandramouli, Prof. V. Subramanya Sarma, Prof. Haribabu Arthanari, Vignesh Ishwar, Goutham Koka, Prof. Juergen Schieber, Aparna Karthikeyan and S. Gopalakrishnan. Prof. V. Subramanya Sarma also conducted tests on the various stones used for the sadam at the Indian Institute of Technology, Madras.

The following people spent innumerable hours carefully transcribing many of the interviews.

Rajesh Garga

Vignesh Ishwar

Sangeetha Sivakumar

G. Ravikiran

S. Hariharan

Prof. A.R. Venkatachalapathy graciously helped us put together the pronunciation guide. Vikram Raghavan structured the family trees and assisted me during research-related travels to Panruti and Thanjavur. The typesetter, Rajinder Ganju, for his immense patience with all the changes we kept sending him. Vignesh Krishnamurthy was just a call away whenever I needed any help in Chennai and recorded my interview with P. Ravikumar.

I would also like to thank Prof. Shiv Visvanathan, Prof. Ravi Subrahmanyan and Raman Research Institute Trust for trying to find information regarding the mrdangam used by C.V. Raman for his research regarding its harmonic properties. And *The Hindu* for looking into their archives in search of an article published in 1920.

It is a privilege to be able to write in places that open one's mind to ideas and words. Dayanita Singh opened the doors to her gorgeous village home in Goa, where I spent a week with just the rains as my companion. And Olivia made sure that everything was perfect. As the monsoons continued unabated, I moved from Goa to the Manipal Centre for Humanities, where Prof. Nikhil Govind and Prof. Gayathri Prabhu offered me a balcony seat to watch the torrential rains. Srijin Deshpande was always there to help. When I came back to my home base in Chennai, the mathematicians at the Chennai Mathematical Institute provided me an office to work out of. And that is where I give this manuscript its finishing touches.

INDEX

liming, 217–219

machine-made instruments, 147
Madhammal, 306, 307, 308, 355
Madras District Gazetteers: Tanjore
   (Hemingway), 7, 12, 351
Madras muttu, 42, 224, 267, 279, 344
Madurai, 6, 8, 15, 37, 178, 206, 252,
   330
Madurai Roman Catholic Mission, 15
Mahalingam, T.R., 152
Maharashtrian cultural influx, 8
male musicians, 9, 140, 143, 146, 221,
   256, 262, 305
Mambalam, 51, 97, 119, 120, 204, 228
Mani, Karaikudi, 47, 63, 64, 83, 94,
   123, 136, 138, 194, 225, 228, 236,
   263, 264, 268, 273, 274
Mani, N.V.S, 119
Manickam, 26
Manikyam, 289, 291, 292
Manimangalam, 243, 244
Mannargudi, 20, 60, 307
Manro, 26
Maraimalai Nagar, 244–246
Maratha-influenced Thanjavur
   tradition, 6, 8–9
Marian shrine in Nagapattinam, 12
Martin, P.T., 21, 71, 73, 171
Melgies, F., 5, 15, 32, 33, 41, 47, 48,
   51, 54–55, 60, 64, 156, 161, 162,
   163, 165–171, 204–207, 224, 247,
   260, 292, 325, 338
mrdangam
   demand, 56, 74, 287, 310
   description, 3–4
   layers of hide, 3–4
   leather membranes, 3–4
   machine, 148–150
mrdangam-making
   chittankallu, 228
   Fevicol, 162, 243, 294–295
   flat nylon webbing, 164
   frame, 3, 4, 146, 149, 150, 164, 176,
      276, 293
   kayaru, 164, 168, 213
      thangukayaru, 167, 350

kattai, 128, 131–142, 144–151,
   167, 176, 214, 256, 263, 339, 349
kattai-making, 144–151
kannu, 167–168, 170, 172, 173,
   198, 199, 200–202, 210, 211,
   237, 251, 255, 258, 262, 348
kavanai, 165–168, 183
keedakallu, 296
kittankallu, 228, 229, 231–233,
   235, 238, 243, 244, 246, 247,
   254, 296, 349
kunnumani (*Abrus precatorius*,
   kunnikuru or guruganji), 294
nut-and-bolt system, 214
padiparkardu, 212, 215, 349
parachute ropes made of nylon
   kernmantle, 164
Plastic Fermit, 226
polyethylene ropes, 164
sadam
   nadu-sadam, 238
   on kottu thattu, 233–234
   on valandalai, 235–237, 241
   ora-sadam, 238
resonance, 4, 47, 62, 126, 179, 184,
   210, 220, 222, 223, 249, 250,
   251, 253, 264, 266, 268, 272, 293
sattai, 171–174, 180, 200, 202, 210,
   350
   pinnrasattai, 171–174, 349
   ul sattai, 171, 173, 174, 180, 202,
      350
shell-making, 126, 129
stretching, 8, 161, 276
suddham panradu, 258, 350
tambalam, 241
thattu, 162–171, 176, 179, 181, 182,
   193, 196–198, 202, 204, 205, 210,
   212, 213, 217, 218, 223, 233–241,
   243, 250, 253–257, 262, 268, 270,
   272, 273, 282, 292, 293, 295, 317,
   349–350
   thattu podradu, 162
   tying of thattus, 168
   okkara thattu, 196–198, 250
   sunnambu thattu, 217, 262
Teflon ropes, 164